Bradley Wiggins has won three Olympic gold medals on the track and ridden in two of the most controversial Tour de France races in history. He is the sport's most trenchant critic of drug taking and has been at the vanguard of the remarkable renaissance in British cycling.

Brendan Gallagher has worked as a sports journalist for the *Daily Telegraph* for nearly twenty years, writing mainly on rugby, athletics and cycling. He collaborated with Brian O'Driscoll on his book *A Year in the Centre* and is also the author of *Sporting Supermen*, an anthology of comic-book heroes.

In Pursuit of Glory

The Autobiography

Bradley Wiggins

An Orion paperback

First published in Great Britain in 2008
by Orion
This paperback edition published in 2009
by Orion Books Ltd,
Orion House, 5 Upper St Martin's Lane,
London WC2H 9EA

An Hachette UK company

9 10 8

A CIP catalogue record for this book
is available from the British Library.

ISBN 978-0-7528-8403-5

Designed in Utopia by Geoff Green Book Design, Cambridge

Printed and bound by CPI Group (UK) Ltd, Croydon, CR0 4YY

The Orion Publishing Group's policy is to use papers that
are natural, renewable and recyclable products and
made from wood grown in sustainable forests. The logging
and manufacturing processes are expected to conform to
the environmental regulations of the country of origin.

www.orionbooks.co.uk

To Cath, Ben and Isabella.
Everything I do I do for you.

Contents

Acknowledgements

Very little worthwhile can be achieved totally on you own. You may occasionally think you are ploughing a lonely furrow and doing it all yourself but always in the background there are people going the extra yard to help and encourage you. I have been luckier than most and there are a fair few people right from the outset of this book I want to acknowledge. Some of the names will mean nothing to the general public but they mean a huge amount me. I won't elaborate too much – mainly to save their blushes – but thank you one and all so very much. The debt of gratitude starts with my mum Linda, of course, Brendan, brother Ryan, Nan and George, my in-laws Liz and Dave, Auntie Karen, Big Dean, Lois, Anton, Dean and Adam, Tailor and Mr Hatch my old PE teacher who saw and encouraged the first glimpses of what sporting talent I have.

Then there are those from my early cycling days: Stuart Benstead, the late Stan Knight, Pat and Len Docker who have both, alas, died as well. Mike and Pat Taylor; Richard and Mick at Sport Publicity; Russell Williams, Dave Creasy, Sean Bannister, Graham Bristow and Eddie Wingrave – the latter taught me never to take my hands off the handlebars when crossing the line; he used to disqualify me to ram the message home. Nor must I ever forget Garry Beckett and the late Ron Beckett for all they have done, not to mention Monty and Grant Young at Condor Cycles.

As I progressed up the ladder and I was lucky to encounter seriously good coaches and back- up staff – so many thanks to Doug Dailey, Steve Pauldling, Marshall Thomas, Simon Jones and of course Peter Keen who played such a big role in setting up the success story that is British cycling. Matt Parker is an exceptional coach who seems to have devoted his last two years to making it happen for me – if you are Matt's wife and reading this, thank you for loaning me your husband – while down in the pits let's hear it for Chief Mechanic Ernie Feargrieve, Mark Ingham, the ubiquitous Spike and all the crew. Thank you guys for all your help.

I must thank all the girls at the World Class programme for all their hard work: Diane Evans for that wonderful big smile she always greets you with which brightens the darkest day, Rose, who very possibly does the best jacket potatoes and filling in all of England, and Steve and Giles who keep the Manchester Velodrome up and running at all hours and in all weathers so the likes of me can get their training fix and some ungodly hour every morning.

Terry Dolan and his family have been great friends and supporters throughout, a real constant in my life and, on the subject of special thanks, where would myself and Cath be without Claire, who is just the best child minder and baby sitter in Christendom and whose complete reliability and love for the kids means myself and Cath can rest easy when we are away. And huge thanks, of course, to Brendan Gallagher, for everything with the book.

And now those who have added the X factor in my cycling career and transformed dreams into reality. Thank you Chris Boardman for being my initial cycling inspiration and then working so hard – with an occasionally difficult pupil! – to ensure I fulfilled my potential in 2004 and beyond. Thank you Dave Brailsford – the GB Performance Director – for being simply the best man manager I have ever encountered in sport. Despite the huge load on your shoulders you have remained a total cycling enthusiast, which I love, and although you are my 'boss' you are also my friend. Thank you Steve Peters for opening my eyes on how to approach my worries and fears and for simply being the world expert in common sense – isn't it odd how extremely rare 'common' sense is? And finally thank you Shane Sutton. You are a men amongst men. A total inspiration as a bloke and coach and somebody whose friendship I cherish so much. None of my recent success could have happened without you Shane, I truly mean that.

I've lost track whether you are an 'Aussie' or a 'Taff' these days but I do know you are the true heart and soul of British Cycling.

Chapter One

It's four in the morning . . .

Saturday 26 January 2008 and it's 4 a.m. at home in Eccleston, a sleepy town in West Lancashire, north of Manchester and west of Liverpool – nowhere in particular, anonymous and unpretentious, which is exactly as I like it. The wind is kicking up outside but the kids are fast asleep in the room next door and my wife Cath is dead to the world beside me, sleeping the righteous sleep of a young mum who has been looking after two toddlers around the clock. Just about everything in my life is good. It is early in Olympic year and already I have half an eye on Beijing and dreaming the dream, although the immediate target is the World Championships in Manchester in March and going for three gold medals in front of my home crowd. I am tired in a reassuring sort of way after another long winter's week logging up the miles on the track in Manchester and a massive fortnight on the roads in Majorca before that. Feeling relaxed, I stretch my long legs carefully as I shift in bed so as not to wake Cath. Somewhere, a million miles away, I fancy that I can hear a phone ringing but I'm almost certainly dreaming. I've been dreaming a lot recently, mainly of Beijing. I ignore it.

I can't ignore it. Cath's grandmother hasn't been very well recently and when it's 4 a.m. and the phone is ringing off the hook you always fear the worst. The shrill call keeps drilling its way into my brain; gradually I come round and reluctantly return to the land of the conscious. It is definitely our phone ringing. Shit! What bloody idiot is phoning me at this time of night? Nobody phones you in the middle of the night unless they're pissed or they've got very bad news indeed. Hoping for the former but fearing the latter I slip out of bed, trying desperately not to wake Cath.

I rub the sleep out of my eyes, pause for a moment to clear my head and compose myself before tiptoeing down to the kitchen to take the call. Another thought flashes through my mind and my heart sinks a little. There was a time when my father Garry – my biological father that is, he cleared off when I was two years old and only made very sporadic and erratic appearances in my life thereafter – used to phone me about this time of night. He would call from Australia after a long day throwing beers down his neck – VBs as I recall – and start crying down the phone with all his woes and remorse about leaving my mother and treating her so badly all those years ago. But he hasn't phoned for ages now; in fact, to be completely honest, I have no idea if he's even still alive. Our relationship has reached ground zero.

I brace myself, snap into action and reach out for the receiver. It's an Australian twang at the other end all right, but it's the friendly and always welcome voice of Shane Sutton – mentor, coach and general inspiration to me and many others at Team GB – one of my best friends in cycling and just about the soundest guy I have ever known. A bloke you would want in the trenches with you, as I have discovered on more than one occasion.

Just for a second I relax, but almost in that same instant my stomach lurches again and I realise that it can only be bad news. Myself and Shane are in constant touch during key phases of the season – we are both unrepentant cycling nuts and talk non-stop about our sport – but he would never wake me unnecessarily in the middle of the night during a heavy stint of training. This must be very serious indeed.

'G'day, Brad, sorry about this, mate, but I just had to call you, I couldn't wait until the morning,' said the usually chipper Shane in a strained voice. 'I've had a message from a guy in Australia – he just said his name was Neil and that he was a friend of your dad's – saying that Garry is very ill. I've got a number you need to phone at the John Hunter Hospital in Newcastle in New South Wales. I'm really sorry about this mate but I just had to phone you straight away. Ring back if there is anything I can do to help.'

I put the phone down. Garry had been in scrapes many times before and had often been in and out of hospital with ill health. I knew for a fact that he had suffered with minor skin cancers from cycling, or old saddle sores that had gone bad and festered and still played up as his general health declined. And if it wasn't that, he would be hospitalised for treatment after various pub brawls that had left him and the 'other fella' battered and bloodied. Nothing new there whatsoever. I am sad to say that Garry Wiggins being in hospital – or even prison, for that matter – had become the norm and not the cause for any particular alarm for his far-flung and abandoned family – only anger, resentment and pity.

So when Shane's urgent message came to call Australia immediately I knew deep down that Garry was already dead. That had to be the logical conclusion. I was a little stunned, but not shocked. In the very back of my mind I had been preparing for this scenario ever since I had been briefly reunited and reconciled with my 'dad' when I was 19. His life had been such a rollercoaster and, for many years, so very unhappy and dysfunctional. For a while I had feared the worst, but, in my determination to pursue my own career and dreams and to enjoy a loving family life, I had consciously put any thoughts of Garry Wiggins on the back burner.

I thank Shane for his kindness and promise to phone back when I've got the full story. I pour a glass of water and stand there for a while, numb, trying to take it all in. What with the phone call from Shane and the house downstairs lit up like Christmas, Cath has stirred and come down to see what's up. I briefly tell her exactly what I know.

What to do? For a moment I seriously consider just going back to bed and going into denial. Do nothing at all. This man had deserted me and my mum when I was a kid, hit her in mad rages when under the influence of drink and drugs, and contributed not a penny to my upbringing. When I did finally feel strong enough to meet him in Australia he was depressed and morose, full of unattractive self-pity. And then, for a few years, he repeatedly tried to dump all his emotional baggage and guilt on me during long anguished phone calls at some ungodly hour. He wanted to turn the clock back 20 years. He just couldn't move on and make anything of his life.

When I arranged to meet up with him at the Ghent Sixes he would happily let me 'sub' him all night so he could go around the nightclubs and bars buying drinks for all his old cronies and acting Mr Big – he would explain to everybody where I was going wrong as a cyclist and what a great Six Day rider he had been. I held my tongue on that occasion, I was still trying to give him the benefit of the doubt, but, if I am honest, he was a complete disaster as a human being, at least in his relationship with me. Other people claim to know another nicer, much kinder Garry Wiggins, who would do anything to help a real friend, but unfortunately I never met him.

I could respect Garry only as a bike rider and could relate to him only as a bike rider. He was an extremely talented and determined

Aussie, who bravely trekked up to Europe to tackle the very best Continental riders on their home patch on the lucrative Six Day circuit. Lucrative, that is, for those very few who made it onto the fabled 'Blue Train' – the small phalanx of top riders, perhaps 12 or 14, who got invites to all the competitions across Europe and were looked after by the organisers. But hell on earth for those who were riding their guts out trying to make it. A nasty dog-eat-dog world. I remember reading once that very few Six Day riders remain close friends after they retire. There is too much baggage between them all, too many old fights and broken alliances, too many old scores that haven't really been settled.

Garry was pretty classy on a bike, with good natural speed and undoubtedly he was a bloody hard case, a hard-driving Aussie warrior who would get into fights not only off the track but on it as well. You didn't cross Garry Wiggins and get away with it. Garry only knew one way to sort out an argument and that was with a left hook. Talking to his old colleagues and opponents I see a look of fear, and occasionally loathing, on their faces when I bring up his name.

Nonetheless, I have always been proud of his achievements and style as a rider, and talking to those contemporaries – male and female – it is clear that, on a rare good day, he could also be a lovable rogue with an undeniable charm: the leader of the pack and centre of most of the fun and all the mischief. But as a partner and a parent he was a car crash – and I was just one of the battered survivors.

The truth is, I didn't like this man one bit as a bloke and, having met him in his declining years and been briefly reconciled in my late teens, I then felt confident enough to make up my own mind as to whether we remained close. My verdict, eventually, was that I wanted nothing whatsoever to do with him. He had never met my wife and our two beautiful children Ben and Isabella, and that was a conscious decision on my part. He was so wild and erratic in his latter drunken years that he clearly wasn't going to be a stable factor in their lives. It could only end in tears and there had been too many of them already.

We hadn't spoken since after the 2003 World Championships, although he left a message after my Olympic success in 2004. He had abandoned me and now I was withdrawing from him, even if occasionally I still wondered if he continued to follow my career 12,000 miles away. Just as I was still proud of him as a bike rider, he apparently was proud of me, although typically he never had the balls to tell me to my face. In fact he used to criticise me non-stop and humiliate me in front of his mates, like that occasion in Ghent or a track meet in Australia once when I took him along and came 'only' second in the Madison.

I stand there in a daze, unable to think straight or decide what needs doing first, if anything. Cath, as usual, brings me back to my senses. She has been doing this since the blessed day we got together in 2002. Of course I had to phone the hospital in Australia. Despite everything, Garry was my father and, just as importantly, the grandfather of Ben and Isabella. There would be formalities to complete; my mother would need to be told of his death and would need support; and there were other members of Garry's extended family – my family – who I needed to bear in mind. Whatever the history between myself and Garry – and there was plenty – I needed to try to do the right thing now so the surviving members of the family could come a little closer.

I take courage and phone the hospital; it is pretty clear they have been waiting for the call. I was immediately put through to a ward doctor who, in a very professional and businesslike way, told me that he was very sorry but Garry has died. The hospital seems to be totally unaware that Garry has close surviving family in Australia – a sister and two daughters, that is, my aunt and two sisters – so later that day it fell upon me, 12,000 miles away, to start making the sort of phone calls you dread.

My first reaction, however, was perhaps a little strange. I suddenly tore up the stairs to wake Ben and 'Bella from their sweet dreams. I just wanted to see them alive, feel them in my arms and cuddle them. It is a big horrible world out there sometimes but nothing could take my little family away from me. I was getting very emotional about it all. Whatever life threw at us they would always have a 'dad' in their lives.

As dawn started to break I phoned my mum, Linda, who understandably was in a state of shock despite the fraught relationship she had endured with Garry. She had loved him once very much and there was a place in her heart that was always his. Then came his older sister – Glenda Hughes – in Australia who broke down in tears before phoning her niece Shannon who was the product of his first teenage marriage. Shannon said she would contact Madison – so named because of his love and expertise in that specialist track cycling event – who was our much younger sister, the progeny of his failed third marriage, to Fiona.

As the day wore on I began to experience massive emotional dips, which really rocked me. I hadn't expected it. Damn. I should have just picked up the phone occasionally and phoned the old man. Why didn't I do that? He was obviously lonely as hell and perhaps it would have made his day, kept him on a more even keel. It would only have taken five minutes, every other week or so. I beat myself up a bit but, as I sipped a coffee or played my guitar out in our sunroom, I rationalised it all and was much kinder on myself. 'Sod it, I tried again and again with you, Garry. You broke my bloody heart but I tried. I kept an open mind despite all the stories I heard around the track. It was me who made the big move and came to visit you in Australia to stay with you and talk through all your troubles, it was me who made the effort to keep in touch. I subbed you while you insisted on standing all your old mates drinks night after night when I was riding at the Ghent Sixes. I couldn't have done more and you kept throwing it all back in my face. You had your chance, Garry, time and time again.'

Time stood still, as it does when there is a death in the family, and gradually new information came to light, none of it particularly welcome or of much comfort. I phoned up Neil – he never offered a second name so I never asked – and thanked him for alerting us to Garry's death, or at least unexplained absence. He was a comparatively new friend, who had met Garry a year or so ago down his local and had taken to yarning most nights away with him. He had become alarmed when Garry hadn't turned up at the pub one night when they had arranged to meet for a drink, had made a few enquiries and had discovered he had been 'beaten up' and taken to hospital and was extremely ill. All he knew of Garry's circumstances was that he was the father of Great Britain Olympic champion Bradley Wiggins. Me.

Neil couldn't think where to start, so, as a long shot, he phoned the Australian Cycling Federation and somebody there – and a heartfelt thank you whoever you are – thought quickly on their feet and contacted Gary Sutton, who is probably best known in Britain as Hugh Porter's sidekick on the BBC's cycling commentaries. Gary Sutton was a fine rider in his day and has close links with the Australian Federation; he is also the brother of Shane, who he immediately phoned. And that's how I found myself answering the phone in the middle of the night.

The more I learned, the more disturbing it became. Garry's sister Glenda phoned back to say she had seen the body in the morgue – he had been beaten to a pulp and there was a huge wound on the back of his head that was very unlikely to have been caused by a fall or an accident. One of the nurses had apparently commented that it was the worst beating she had ever seen. It sounded horrible. New South Wales police seemed to concur; they set up a special homicide unit – Strike Force Durbin – combining local officers and detectives from the New South Wales Homicide Squad. These units are only ever formed to investigate suspected murders and unexplained deaths. At the time of going to press their investigations are ongoing, so although we know some of the circumstances surrounding Garry's death, we are not at liberty to say much. What is known is that Garry was found unconscious and bleeding at 7 a.m. Australian time on Friday 25 January, in Segenhoe Street, Aberdeen, which is a small town some way to the north-west of Newcastle. The medics estimated he had been there for some nine hours. Initially he was taken to the local Muswellbrook Hospital but later he was airlifted to the John Hunter Hospital in Newcastle where he died.

Soon after I took the call from Shane Sutton the press and media – in Britain and Australia – got whiff of the story and the phone started ringing from dawn to dusk. In my confused state of mind I told one or two reporters exactly where they could stuff their questions. I like to think I get on pretty well with the press but certain individuals overstepped the line that day.

Dave Brailsford – the GB performance manager and, much more importantly in this moment of crisis, a good friend as well as my 'track' boss – got through and immediately offered to finance a business-class flight to Melbourne and organise every-thing if I wanted to go down to Australia for the funeral. It was good of Dave – solid practical help at a time when my mind was all over the place. Glenda and Shannon both rang back and Glenda said that when she went to clear up his housing unit in Muswellbrook – it was a complete pigsty apparently and she had to burn almost everything – there was one neatly arranged shelf, with framed pictures of myself, Shannon and Madison.

There was also a pile of carefully arranged cuttings covering every aspect of my career from my early wins as a junior to the events of 2007 – two gold medals at the World Track Championships and that momentous weekend of the *départ* of the Tour de France in London, when I got plenty of column inches for being a Londoner riding on his own patch. It was nice to think that Garry was proud of us but confusing as well – why could he never show that when he was alive?

Glenda asked me to come down to view the body and carry the coffin. Initially I was up for it but in the end, on the way to the airport, it just didn't seem right and I bailed out. Perhaps I will regret the decision but it seemed right then and still does. I know Shannon, down in Australia, had to think very seriously about going as well. This was a time of very mixed emotions; Garry had caused so much chaos and turmoil in my life I couldn't stand the thought of any more. I had handled everything he had thrown at me so far but this could tip me over the edge emotionally. This was the biggest year of my sporting life and I wanted to feel I was in control – well, as much as any sportsman can be.

In the end I did what I have always done. Secure in the love and support of Cath on the home front, I lost myself in training and riding my bike. I put in some huge sessions down on the track – the World Championships were only seven weeks away and I was deep into heavy conditioning work – and when the weather was clear enough I went on long mind-clearing rides around the narrow lanes of West Lancs and far beyond. Usually you invent mind games or hum your favourite pieces of music to help the miles go quickly and counter the fatigue, but this time I had more than enough to mull on. If the weather was icy or just too wet to make it fun I took myself off to my cluttered garage, cleared all the kids' toys out of the way and put my bike on the rollers. The turbo as we call it. Then I plugged into my little DVD player, turned on the fan to keep me cool and just pedalled away for two, three, sometimes four hours.

I am much more of a 'doer' than a thinker but this was a reflective time – a tragic start to possibly a career-defining year – with a thousand thoughts rushing through my mind and competing for attention. What were my feelings about Garry and his chaotic life? How had I got to this point in my own life where I was grieving for a man I hadn't met for five years? What exactly happened down in Australia? How have I managed to avoid the pitfalls that blew Garry's life to pieces? Have I achieved everything I set out to do as a cyclist or have I got the hunger to take it to another level? How could I ever cope without Cath and the kids? And how could Garry ever leave his wives and children – not once, not twice but three times? Big serious stuff that perhaps you only sit down and address properly once or twice in a lifetime. This was one of these occasions. How did it all come to this?

I came to a striking, perhaps shocking, conclusion. I examined my emotional reaction to his death honestly and, once the fog had cleared, I realised that, deep down, I was almost glad he had now gone. Or at least relieved there would be no more suffering. Glad that Garry couldn't hurt himself any more and have to endure the life he was living and what he perceived as his disappointments and failures; glad that his struggle was now over and he was safe from the demons that seemed to haunt him. And just glad that myself and my two half-sisters – who I didn't meet until I was 19 – could be free of the black cloud that has always hung over us. He was free ... and so were we.

—

Chapter Two

My father's son

During those long training miles I decided that my story – such as it is – and certainly the account of how I became a World and Olympic cycling champion, has to start with an account of Garry, warts and all. He may have gone AWOL for most of my life but his achievements as a cyclist and almost 'legendary' hard-man status on the circuit undoubtedly helped propel me towards a competitive career in the sport. Our shared DNA is at the heart of the story.

You will have to bear with me a little because there are significant gaps in Garry's story – he left such a trail of devastation and alienated himself from so many people that we may never know the full truth. At various times he lost touch completely with just about everybody who cared for him or had loved him. There are considerable periods of his life that are unaccounted for.

The trail starts in Yallourn, Victoria, where he was born, and then just down the road in Morwell where his family lived – both towns are a million miles away from the beachside paradise you often conjure up when thinking about Australia and the rippling tanned athletes it seems to produce in all sports. Morwell existed for one reason only and that was to provide housing units for those working at the huge Yallourn power station and the old open-cast coalmine that used to operate nearby. On 20 November 1952, when Garry was born, it was a pretty rough, tough, male-dominated 'bush' town, with very little of the sophistication of the state capital Melbourne some 90 miles to the west. It definitely was not the Australia you read about in the tourist brochures.

As far as I know, Garry's early years were far from unhappy or troubled and his folks – his father Roy is still alive aged 90 – were supportive. He soon showed an aptitude for bikes and his mum and dad used to drive Garry and Glenda in their camper van all around Victoria, and sometimes beyond, to attend various cycling competitions. The original Aussies on tour – fiercely self-sufficient and independent. Garry quickly became a National Junior Track champion and was an outstanding prospect, but he was very ambitious and had no intention of simply becoming the best in Australia and scraping a living.

He was thinking big, but generally life was far from glamorous in Morwell. From what he used to tell me, every Friday night without fail finished with a frenzied Wild West free-for-all down the pub. Garry was very useful with his fists even then – a Victoria junior champion according to his own claims – and a fanatical love of boxing is about the only thing I have ever had in common with him apart from cycling.

Sport was one of the few ways you could hope to better yourself and escape from the small-town drudgery. Garry very quickly saw cycling as his passport out of Morwell and started making plans to move to Europe and to compete in, if not the Tour de France – he had no experience or background as a road racer – then at least the highly profitable winter track circuit, for which he was very well suited. He had made a big splash with the local Latrobe City Cycling Club and was ready to move on. He wasn't the only one. Another young lad from Morwell, John

Trevorrow – who became the Australian road cycling champion and a well-respected correspondent for *Cycling News* – chose exactly the same path just a couple of years earlier.

Garry was ruthless in his ambition and not even a teenage marriage and a doting young daughter, Shannon, was going to thwart those ambitions. Loads of young Aussies trek up to Britain as part of their life experience but they don't usually ditch a wife and daughter to live their dream. Some would argue he was running away from his personal problems, but to my mind nothing was ever going to stop Garry from taking his shot at fame and fortune. That was what drove him on. Nothing else mattered. He didn't think twice about doing a 'runner', and, having scraped the airfare together, he headed for Heathrow in 1974, first stop the well-known Archer's Cycling Club at Herne Hill.

Herne Hill, in south London not far from Dulwich, was the venue for the track cycling events at the 1948 Olympics, when Britain's Reg Harris won two silver medals. In fact it is the only venue from those games still being used, with its Good Friday meeting remaining one of the institutions of British cycling. A long concrete track – 430 metres, with gently sloping banks of no more than 30 degrees – it has always been something of a Mecca for track cyclists in London and is very much the home for Archer's Cycling Club, a thriving club which was then sponsored by Cutty Sark and slightly more affluent than most, although that isn't saying much. There was never a fortune to be made in British track cycling.

Like any sporting club in this country it is run by a band of dedicated stalwarts and one of those – then as now – is Stuart Benstead, who was the first point of contact for Garry. Stuart is half-Australian himself – his dad was from Alice Springs – and he always kept an eye open for hungry and talented young Aussie and Kiwi riders looking to travel and gain experience in Europe.

In a short period of time he recruited the likes of the Sanders brothers – Dave and John – who were both classy performers and Australian champions, New Zealander John Mullan and Garry. Initially Stuart put Garry up for the first month or so at his home in Heston, before Garry found more permanent lodgings for 18 months with Graham Temple in Shepherd's Bush. Robin Croker was another 'Aussie' who dropped into the British scene around this time, although he had British parents and had qualified to ride for GB at the 1976 Olympics, where he took a bronze medal in the Team Pursuit.

Garry adapted quickly, earning enough prize money at the thriving Monday night 'comps' and the open meetings every Wednesday, where up to a thousand die-hard spectators would often create a bit of an atmosphere. Companies like Cutty Sark, Charringtons, Philips (the shaver company) and EMI used to put up decent cash prizes, and the competition was fierce. Some of Britain's best young riders, like Ian Hallam – twice an Olympic bronze medallist – and Steve Heffernan, often used to compete. Garry must have been pretty useful to hold his own in such company, and he was able to pay his rent from his winnings, and subsidise what was already a voracious thirst and a party lifestyle. At this stage he seemed well able to handle the grog and, although he was an extremely tough gung-ho Aussie, his behaviour while living and riding in England caused no particular alarm, although I suspect it will be news to many of his contemporaries that he had already abandoned a wife and young daughter.

Garry was a busy rider, always ready to accept a challenge. At very short notice he rode the nine-day Tour of Ireland, which included plenty of punishing climbs – his first stage race. He won an Australian Handicap up at Leicester and was also a regular racer at the old Paddington track as well as Herne Hill. At one time I understand he and Heffernan used to combine forces a little in individual races they ostensibly entered as individuals, but then spilt the prize money when they got on the podium.

Garry was pretty formidable on a tandem apparently – I can imagine him giving his partner absolute hell if he slacked at all. His reputation as being a hard man was already in place. You still hear tell these days of the morning he and Mullan – his regular training partner – fell out violently on a ride and Garry chased him across the fields to administer his usual brand of justice.

At the end of 1976 he turned professional with the Falcon team, and during this period he was also periodically returning to Australia in the winter to compete in their track season. He was pretty successful down there, winning the Australia Kilo championship – a 1000 m time-trial and the event Britain's Chris Hoy dominated for so long in recent years – and helping the Victoria quartet to take the Team Pursuit title.

Meanwhile back in Britain he had met my mother Linda just a matter of months after he had arrived. Garry didn't waste time. She lived in a block of flats close to the Paddington track and used to avidly watch all the meets, and they soon clocked each other. She was a very independent and, dare I say, feisty 17-year-old, who knew her own mind, and he was a handsome Aussie, seemingly a man of the world, albeit he was only 22 and had recently ditched his wife and child. The attraction was fairly instantaneous and by 1976 they had moved in together in West End Lane nearby.

He married Linda at St Augustine's church in January 1979 and immediately departed for Ghent in Belgium – a major cycling enclave on the Continent – moving Mum over as soon as he found a small apartment. He was going for broke and, as he reached for the top, was increasingly out of control

Garry pursued his career remorselessly and was moving into

dangerous territory. He was good enough to harbour hopes that he might make it but, in the cold light of day, he wasn't quite good enough to get to the very top on sheer talent alone. He would need to be stronger, nastier and more ruthless than anybody else. He would have to train longer and harder than anybody else, learn all the dirty tricks and use his fists regularly to intimidate other riders. A generation of riders felt the full force of his fists, including his team-mate and friend – former Olympic 4 km champion Robert Dill Brundi from Switzerland – who he hospitalised with one punch after they crossed swords in the interval at a Six Day race in Cologne. Garry was a man living on the edge.

It was bloody hard out there. I accept that, and a large part of me admires Garry for having a go. At one stage, during the summer season, he would often work a night shift in a warehouse and then ride in a 200 km Kermesse – Belgium's own unique version of a small-town Criterium around a tight closed-roads circuit – as a *domestique* for a small team. And all this for a pittance. He might do three or four days like that a week and he gradually climbed up the ladder. He had his successes as a Kermesse rider and once famously beat Lucien van Impe at a race at Eeklo in Belgium in 1981, and these successes were enough to just about keep the dream alive.

On the track he was giving it his all – no half measures in anything with Garry. Remember there were about 150 resident professionals in Belgium, Holland and Germany chasing 28 starting places on the Six Day circuit. Just over half of those were nailed down by the elite 'Blue Train' members who attended all the meets. At some of the big events, like Berlin or Munich, upwards of 80,000 paying fans would go through the gates during the six nights and they would party until the early hours at the bars, restaurants and nightclubs. It was and is a huge business, and to be one of the chosen few riders to attend every race was to have made it in a big way. That was the ultimate. Another ten or so places were distributed to reigning World Track champions, who were a big draw in their own right, and the local heroes of whatever track you were at. That left everybody else scrapping – sometimes literally – for the few remaining invites. It was dog-eat-dog because the rewards were very good – you could pay for a house with one decent winter on the circuit. Five or six good years and theoretically you should be made for life.

For a while Garry was a 'reserve' or extra man, which meant he was the lowest of the low. He had to be permanently on call – bag packed, track bike stripped down – to be parachuted in if one of the first-choice riders suddenly fell ill or crashed and a replacement was needed. It was nerve-wracking stuff but gradually he began to earn a few invites as of right. One of his early colleagues was Maurice Burton, a powerful British rider and the first Brit to really have a concerted go at the Six Day scene. Maurice was the first black rider to emerge from Britain and was a tough guy who took no nonsense from Garry, so there was a lot of mutual respect between the two. Looking back, it was the strong guys who stood up to Garry and refused to be bullied by him that brought the best out of him and probably have the fondest memories of him. But they didn't have to live with him.

Right in the middle of this I came along. Born in Ghent, a beautiful historic old city in Belgium, on 28 April 1980. I definitely wasn't part of the master plan. Just as Shannon's arrival in Australia a few years earlier had seriously cramped his style when he was looking to spread his wings and move to Europe, Garry was now hell-bent on becoming one of the greatest, and wealthiest, track riders in the world; and, frankly, starting a second family was bloody inconvenient and bad timing, to say the least.

Trying to understand my dad now I can see he was a man under immense pressure, although a lot of it was self-induced. He was rapidly heading towards 30, had a second wife to support and a young son on the scene, and he hadn't really made the big breakthrough he wanted and expected. Having spoken to him and Linda there is not the slightest doubt that, along with some other riders, he was using amphetamines to keep going during his hectic racing schedule.

It was pretty unsophisticated drug use and during that era it was still semi-acceptable, or at least tacitly ignored. After the Second World War, over 80 million amphetamine tablets had been dumped in Europe and other theatres of war by departing American forces, who had used them to keep their troops awake in combat situations. A black market sprang up and cyclists, who had been using and abusing various strange potions for decades, soon monopolized that market. The early 1980s was the tail end of that phase, before more sophisticated performance-enhancing drugs came to the fore, and the situation became almost comical occasionally – at one stage Garry flew us down to Australia to meet his family and, on the way back, smuggled more drugs back into Belgium, hiding them in my nappy.

Garry had earned the nickname 'Doc' on the circuit – I will let you draw your own conclusions – and not only used amphetamines but also dealt. My mum has vivid memories of local riders queuing up at our apartment in Ghent on Friday evenings to get their fix for their weekend racing. And, worse still, the pills were gradually changing his personality. We now know how amphetamines – speed – accentuate the psychotic and extreme sides of your personality, and when you combine that with the industrial quantities of booze Garry consumed most nights it wasn't a pretty sight. He started to smack Mum around when he came back from the racing, high on booze and drugs. Maurice Burton pulled him up about it one day, much to Garry's embarrassment, when he noticed Linda was trying to disguise another black eye. Garry and Linda fought like cats and broke up a couple of times only to get back together again.

The big split eventually came over the Christmas holidays in 1982. Mum had brought me back to her parents' flat in Kilburn and Garry was to follow when he had finished his latest Six Day event, but, just before Christmas, he phoned Linda up to say he was leaving her and she wasn't to bother coming back to Ghent. He had 'met' somebody on the circuit – Miss Dortmund, to be precise, who went by the name of Enid – and we were history. Shortly afterwards he threw all our belongings into four black bin-liners, took the ferry back over to Britain and left them at the foot of the stairs in the block of flats where Grandad and Nan lived.

Garry refused point blank to see Linda, but insisted on taking me to London Zoo where he even asked a passer-by to take a rather poignant picture of father and son apparently enjoying an idyllic day out together. It was the last time I saw him for nearly 17 years, although of course I don't really remember the day itself. I've just got the picture from the zoo, around which I tried occasionally to create the fantasy that I had a father. A child's bike appeared a few months later, by way of a third birthday present, but then the door was slammed firmly shut on Linda and myself. As far as Garry was concerned we didn't exist.

Garry's subsequent Six Day career fell just short of greatness but, in fairness, he emerged as a mighty competitor and for three years or so got onto the Blue Train and made some very decent money – enough to buy himself a flash Mercedes at one stage, as he told me later, although not enough apparently to ever consider sending a few quid over to help with the upbringing of his son. In a highly competitive arena he was 7th overall in the

1983–84 series off 13 starts, 8th the following year again off 13 starts and 11th in 1985–86 off just ten starts.

In the 1983–84 season he achieved good results with Britain's Tony Doyle – who twice won the World Pursuit Championship – in Munich (4th), Zurich (4th), Henning (4th), Bremen (2nd), Copenhagen (4th) and Milan (4th). The following season they won the prestigious Six Days of Bremen together and clocked up good results in Zurich (3rd) and Maastricht (4th). In 1985 they took the European Madison crown in Zurich, having also finished runners-up the previous year. That was the pinnacle for Garry – all the world's best Madison riders contested the European, which was effectively the World Madison Championships even though it didn't boast that title. I hope Garry was truly happy that evening. It was his crowning achievement. He certainly looks genuinely pleased with life in the pictures. Later that year he won the Melbourne Cup on wheels back in Australia and the Griffin 1000, which is a five-day road stage tour of Western Australia.

It was the final, brightest, flame before the fire was extinguished. He had burned the candle at both ends for too long and his determination to enjoy the fruits of his success lured him away from the training rides and endurance work that are the foundation for a successful Six Day rider. In no time at all he plunged into a steady and depressing decline. By the 1986–87 season he had plummeted to 53rd in the rankings, only racing on seven occasions, although he did pull it around enough to make a brave defence of his European crown with Doyle, winning the silver medal in Copenhagen.

In fairness, was it any wonder? Given the schedule, it is not unknown for Six Day veterans to suddenly crack. There was one point at the very height of the Six Day circuit when the bikers would compete on 42 out of 43 consecutive days at Berlin,

Dortmund, Geneva, Munich, Ghent and Zurich. It was a totally insane schedule, with racing often not finishing until 3 or 4 a.m. – a three-hour 'matinee' shift in the afternoon was followed by the main event at 8 p.m. every night. Garry hit the wall with a mighty crash and he rode his last Six Day race in January 1987 in Copenhagen. The dream was over and the true nightmare was just beginning.

Along with Enid, who by all accounts was very supportive and tried, like all of Garry's women, to make their relationship work, he opened a bar in Bremen; but it was the worst possible move, like putting King Herod in charge of child welfare. Within 18 months he had drunk all the profits, ruined the business and destroyed his relationship with Enid. At which point he did what he always did and cleared off, this time back to Australia – having written to his sister for the fare home – where I think we shall leave him until he decided he wanted re-enter our lives towards the end of the millennium. The Garry Wiggins saga was far from over.

Chapter Three

Boy racer

am not a great one for reading about somebody's early childhood – it's the part of a book I usually skip if I am honest – so I will keep this bit short and hopefully relevant to the rider and adult who emerged in his late teens with more or less the same dreams as his absentee dad.

So, post-Ghent, there I am growing up in a single-parent family in a flat in Dibden House in Paddington, although some people prefer to call it Kilburn. There wasn't a lot of money around and Mum had to work hard all hours. As well as her love and support I was lucky to have brilliant grandparents who stepped in to provide a stable family background. Considering the dramas over the split between Linda and Garry, my childhood was remarkably free of angst and was pretty normal in a London working-class sort of way.

Garry was rarely mentioned, but when he was there was no slagging off from Mum or my grandparents – George and Maureen – even though I know that George, in particular, absolutely despised him for what he had done. Mum would simply say that Dad was a brilliant bike rider who used to race for money on the indoor tracks in Europe. She didn't try to turn me against him in any way. She probably knew that at some stage in my life I would have to make up my own mind.

Initially, after the split, we lived with my grandparents. As Linda's two sisters were both at home, this made for a fairly crowded flat – myself and Mum sleeping on the settee in the sitting room. For such an independent girl it must have been a setback for Mum, but she always remained positive. She had soon got herself a job as a booking clerk for a freight company behind Marylebone Station and, at the earliest possible opportunity, we moved into our own Church Commission flat at Dibden House. It only had one bedroom so it wasn't exactly the lap of luxury, but it was from there that Mum started to rebuild our lives.

She would take me to school every morning – initially nursery school in the Harrow Road and then St Augustine's junior school. Grandad would pick me up after he had finished work with London Electric. We used to walk everywhere and became very close. George was the nearest thing I ever had to a father figure, and I was the son he never had, I suppose, although we have never spoken directly about it.

We became mates as much as anything. We would go to 'the dogs' together a couple of times a week – Wimbledon, Wembley, even once to the old White City track at the stadium built for the 1908 Olympics, before they knocked it down. I was never into betting – 50p each way was the limit of my resources and ambition – but I loved the ambience and the mad collection of characters playing their specific parts to make the entire scene. I used to look on fascinated – and it's part of what I also love about the cycling scene I eventually found myself embroiled in. So much going on, so many people claiming to be in the know. Flash individuals who stand out and make a lot of noise, and others who lurk around a little in the shadows. A close-knit, smallish world, all depending on each other.

With Grandad as my mentor I lapped it up, along with our

frequent visits to the 'Legion', where I spent countless hours playing darts, pool and cards. I should have ended up a right geezer after such a glorious misspent youth – thanks to George my childhood days were rarely boring.

As the crow flies, our home was probably a mile and half from the Houses of Parliament but it was a different world from the glitz of Westminster. There was an amazing ethnic mix ranging through all the Indian subcontinent to war-torn Somalia and Sudan, to my good self, an Anglo/Aussie hybrid from Belgium. I wouldn't have been the only product of a single-parent family either.

Essentially I was shy, but there was also an extrovert side to me that liked to entertain, act the class clown and mimic the teachers. This really started to emerge once I moved up to St Augustine's secondary school. Looking back, it was a defence mechanism, a way of earning popularity and keeping out of trouble. I was good at most sports we tried – football, baseball, cross-country running – and the PE teacher, Mr Hatch, was the one master I developed a rapport with. He was ex-army – or at least he had the bearing of an ex-army man, I never actually asked – and at parents' evenings I would always steer Mum in his direction in the sure knowledge he would sing my praises. I was certainly no academic and praise was going to be in short supply elsewhere.

I had one little mad spell when I and another kid for some reason thought it was clever to start stealing money from the masters' common room. For my part it was simply for the challenge, to see if we could do it and not get caught – our own Mission Impossible with me as the heroic super-agent – but in reality it was just bloody stupid and could have got me expelled. I was on a bit of a knife edge at the time and I could have tipped over the wrong way and become a right little thug. Many others did.

Mum eventually got a job as secretary at the school which helped sharpen up my good behaviour, and by this time she had also settled down with a new partner – Brendan – who became my quasi-stepfather. We never had a father-and-son relationship but Brendan was sound and was totally supportive of everything my mum and I did. They produced a son of their own, Ryan – my half-brother – who is seven years younger than me and with whom I have always got on. Until Mum and Brendan split up in my late teens that was the family unit and we rubbed along fine.

Football was my first passion – we used to spend every daylight hour kicking a ball around outside the flats – but I had a serious dilemma. I was an Arsenal fanatic but all my mates supported the enemy – Spurs. I enjoyed their friendship and didn't fancy going up to Highbury on my own when I could afford it so I started going to White Hart Lane with them.

This is not normal behaviour at all and I started to develop a split personality – an Arsenal diehard who nonetheless listed Gary Lineker and Paul Gascoigne as his football idols and had the posters in his bedroom to prove it. I even adopted Gazza's eccentric hairstyles, a harbinger of things to come, perhaps, as I was later to become well known in cycling circles for my own 'interesting' hair.

Poor Gary Lineker. We started to stalk him, for want of a better word. We discovered where he lived down Abbey Road and used to hang around behind bushes and dustbins like paparazzi. Once I bumped into him after he nipped out to get a couple of pints of milk and another time I got really bold and went up to his front door and rang the bell. His then wife Michelle opened the door and didn't seem at all phased when I asked if Gary was in. She reached over to a pile of postcard photos signed by the great man that she kept just inside the door and gave me a couple. Somehow I got the impression I wasn't the first nutter she had dealt with trying to knock down her front door wanting to meet her husband.

But then came the parting of the ways. I fell in love with cycling. I had spent the entire summer of 1992 down at the West Ham Soccer School at East Ham, which, if nothing else, kept me out of Mum's hair for six weeks. I fancied myself as a goalkeeper and I was okay – by no means out of my depth – and despite being an Arsenal fan who went to Spurs home games I wanted to be Peter Shilton, who played for neither team. But then one evening I was enjoying a final kick-about with the lads outside the flats when Mum frantically called me in and said there was something I needed to watch on the TV.

I reluctantly trooped off but soon shelved all thoughts about football as I sat in front of the TV and watched Chris Boardman getting ready to tackle Jens Lehmann from Germany in the final of the 4 km pursuit at the Barcelona Olympics. Mum was talking away – 'This was one of the events your father was very good at, it's the Blue Riband event of track cycling, it's the race that all the best riders like to win' – so I sat down and was transfixed as Chris cruised around on that beautiful, specially produced, 'space age' Lotus bike of his. He and the bike seemed from another planet.

Bloody hell, this was fantastic. I got a real buzz from watching Chris win his gold medal – 12 years later he helped me to do exactly the same in Beijing – and the next night I abandoned the football again to watch the action from the athletics track. This time it was Linford Christie racing to gold in the 100 m and Sally Gunnell doing exactly the same in the 400 m hurdles. Fantastic, and not just the pure sport. Again I loved the theatre of it all – the build-up, the preparations, officials running around, Linford going into the zone and prowling around, refusing to acknowledge anybody and making everybody wait on their marks until he, the great man, was ready to race. The flash of cameras as the gun went, the press and media interviews afterwards and the medal ceremonies with the Union Jack going up the pole and everybody trying not to cry. It was the entire package that mesmerised me.

Then, a couple of days later, came Redgrave and Pinsent in the rowing and another gold for Britain. Wow! It wasn't just cycling I had fallen in love with, it was the Olympics itself and the sheer glory and achievement of trying to win medals for Britain. I used to almost get sick with the excitement and nerves of watching the British competitors line up. That week or so in front of the TV watching the pictures from Barcelona changed my life, and I hope there are kids out there today who still get as excited about sport and competing for your country as I did. We are in serious trouble if there aren't. After each British gold I used to get my old bike out and go charging around the flats, working off my excitement. This was what I wanted to do. Ride a bike and win medals for Britain.

I went down the Serpentine in Hyde Park – the nearest place where you could race around on your bike on closed roads, which was great – and a little bit of local knowledge gleaned then did no harm 15 years later when the Tour de France prologue used part of that exact same route – but I had to find a permanent base for my sport.

My mum picked up on this new-found enthusiasm straight away – in fact I suspect she had half planned it, or at least hoped for something to really fire me up and give me a chance of bettering myself. I wasn't going to achieve that by studying, we both knew that, and she clearly wasn't convinced by my abilities as a footballer – she used to point out frequently how few youngsters actually made it to the top. Which is actually excellent advice but not at all what the next Peter Shilton wanted to hear.

But she was full-on in her support of my cycling from day one, which is interesting seeing how much heartache the sport had given her in her relationship with Garry. Being Mum she immediately wrote to the British Cycling Federation requesting information as to the nearest cycle club and track. She was on my case with a vengeance.

They pointed me in the general direction of the old Hayes bypass, which was a curious unused bit of dual carriageway waiting to be completed while the politicians made up their minds as to whether it was really necessary, or even if there was actually enough money to complete it. In the meantime a bike club had been formed there.

Mum learned that there was something called the West London Challenge 92 being held there so we rocked up and I raced with my old Halfords bike – all cables and toe-clips – in old trainers and an ancient cycling hat of Garry's, one of those prehistoric hairnet things that Mum had found in Grandad's shed. I finished way down the field in the 3-mile handicap but the next Tuesday we turned up again and this time I finished third in the handicap. 'That will get you a mention in *Cycling Weekly*,' said Mum knowingly, having spent much of her early years collecting clippings for Garry. She still has that first ever press mention somewhere, along with everything else that has ever appeared in the press about me.

The die was cast. At one of the meetings at Hayes my mum spotted Stuart Benstead, the guy who had helped Garry come over from Australia. Mum approached him and pointed me out as Garry Wiggins's son. The autumn was approaching and Stuart suggested I should train and race at Herne Hill, where Garry had cut his teeth in the late 1970s. During the winter months the Archer Road Club also had a club night on Fridays, when they used to sit around in the sixth-form room of a local school on

Ealing Common Broadway to discuss cycling and plan weekend runs and the like. It was a bit of a talking shop really, but it was cool and I made every effort to attend. I was totally smitten by my new-found love. Cycling was going to be my road to success and I don't write that retrospectively. I was dreaming the dream even then.

—

Chapter Four

Early success

My life was on track but it wasn't long before I had my first bad crash on a bike. Strangely it proved a blessing in disguise, not that it felt that way at the time. It was pitch black one Friday night late in the autumn of 1992 and I, aged 12, was determined to cycle across town for the club meet at Ealing Common Broadway, because that was what you did when you were a proper cyclist. Mum, for all her support, wasn't keen and we had a blazing row which resulted in me stomping out and heading off without her consent. I had no cycling gear, was wearing a pair of Mum's leggings to keep warm, and headed out into the Friday night rush-hour traffic with a strop on. I was in the Shepherd's Bush area when I went around a bus and a woman driving a car went to turn right into Kwick Fit and smashed straight into me. She clearly hadn't seen me. I went over the top of the car, hit the ground hard and was knocked unconscious. I had also broken my collar bone and was rushed off to a hospital next to Wormwood Scrubs, as I remember. As you do when you are dazed, my first thought when I came around was whether I could still make it to the club night, but I was in no state to go anywhere. Mum arrived after a few frantic calls to Grandad's flat and she was surprisingly good and understanding about everything. Eventually I was let out and went home to lick my wounds.

It's an ill wind that blows nobody any good, as I was soon to discover. Mum was incensed at the carelessness of the woman driver and decided, in her usual determined way, to sue her and get some compensation for her poor battered boy. It involved all sorts of tests and X-rays at Harley Street and a mountain of correspondence on her part, but eventually – a year later – I was awarded £1700 compensation. I gave mum £700 to thank her for all her help and the rest I used to buy my first proper racing bike.

In the meantime – while I dreamed of getting the money and my bike – I was cutting my teeth down at Herne Hill and beyond. I was a busy boy. On Sundays when the weather was better a group of us would train down at the track with Russell Williams, or I would meet another coach, Stan Knight, at Acton Station and we would cycle out to Burnham Beeches to get some road miles in my legs. Stan must have been 70-odd but was a complete cycling nut who was happy to do his bit to encourage a young hopeful. Monday night was the track league down at Herne Hill and I used to compete in all sorts but I particularly remember the U16 Handicap ten-lap points races everybody used to enter.

By Tuesday we switched to Crystal Palace and the park around the national sports centre and athletics stadium where they used to hold road races on the closed road around the complex. I wasn't any good on the roads at this time – no real strength in my long legs – but it was all good conditioning work. Running me around was a massive commitment for Mum and Brendan, who used to finish work as a panel beater at tea-time and immediately start ferrying me around south London. It is only now, as a father myself, that I realise the effort they put in.

It was an enjoyable summer and the icing on the cake was when the accident money eventually came through and I set out in October to buy my new bike. Those of you who have done the same will appreciate the rising excitement. By coincidence I had won a regional pool competition down at Pontin's on Camber Sands and had been invited up to Pontin's at Prestatyn with the family to play in the national final. All those misspent hours down the Legion had paid off. I got knocked out in the second round but the supreme moment was calling into Ribble Cycles on the way home and buying my first racing bike. No more tractor tyres and comical cables that could hold up the Forth Bridge. The Real McCoy, as befits one who intended to make cycling his life!

The year 1994 saw me learning my craft. I raced a lot and won regularly locally but was a year too young really to compete nationally at juvenile level. I still went up to the British Championships at Leicester though, just for the experience, and loved every moment. Again it was the scene and setting I loved. Announcements on the tannoy that you can't really understand, official programmes with your name and club in, proper medal ceremonies, officials walking around importantly in uniform, time-keepers hunched up by their table comparing sheets and looking stressed, one or two journalists scurrying around, old copies of *Cycling Weekly* on their stand to leaf through. I felt very at home in this cycling family. I came tenth and fifteenth in the Schoolboys' Scratch and points race, and surprised myself with a seventh in the sprint, but I was there to soak it all in and generally enjoy, which I did.

By that winter I was training hard, had started to watch my diet and was already dreaming of championships and making money from this sport. I had quickly gone through the stage when you dip your toe in the water and are just larking about. I was in this sport for real and intended to be a major success. I loved the physical sensation of riding a bike and the entire ambience of the sport, but I also intended to make this love affair with cycling give me a professional career and pay the bills. That was my mindset from the start.

The following year I dominated locally and was pretty confident and cocky when I travelled to the British Championships, which were being held this time at Manchester, at the spanking new velodrome that had been opened the previous year. It didn't start well at all – I got knocked out of the sprint, bombed in the 500 m time-trial, but then against the odds I took the points title. I was a British schoolboy champion for the first time, although the schoolboy bit was inappropriate really. Nobody at school even knew I was into bikes, let alone took an active role in encouraging me. I had done this on my own, with the help of my family and the Archer Road Club. It was tempting to try to win the pursuit title the following day but I also had my eyes on the Road Race Championship which was being held at Southport a few days later. I withdrew and was rewarded with a second place behind Gareth Hewitt.

Happy days. I returned to Herne Hill and enjoyed strutting around a bit – racing in my British champion's jersey. I started competing against a few seniors – at Herne Hill and at the Reading Track League – and by the end of the year, at the age of 15, I had claimed a win in the 20 km open scratch race at Reading. From this moment I never doubted I was going to make it. Some would call it arrogance, I would term it self-belief and if you don't have that as part of your make-up you probably won't make it. You don't have to ram it down everybody's throat but you have to believe, deep down inside, that you are the best and that you are going right to the top no matter what gets thrown at you.

The year 1996 hoved into view. Could I step up and compete regularly as a 16-year-old against the best juniors in the country? Was my self-belief that strong? I was the top dog at my local tracks but the British Championships – back at Leicester again – were going to be tough. Despite my slightly cocky – or gauche – exterior

I was nervous, but was delighted to win the 1 km time-trial (kilo), take silver in the sprint and bronze in the points. The local press latched on to me and I thought I was it. Three national medals – including one gold – and two more years to go as a junior.

The British selectors had also noticed my achievement and invited me up to Manchester for training weekends with the national junior squad. I couldn't get enough. I trained hard and raced hard. I ate, drank and lived cycling. At home I became a complete cycling recluse – I wasn't bothered with girls or going down to the football with mates or keeping in touch with friends at school. I was totally absorbed with the sport and aiming for a very big year indeed in 1997.

And that's exactly what happened. I was so focused on a cycling career that any thoughts of completing my education were abandoned. After leaving school I bizarrely had one unlikely spell working as a trainee carpenter down at the plush Lanesborough Hotel in London. That was always destined to end in tears and I then embarked on a BTEC foundation course in business studies, but it was getting in the way of my cycling. Things came to a head in January 1997 when I absented myself for a week to compete for Great Britain in Denmark and was chucked off the course when I returned. That was fine by me; in truth I had probably been trying to engineer that situation anyway.

The racing year started with a win in the Peter Buckley Junior Road Race series, and I went on to claim a grand slam of titles at the British Junior Track Championships – pursuit, points, scratch and kilo. This was pretty rare, although Phil West, a super-talented young rider from Middlesbrough, had pulled off the same quartet of victories the previous year. Great things were predicted for him and I was very proud to equal his record. I couldn't get enough cycling and am glad also that I hadn't started to specialise at this stage. I gave every event and discipline my all and picked up lots of experience and tricks of the trade along the way, as well as developing an all-round cycling fitness. I could turn my hand to most things and that versatility has served me well throughout my senior career.

All of which led to selection later that year for Great Britain in the World Junior Championships in Cape Town. This was a big thing in all respects – Great Britain rarely even sent competitors to the junior Worlds at the time, so the decision to send me, as a first year junior, was a big honour. I had never even been out of the country and suddenly there I was heading for post-apartheid South Africa and its most spectacular city. It was the start of my international career proper and a few riders I have regularly competed against in subsequent years were also flexing their muscles, such as those tough Aussies Graeme Brown and Michael Rogers. The latter – who was to become a colleague at Team Columbia – was an outstanding junior on the track and he won two gold medals in South Africa – in the points race and Team Pursuit – and he also took a silver in the Individual Pursuit as I recall. I was on my own as a competitor and felt a little bit overawed but did okay. I finished 16th in the pursuit, which I didn't really consider my event at the time, and took a very pleasing fourth in the points race, missing bronze by one point. It was the nearest GB had got to a medal at the World Juniors for an age and my efforts were well received.

Even more success followed in 1998, I was on a roll. I trained like a dog that winter. Shaun Bannister – one of the best coaches locally – had taken over my training and cycling had consumed me totally. I trained like a professional, watched my diet closely and read up on everything to do with performance and endurance training. I was supremely confident as I collected my GB kit to fly out to Havana for the World Juniors, but got a rude surprise as I tried to acclimatise to the 36-degree heat and debilitating humidity. This was a new set of problems and to start with I was disorientated and struggled.

Finishing fourth again in the points was a massive disappointment and a bit of a wake-up call – I was a year older and fitter than 12 months before, yet I had been unable to improve on my placing – and I fumed for a while before the GB management suggested that, as I was there and it had cost a fair bit to get me over to Cuba, I might as well ride in the Individual Pursuit, which at that age group is over 3 km, or 12 laps of a standard 250 m track. I shrugged without any great enthusiasm. Why not?

I was relaxed to say the least, there was no tension in my body, it wasn't quite as hot as it had been and suddenly I really got the bike moving smoothly. It felt great and before I knew it I had won the bloody title, a Junior World champion at 18 and the first Junior World title holder from Great Britain in decades. I couldn't stop laughing to myself, but I was intensely proud to pull on the rainbow shirt that denotes a World champion and listen to the national anthem on the podium. I had arrived. Six years after that crash on the Uxbridge Road that miserable night I was a world champion.

Around this time I felt invincible. The week after I came back from Cuba I took another four titles at the Nationals and then took the 25 km time-trial. As a result of this I was drafted into the senior England squad for the Commonwealth Games in Kuala Lumpur in Malaysia, which was even hotter and steamier than Havana, but I was well acclimatised and rode strongly. I finished fourth in the Individual Pursuit – 4 km at senior level – after losing to a red-hot Bradley McGee in the semi-finals – and was then a member of the England quartet that took silver in the Team Pursuit, my first senior medal.

I was definitely on my way and it was my good fortune – and

that of every elite sportsman and woman of my age in this country for that matter – that at this precise time in our sporting history Lottery funding began to kick in. On the back of my performances in Cuba and Malaysia I was put on a full Category A grant of nearly £20,000 a year, which took all the financial worries out of my life and provided a complete vindication for all the time and effort I had put into my cycling career. Of course I felt pretty pleased with myself. I would be in the local Tesco's and see contemporaries from school – who were academically much brighter than me – bored to distraction working on the counters or stacking goods. I was 18, had already been to Cape Town, Havana and Kuala Lumpur. I had money in the bank and a secure income. Everything had come together in a rush. I was on my way.

Chapter Five

—

Heading for Sydney

The moment I returned from the Commonwealth Games with my silver medal I started thinking about the Sydney Olympics. Just about every sportsman in Britain did. The Atlanta Games had been a disaster for Great Britain – just one gold medal from the ever reliable Steve Redgrave and Matt Pinsent – but the Lottery funding had arrived soon after and there was a feeling that, for the first time in decades, we would be competing on a level playing field. To be honest, most competitors believed it would be Athens in 2004 before the Lottery effect really kicked in with big medals across the board, but we were determined to make a much improved showing and show the public what they were getting for their money so to speak.

Track cycling, a comparatively small but well-established Olympic sport, was at the forefront of this. Given investment in facilities, proper talent identification and scientific coaching, those at the top quickly realised that the extra funding could quickly reap rewards, sooner rather than later. In the years that have followed track cycling has become an object lesson on how to run and optimise the potential of a small sport.

Aside from this urgent need to improve Britain's medal haul, my biggest motivation was still overwhelmingly that I had fallen in love with the Olympics in 1992 and simply wanted to be there in Australia. I had to be involved in Sydney – wear the national colours at the Olympics – and then I could finally turn my full attention to the road and become a Tour de France rider. That was still the master plan. It was all written on tablets of stone.

So 1999 was a tough and testing year, deliberately so. I trained with the GB pursuit squad throughout, starting with a camp in Australia and then back on the track at Manchester, I rode the British Pru Tour – the old Tour of Britain which used to be called the Milk Race and then the Kellogg's – that summer and finished it, which was a big boost to morale. I was never going to threaten winner Marc Wauters from Rabobank but I got around fine and on the road this was a level above any I had raced at before. It was brilliantly organised and had the feel of a big 'Tour'.

Onwards and upwards, and we started concentrating on the World Tracks in Berlin and the GB squad of myself, Paul Manning, Rob Hayles, Bryan Steele and Matt Illingworth. We came fifth, our best performance for a while, and I rode strongly to cement my place, barring injury, in Sydney. I also teamed up with Rob Hayles in the Madison and achieved a credible tenth in a bloody hard race. Enjoyable though.

The Madison is probably the most fun you can have on a bike on a track and of course it was the event that Garry specialised in, so I assumed it was in the genes and I would excel without any problems. I definitely had an aptitude for the Madison but I was very inexperienced at that level so was glad to have Rob show me the ropes. Tenth was good enough to qualify us for the Olympic Madison, which was good news as well, another string to my bow.

Having qualified for the Sydney Madison it made sense to race a bit on the Sixes circuit that winter – Ghent, Zurich, Berlin – a strange case of history repeating itself as I followed Garry's footsteps 13 years after he had last been seen on the tracks of Europe. I started to hear all the old stories – some of them a little unsavoury – and lots of the back-up staff remembered him well and were curious as to how his son would do. Riding in those races was an eye-opener, and a valuable insight into the tough macho world in which he had existed.

The new millennium dawned and I was full of hope: 1999 had been a solid year of achievement and, barring an accident, I was going to the Olympics. After the new year's toasts it was on the plane to Australia the next day and another massive six-week block of training to lay the foundations for the pursuit squad. We moved together as one that year – Paul Manning, with whom I have always been particular friends, Chris Newton, who had come into the squad, Bryan Steele, Rob Hayles and myself. Rob was also going to do the Individual Pursuit. Simon Jones was coaching us and masterminded the entire operation.

First, though, I had to overcome a certain local difficulty. Travelling to Manchester by train with my bike and bags for national training was becoming a pain and embarrassing for a 20-year-old tyro who wanted to appear cool at all times. Everybody else arrived in style by car and I was determined to do likewise. Unfortunately I had failed my driving test, although I blamed the instructor, who, it seemed to me, had deliberately set up his car with a sticky clutch to ensure lots of failures and, presumably, more lessons as punters returned to practise for their retakes. That's my excuse anyway.

When I asked to drive Nan's car I was amazed to find out how easy it was to drive a normal car (with or without a properly adjusted clutch!) and, with a two-week camp beckoning in Manchester, the temptation was just too great. I 'borrowed' the car, drove at a sedate 60 mph in the slow lane all the way up the motorway to Manchester and sauntered around Manchester in third gear for the next fortnight. I didn't have a licence and of course I wasn't insured. Not something I am particularly proud of in retrospect. Mum was livid and, after I retook and passed my test, Grandad made me feel even worse by insisting on paying the £1000 deposit on a new car he had always promised me since I was a toddler. I could have well afforded it myself but he was adamant. I suppose it was a kind of rites of passage moment he wanted to mark. Whatever, it was very generous.

It was a pretty shameful episode but that's how focused I was on Sydney. Absolutely nothing else mattered and, after a series of gruelling road races in Belgium to get the final conditioning into our legs, the big day was eventually upon us. We were all fitted out for our official BOA uniforms – I love all that kind of patriotic stuff – and suddenly, after flying for a day or more, I found myself waking up at the holding camp on the Sunshine coast outside Brisbane. There could not have been a more excited and proud 20-year-old in the world of sport.

We put the final touches to our preparations and then it was off down to Sydney. Then the enormity of it finally hit me and for a few days I became very nervous and agitated. It was bad enough strolling around the British quarters and bumping into Steve Redgrave and Matt Pinsent – my all-time sporting inspirations – but then, when I stepped out into the village, I was blown away by the vast array of household names. I had to get my head together quickly, this was all too much.

Luckily, we were quickly into competition on the first Monday of the Games and as a pursuit squad we had decided not to attend the opening ceremony – from my point of view it could have been one star-spotting fest too many. You start clocking all the world-famous names milling around and that gets you wondering what on earth you are doing there! We had the heats of the Team Pursuit to nail down and had come too far as a squad in the last 18 months to freeze on the day.

We wanted to give a good account of ourselves and, in any

case, Jason Queally had already set the tone for the British team – not just the cyclists but the entire GB Olympic squad – by grabbing a superb gold medal in the Kilo on the opening night. I sometimes think British sport generally has not looked back since Jason's dash for glory that night. In just over a minute he seemed to bury all the disappointments of Atlanta and show to the world that a new, confident breed of Brit had entered the sporting arena.

But it was our turn now and we tore into the competition to qualify fastest with a 4 mins 4.030 secs to break the Olympic record, albeit only temporarily. After a few whoops and shrieks, we beat a retreat to the village to quieten down and get our race heads on for the quarter-finals that night. An Olympic quarter-final – this was getting weird and a little scary. My dream was beginning to come true. This wasn't meant to be happening to people like me.

That evening we beat the Dutch comfortably enough and now I was looking at a semi-final against the crack Ukraine outfit the following day. They did us in the semi-final, riding an outstanding then world record of 4 mins 00.720 secs, with Great Britain just over two seconds behind with another British record. We fought like dogs but were outclassed in that race; but we still fancied our chances against France, a team we had consistently beaten, in the bronze medal race-off.

We had, however, pretty much taken it to the limit in our three races to give ourselves a chance of medalling, so we took the tactical decision to bring in the fresher legs of Chris Newton and Bryan Steele for the ride-off after great contributions from Rob Hayles and Jonny Clay when we had gone so fast but lost to the Ukrainians. It paid off handsomely: we were always in charge and broke the British record for a third time with a very swift 4 mins 1.979 secs. The Ukrainians, incidentally, had left their best race on the track and failed to get on terms with Germany in the final, and the Germans became the first team ever to come in under four minutes, with a cracking time of 3 mins 59.710 secs.

The excitement of that bronze medal still remains one of the highlights of my career, right up there with World and Olympic golds. It was the novelty of it all and just being part of that great Sydney buzz which made for one of the greatest Olympics on record. To be there competing was fantastic, to actually help claim a medal for Britain was unbelievable. I distinctly remember standing on the podium with the boys and thinking that if I stopped now and packed it up I would be very happy. Many superb cyclists have raced for a decade or more and never won an Olympic medal.

A couple of days later I nearly had another bronze medal to celebrate. I was riding with Rob Hayles in the Madison and all our hard work on the tough Six Day circuit the previous winter seemed to have paid off when we were approaching the latter stages of the 240 laps in third place and looking good. Unfortunately, Rob then suffered one of those mishaps that makes the Madison so frustrating and exciting. The Austrians – not really in medal contention – messed up a change and crashed into the Spanish rider, who then crashed into Rob who was sent sprawling. No medal, although I managed to hang on and finish in the pack to ensure fourth spot.

It completed an unlucky Games for Rob, who just missed out on bronze to Brad McGee in the Individual Pursuit after a fine ride and then faced the prospect of not being awarded a medal in the Team Pursuit after he and Jonny Clay had been rested for the final. Happily, the authorities intervened on that one and ensured that everybody who had ridden in either the semi-final or final got their appropriate gong.

Once all the emotion concerning the medal and the podium

had died down, not to mention the endless round of parties that followed at various fabulous venues across Sydney, I had a chance to radically reassess my career. The Olympics, a little to my surprise, had usurped my sporting ambitions. My master plan – to move seamlessly on after Sydney and pursue glory for the next decade on the road, and in particular in the Tour de France – was not looking so black and white. Sydney could never be just a glorious one-off – I could never walk away from the possibility of representing GB at the Olympics. Athens had to become my focus and, although the bronze was bloody marvellous, in the sober light of day I soon admitted to myself that I wanted much more.

I was deluding myself to think a bronze medal was enough to satisfy me. That was a momentary thought on an elated and confusing evening. What I really wanted from life was an Olympic gold medal around my neck. And, if possible, more than one. With the rest of you I had cheered Redgrave and Pinsent on in the Coxless Four and caught a sense of what these truly great competitors were all about and how much it meant to them – the pride and dedication they put into their sport and representing their country at the Olympics.

I don't have sporting heroes as such – if you put individuals on a pedestal you are saying that you can't emulate them and you are also giving yourself a get-out clause and excuse for failure. Only 'special people' with 'God given' talent or extraordinary capabilities can achieve such things. That is a nonsense. We can all 'achieve' if the motivation and mindset is right. But I do have a few sportsmen I find inspiring and role models in how they conduct themselves, and at the very top of my relatively small personal list are Steve Redgrave and Matt Pinsent. Their achievements will be proudly talked about in 100 years' time. That's an incredible sporting legacy to leave.

—

Chapter Six

'Hello, I am Garry Wiggins, I am your father'

n the build-up to the Sydney Olympics I had not allowed anything to derail my efforts to earn selection and then compete for a medal, but it would be untrue to say life was devoid of all dramatic episodes en route. As you have probably guessed these tended to revolve around my father.

One morning in 1997 the phone rang – we had a phone at home by then – and, suspecting nothing unusual, I picked up the receiver. It was a Garry Wiggins phoning from Australia. I hadn't seen or heard from him since our afternoon at London Zoo in January 1983, when that picture was taken of us together feeding the ducks by the lake. Not that I remember the day, the photo was all I had. Since then nothing – and no effort whatsoever to assist in any way with my upbringing, even when he was making good money in the 1980s at the Six Dayers and driving around Bremen with his blonde girlfriend in a new Mercedes bought with his winnings.

Tales of his racing exploits had undoubtedly helped feed my interest in cycling, although the true inspiration was that Olympic gold medal won by Chris Boardman in Barcelona. I also had a few other pictures of Garry that Mum had given me, but I felt absolutely no emotional attachment or connection to him.

My family was Mum and my grandparents, my aunts and Ryan

my half-brother. I also had respect for Brendan, and appreciated the efforts he had made to support me and encourage my love of cycling, even though I never saw him as a substitute father and his relationship with Mum had recently foundered.

So Garry phoned and, after introducing himself, didn't waste time with small talk. He was in a mess and very tearful and just hit me with everything on the emotional front. He was sorry how he had treated Mum, sorry he had run out on us, sorry he had ignored us and just sorry for everything. If he could he would turn back the clock and change it all.

He was sorry? Nothing for 14 years, not even a bloody Christmas card, and now this. I wasn't wildly impressed and acted cool, which wasn't that difficult because I was cool. I felt nothing for this stranger at the end of the phone. And anyway, I was 17 and you just do act cool when you are 17; it is adults who are emotional basket cases and can't handle stuff. That was my attitude anyway.

So I just nattered away, wondering where this phone call was going: 'It was fine, no problem,' I said. 'My mum told me about you although we weren't sure if you were still alive any more because, well to be honest, we never hear from you. What is done is done. No use crying over spilt milk. We have all moved on now and life is good and I am hoping to make a career as a cyclist, road and track. I've won a few national junior titles and am beginning to take training seriously. Lottery funding is beginning to come in and apparently we will be able to make a decent living from being a GB team member. That is my aim, I want to break into the GB squad and one day be selected for the Olympics and win a gold medal just like Chris Boardman. How's life with you, Garry? Good I hope?'

I can't imagine any of this made Garry feel a whole load better, but at least our conversation wasn't unfriendly and when eventually we said our goodbyes, we agreed to keep in touch – which for a couple of years is exactly what we did, probably on a fortnightly basis, certainly at least once a month. He was 12,000 miles way and couldn't harm us from down there, and actually he sometimes didn't sound too bad on the phone. Garry, I now appreciate, was going through a rare stable period in his life. He had married a lady called Fiona and they had had a daughter, Madison, the previous year. He was employed as a removals man and Fiona had persuaded him that it really was time he started to get to grips with his chaotic past and at least make contact with myself and Shannon, if not our respective mothers.

We struck up a low-level friendship and of course were happy to talk 'bikes' together, although he never let you forget what a great rider he had been on the Six Day circuit back in the old days. The conversation always seemed to work its way back to that. Still, he wouldn't be the only dad like that, would he? He was tolerable and we must have been getting on pretty well because I distinctly remember phoning him in a state of excitement after winning the pursuit gold medal at the World Juniors in Cuba in 1998.

By January 1999 I was a full-time Lottery-funded professional cyclist and by chance I was out in Australia at a GB training camp when an unexpected call came from Garry. Could I find a way of breaking off for a day to meet him for a special lunch at St Kilda, a distinctive rambling Victorian seaside resort and suburb of Melbourne, which you can reach on the trams from the city centre. Loads of little relaxing cafés and restaurants, just what the doctor ordered. It used to be the city's red light district but now it is very chic and Garry sounded very keen.

Why not? Sounded interesting. So I went along to what was a bizarrely memorable and unique lunch, even though it was only in a modest pizza joint just off the famous Esplanade. For the first and only time Garry Wiggins – so called Aussie tough nut, itinerant cyclist, absentee father, disappearing husband – sat down to break bread with his three children by three different wives. Amidst the clatter of other normal families on holiday there sat the four of us – Garry, Shannon, myself and little Madison meeting each other for the first time. Complete and utter strangers related only by blood. It was utterly surreal – you could write a play about it but it would get too complicated and nobody would believe you.

Garry was not in good shape. He was beginning to fight with Fiona by now, and his latest marriage was heading for the rocks. He was back drinking heavily but he just about held things together for the lunch. You could sense trouble ahead, however. A few months earlier he had started this entire reconciliation process by getting in touch with Shannon on the phone – and explained his desire for this family reunion – but that relationship was already going sour again. Shannon was engaged to be married and Garry, on the strength of the briefest of acquaintances with his daughter, was already demanding that he be the one who give her away. She was horrified at the thought – as with me, Garry had played absolutely no part in her life – and sure enough they fell out again in the coming months as he continued to insist that he play the role of her father at the marriage. Shannon pointblank refused and that was that. I don't blame her for one second.

It was all extremely odd but I was consciously trying to take it in my stride and act cool at the pizza restaurant. I reasoned that if you tried to go into this too deep you would end up an emotional mess like Garry. None of this was my doing and the responsibility to sort the mess out was not mine. And in any case I was in a bubble. I had just got on the Lottery scheme and I was already aiming for the Sydney Olympics, in fact that is why I was down in Australia in the first place on the GB training camp. I simply refused to allow this totally bizarre and emotionally loaded occasion to unsettle me. In denial, perhaps, but I prefer to call it looking after number one. Too many lives had already been decimated and I had no intention of becoming another victim.

At one stage, when Garry trooped off to the gents, a bewildered Shannon started shaking her head: 'How do you feel about all this? Are you okay with this, Brad? It's just too strange for words, I can't get my head around it.' It was freaking Shannon but I just didn't feel like that. I was free of any emotional attachment to this man. At this first meeting I felt much more of a bond with my sisters – victims of this situation like me – and wondered what they had been going through over the years, particularly Shannon, who has shared much the same experience as me.

Eventually we broke up and went our separate ways, promising to keep in touch, as you do. Looking back I realise that probably Garry had wanted much more from the lunch, something akin to a formal reconciliation and an agreement for us to all put the past behind us and behave much more like a family. In that case he would have been sorely disappointed. Did he really expect me and Shannon just to forgive him everything and embrace him? His life appeared to go right off the rails again soon after.

The following January – 2000, Olympic year – Great Britain were again heading 'down under' for their winter training camp and this time, having thought long and hard and possibly mellowed a little since that first meeting, I decided to be proactive and phoned Garry to say I would be willing to come out three weeks in advance of the camp and stay with him to really make an effort to get to know him. Father-and-son bonding and all that. I was very uneasy at the prospect but, after the meeting in St Kilda and his belated arrival in my life, I had eventually come to the conclusion that it was probably something I needed to do or I might regret it for the rest of my life. From the brief encounter the year before I knew I could never accept him as a father, but maybe we could be proper mates.

It was a disaster. He was disintegrating fast. Garry had started using his fists again and he and Fiona had finally split up for good; he was only getting to see Madison at weekends, which understandably depressed him. He was drinking for Australia and, bloody hell, could he put the grog away. He rarely got slobbering, falling-over drunk, but at a certain point he suddenly underwent a massive personality change and became a nasty, threatening drunk who went looking for trouble. I don't think he ever remembered much of his conduct the following day. He was still just about holding down his job with the removals company at this stage, but most of his days seemed to consist of buying a couple of crates of VBs, dragging them back to his 'unit' and steadily drinking himself into an angry stupor.

Before he got completely bladdered we would enjoy watching a couple of boxing videos – all the great Ali fights, Sugar Ray Leonard, Marvin Hagler. He really knew his stuff and we would swap opinions and banter. At that time boxing was a big passion of mine and, apart from cycling, it was one of the few subjects he could ever engage over and have a proper conversation about. But once he tipped over the edge – and because he had no control that would be virtually every night – all the old anger and self-disgust would come pouring out, over and over again. And the contempt for the people who had done so much to help him and had loved him. He would go into a rage and I would just sit there and wait for it to die down.

In retrospect, he was probably clinically depressed – I was just 19 and wasn't really sure about these things. And he wasn't the sort of guy I could just go up to and say, 'Garry, you're depressed and you badly need medical help.' He wouldn't have taken that from his 19-year-old 'Pommie' son. And if he had already acknowledged the problem privately and was on medication, he certainly shouldn't have been pouring beer down his throat all night. I tried to entice him out on a bike again, and we did manage it once for a short spin, but he was clearly unwell and unfit.

One afternoon, Garry came to a big Aussie track meeting with me. I had entered the Madison for a bit of fun, to add some variety to my training before the GB camp. He hadn't been down to any track for a decade or more – he had been something of a recluse as far as cycling was concerned and turned his back on everybody – and his arrival became a huge event and caused much excitement. They announced his presence on the stadium tannoy and old cronies were soon forming a queue at the bar to buy him a few drinks. By the end of my race – we finished a very credible second – he was surrounded by a pile of 'tinnies', absolutely hammered and intent on slagging me off in front of everybody and telling me what I had done wrong and how he would have done it differently and won. 'You got it all wrong, sunshine, your old dad would have won, Brad. No worries. We used to beat everybody in Europe. I was champion of Europe. Did I ever tell you that, Brad? We were the best, nobody could bloody touch us.'

I was beginning to seriously dislike this man but had vowed to stick out the three weeks, like I said I would, in the hope that he might 'come good' and I might see the nice generous side that other people occasionally talked about. I waited in vain. When it came to leaving time he started crying again and sobbed that he wanted to make up for the last 20 years and be my father. He wanted me to be his son.

I had to swallow hard and tell him exactly how it was. I didn't want any of this, I didn't want to be his son. Let's just leave it as it was. We could keep in touch and stay friendly but we were way too far down the line for anything like a normal father/son relationship to develop. It was just too late, Garry. We parted on those terms.

Although the Olympics were in Sydney he made no effort to attend, although we did speak briefly on the phone after I won a bronze medal in the Team Pursuit. After the Olympics, when I got home, he suddenly started phoning up again, this time in the middle of the night, invariably drunk and in very bad humour. This man was haunting me and I consciously started to withdraw from him. I couldn't take it any more. There was also a good deal of jealousy, or perhaps envy is a slightly kinder word. I was actually living his dream – at the age of 20 I was already earning a decent living from cycling, travelling the world with my sport, a junior world champion who had won senior Commonwealth and Olympic medals before the age of 21. And, what's more, what probably hurt more than anything, I had done it all without his help and assistance. He might have been a big shot in his day and a bit of legend among his friends, but I had done it all without him. It must have stirred up all kinds of emotions within him and by 2001 he had got the message and we weren't talking. I didn't take his calls and gradually he stopped ringing. We were back to square one.

—

Chapter Seven

Team on the run

was on a high from Sydney and the cycling world seemed my oyster, but life was about to become very interesting indeed, and a little fraught. The assumption that I would switch to the road with instant success before effortlessly switching back to the track whenever I fancied was wrong. Everything was to prove much more complicated than that. At the time, late November 2000, joining the Linda McCartney Pro Cycling team seemed the most important thing in my life and the subsequent folding of that team seemed a disaster, although looking back now it was a smallish diversion that didn't sidetrack me too much. I know now that cycling teams come and go, money men come and go, contracts are not always fully honoured, riders and management fall out, and that despite everything the sport continues and we move forward. Cycling has always had more than its fair share of behind-the-scenes chicanery and madness.

Initially it was all good. I could do everything and, although my major long-term goal was now the four-yearly Olympics, I had a couple of years to indulge my road-racing objectives. The Linda McCartney team seemed the answer to all my prayers and it needed little persuasion from their Directeur Sportif Sean Yates – one of the biggest ever names in British cycling – to get me on board once the dust had settled when I got back from Australia.

The origins and the ethos of the team were British, with a maverick British would-be entrepreneur Julian Clark putting forward the idea back in 1997 that the newly created Linda McCartney Vegetarian Foods should sponsor a team of vegetarian cyclists around Europe, hopefully ending up with invitations to compete in the Giro D'Italia and Tour de France. Against all the odds, it seemed to be working in spectacular fashion.

Despite Linda McCartney's death in the first year of the project following her battle with cancer, Paul McCartney seemed to show a continued interest and of course his name was a great draw. Even if the McCartney organisation didn't put huge sums into the team – that remains a subject of much debate about which I know nothing – they allowed the McCartney name to be used for the team, which appeared to be attracting other sponsors. In 2001 I was told that Jaguar, no less, and Australian wine giants Jacob's Creek were on board to take the team to the next level, to earn a Tour de France ride and to be truly competitive in the world's most famous and most watched race.

Clark was the inspiration and the energy but was eventually exposed as something of a Walter Mitty character. Although a talented motocross rider and a fit guy – he used to run a gym near Brands Hatch – he somehow convinced himself he could be a professional road cyclist and used to ride in the team itself! Despite that the Linda McCartney team soon took off – they had enormous support and goodwill in Britain and home-based riders were keen to make it happen – and incredibly they began to make an immediate impression.

It became the first British team to compete in the Giro D'Italia, bagged a stage win and were pretty competitive wherever they rode. The Linda McCartney team were becoming significant players in the sport. There also seemed to be a great team spirit along the lines I had already been experiencing at Team GB. If ever I was going to make the leap into Continental road racing this seemed to be the perfect vehicle. The language and cultural difficulties would be minimised in an English-speaking team – or so I thought – and of course who wouldn't want the chance of competing under the guiding hand of Sean Yates, one of the greatest *domestiques* the sport has ever produced and a veteran of 20 major Tours? A man who knew everybody in the sport and was respected by everybody in cycling. Frankly, I couldn't believe my luck.

I signed soon after returning from Sydney and was on such a high that I moved straight into a busy autumn, helping Great Britain to go one better than the Olympics and take a silver medal at the World Track Championships in Manchester – very much after the Lord Mayor's show I suppose, but it was fun competing at home – and then I went off and did some of the Six Dayers with Rob Hayles and enjoyed quite a bit of success. I was flying and even in December was putting in some hard miles training ahead of my first big break as a professional on the road.

The holidays came and went and after Sydney – and feeling so good – I gave it a bit of a blast but by 3 January it was back on the treadmill. I loaded up my little Fiesta with all my possessions and set off at 4 a.m., destination Toulouse, which had become the Linda McCartney team's home from home on the Continent. It's a bloody long drive but I made it in just over 16 hours including the crossing, which must be some kind of a record, in a Fiesta anyway. I stopped only for petrol the whole way.

Waiting for me there was Julian Clark, the only time I met him in person, and he put me up in his family's place that night before taking me to the apartment where I would be based. It was a bit of a hole. He gave me some team kit, I unpacked my stuff, and that was it. Officially I was a professional road racer in Europe. It was totally underwhelming and a massive anti-climax after Sydney.

There was absolutely nobody around – the team were racing in Australia in the Tour 'Down Under' – and I didn't know a soul. Toulouse, the so-called red city because many of its older buildings glow in the sun, is gorgeous in the summer but its winters are harsh and wet. I was lonely and bloody miserable but made myself go out and do some training because I didn't want to lose my fitness and that's what professionals do, isn't it? Ride every day. I was down there for three weeks and did eventually hook up with another new signing – the Czech rider Ondrej Fadrny – so training became slightly less monotonous and there was at least one person a day to see and speak to.

Together we travelled back at the end of January to the Cricketers Hotel in Bagshot, where the entire McCartney team was gathering for a couple of days for a pre-season meeting and the official team photoshoot. There were also a series of press interviews planned before moving on to Trafalgar Square the next day for the official team launch, which sounded very glamorous and 'Hollywood' and guaranteed to whip up interest.

I was excited again. It was a very decent team, with a lot of potential and a stack of goodwill. There were hot young Brits like Russell Downing, Matt Stephens and myself; Great Britain's Olympic bronze medallist Max Sciandri, who was reared in Italy where he learned his craft; Ciaran Power and Mark Scanlon from Ireland – the latter a World Junior champion in 1998; Danish sprinter and Six Day rider Tayeb Braikia; Australian David McKenzie, who had won stage seven of the 2000 Giro and had just taken stage seven of the Tour Down Under; and his countryman Peter Rogers. Then there was Marlon Perez, a climber from Colombia, and a clutch of Spaniards – Inigo Cuesta, a former winner of the Tour of the Basque Country, Juan Carlos

Dominguez and Miguel Martin Perdiguero, who had won the Grand Prix Miguel Indurain the previous year.

But that excitement didn't last long. As soon as we arrived from France it was impossible not to pick up the apprehension and barbed comments from those returning from Australia, where it appears none of them had been paid. Indeed, some were claiming they were still owed large amounts of money from the previous season. The alarm bells began to ring.

Sean Yates and Max Sciandri, the team leader who was allegedly owed more money than anybody, were nowhere to be seen. They were away at unspecified meetings all day but eventually they returned and Max gathered us together in a meeting room. The message was stark. Jaguar were not on board, there had been a dreadful misunderstanding and at no point had they committed to the project despite a lot of our gear having already been designed and manufactured to incorporate their logos, and there was now a very serious cash flow problem indeed – i.e. there was none.

It was bloody depressing but there was still a lot of brave talk about battling on and achieving such good results that another big sponsor would be tempted when Sean took a phone call on his mobile and this time it was terminal. Jacob's Creek were not on board either. We had been led to understand that they were putting £1.7 million into the pot but again there had been a breakdown in communication and they, it would appear, only wanted to be involved in the recent and successful foray down to Australia for the Tour Down Under. We were scuppered. All bets off. There was no way the team could continue. We were, as of that night, all out of a job and throughout all this there was no sign of Julian Clark.

I was disappointed but actually I took it in my stride. Maybe it was the innocence of youth – I was still only 20 – or maybe I was still on an invincible high after Sydney. The fact that I wasn't owed scores of thousand of pounds also helped, and I felt sorry for the guys in that situation.

Instinctively I ran for home, which in cycling terms meant Team GB, who were fantastic, immediately got me back on the programme and secured me the Category A Lottery funding again. They could not have been more supportive and they helped ensure that a drama didn't become a crisis. Everything they do is world class and you never spend any time wondering if the opposition have got better facilities and back-up; everything is laid on to maximise the cyclist's performance. People wonder why cycling has been such a success story in Britain in recent years: well, there you have one explanation in a nutshell. Loyalty.

And great man management.

So very soon I was back training and racing with the lads and enjoying a great summer, placing well in a stack of road races here and abroad, including a stage win and General Classification in the Flèche du Sud, third in the Tour of Rhodes and GC in the Cinturion de Mallorca, which included the prologue and a stage win. I was in very useful form, so much so that the French team Française des Jeux, who are sponsored by the French National Lottery, started to register an interest. That was nice to have in the background, but I was having fun and, for the time being, committed to the track boys and training with the World Championships in Antwerp in mind, and in particular a first tilt at the Individual Pursuit title.

Two weeks out and I was in as good a shape as I can ever recall in that early part of my career. I was tearing it apart in training and heading for something special, at least in my own mind, when I had a nasty accident on the Harrow Road and smashed my right wrist into a hundred pieces. There was a tarpaulin draped over a rubbish skip which hadn't been tied down properly and just as I raced past there was a strong gust of wind and the tarpaulin snagged in my handlebars and I went flying.

It was a mangled mess and incredibly painful and required a four-hour operation and two metal pins to put right. The sensible thing would have been to call a halt to the season let alone the impending World Championships there and then but I was in denial. And cyclists are not known generally for doing the sensible thing. If we stopped every time our body ached or seemed to give way we would hardly finish a race. A bit of pain is par for the course. One day I was in the form of my life and now this accident. I tried to pretend it hadn't happened. Five days after my operation (four hours on the slab under anaesthetic) I was down at the Manchester velodrome doing flying kilos at training with a massive cast on. I actually felt better then than a week later when we flew to Antwerp.

I wanted to do well in the Individual Pursuit but I was feeling rubbish and eventually had to settle for seventh. Not a disgrace, and not bad for a man nearly passing out with the pain, but not a patch on what I could have done two weeks earlier before the crash. Somehow, I managed to convince the management that I was okay and I kept my place in the Team Pursuit. I rode a little better as we again came in with a silver medal, but that was it for me, season's end. In much more pain than when I had started the Championship week, I headed home and didn't look at my bike for two months. My body needed time to mend and heal, and in the meantime I would encourage it by eating and drinking for England. I got stuck in and piled on well over a stone before I felt ready to get back on a bike and get serious again as the winter approached. Almost the last thing I had done in Antwerp before coming home was to sign professional forms for Française de Jeux and this time I had no doubt that my career as a professional road cyclist would get under way.

—

Chapter Eight

Lost in France

As often seemed the case in those days, I completely overdid the training coming back from my long lay-off and struggled to shake that off for most of the season that followed. Although there were some good days, mostly I felt lethargic and just plain tired. After enjoying myself after Antwerp I had some weight to lose; luckily, I always shed that quickly. Nonetheless, I was feeling a bit guilty for over-indulging during the rehabilitation after the injury, which is silly and illogical, but led me to beat myself up in training. I also wanted to make a massive impression with Française des Jeux, which is natural enough. You never get a second chance to make a first impression, as the advert says. There would be no familiar English faces in the management and team to smooth my way this time; I would be on my own among a group of strangers in a foreign land with, initially, average French to get by, although I was determined to learn. Instinct told me that one way of surviving and flourishing was to arrive in Olympian form and make a massive impression on the bike.

Come the new year, I was full of hope as I packed my Ford Fiesta again and this time headed off for Nantes on the Atlantic seaboard of France. As usual there was the somewhat haphazard arrangement of meeting a team official at a designated petrol station miles from anywhere at a given time to hand over the key of my apartment – a rather grand term for what turned into a prison cell in a poor part to town – and to give me my team gear and bike.

For the second time in a year I disconsolately unpacked my gear and sat on the bed, waiting in vain for somebody to call or drop by. It was just a million miles away from the world-class set-up with Team GB, but something I had to get used to. Sink or swim. Although I wanted to rant and rave, the thinking at the time was that this was a sort of rite of passage that every young rider – and especially every non-French rider – had to undergo. Even in the few years since then the thinking has changed radically and teams are becoming much more rider-friendly in their attitudes, but that came a tad too late for the young Brad Wiggins. It was an incredibly depressing and demoralising introduction to the so-called glamorous world of professional road cycling in France. The only way I can rationalise it is that such a process possibly sorts the wheat from the chaff. Those who really want it find a way of getting through; the hungriest riders emerge and start getting results for their team, and after that there is some money to be made. At this point, incidentally, I was taking home £700 a month after tax, and of course I had my monthly rent and living expenses to pay out of that. I had been much better off as a member of the GB elite training squad and occasional calls to mates like Steve Cummings didn't bolster my morale much as they spoke about the great set-up back home.

I didn't even have a proper training programme, for God's sake, and I had already made a rod for myself by going too hard too soon back home. It seemed hopeless but, out of habit more than anything, I dragged myself out every day for a ride and tried to pretend I was living the dream. I was probably doing more harm than good, but after a while I did at least make contact with a fellow team member, Jean Cyril Robin, which meant I finally had somebody to talk to occasionally – which was as close to a social life as I had at the time. He was a bloody good rider who had finished sixth in the 1998 Tour de France and won a bronze in the World Championship road race in Verona the year after. He was friendly and sympathetic but there was very little training we could usefully do together. I was a raw kid who had been signed to learn, do a few prologues and act as a workhorse for others. He was a major rider coming towards the end of his career but with a guaranteed Tour de France place that summer. The team possibly thought he could be a mentor, but we had completely different agendas and were riding different training schedules and races.

A vicious circle set in once the racing season started. I was homesick, lonely and prone to pick up every virus going, having trained too much. I would be up before dawn, fly to some regional venue in France I had scarcely heard of, get my head kicked in during the races or fail to finish altogether and then head for the nearest airport for the last flight home to Nantes. I would grab some airport food there in the evening – my only proper meal all day – get into Nantes about 11 p.m., unload my bike, which always took ages to arrive on the baggage reclaim, grab a taxi and arrive back at my apartment well past midnight.

There was no fridge, no home comforts, no fellow lodger or girlfriend to welcome me back home. Nothing. The loneliness of the long-distance cyclist. And the next morning, because I was anxious and determined not to fail through lack of effort, it would be back on my bike and the next day after that there would be another race on the other side of the country with and against people I had never met before. I was totally pissed off, disillusioned and very lonely. And because everybody was having such a good time at home I stopped phoning them and felt even more cut off. I was totally lost in France.

There was only one option, get my head down and get on with it, which is exactly what transpired. I wasn't riding well, but I rode nonetheless. I wasn't happy but I didn't quit and there was a certain satisfaction in that. I wasn't riding remotely well enough to get selected by Française des Jeux for the Tour de France but that had its own advantages. I wouldn't be needed for the second half of June and all of July. I could creep off home, albeit with my tail between my legs, and start training with the GB squad again. The Commonwealth Games were starting in Manchester early in August and perhaps it wasn't too late to salvage the season.

I slotted straight back into training and the joy of being involved again with a hands-on professional outfit who worked with you rather than against you almost made me weep. To enjoy a coffee and laugh with mates after a session was another long-forgotten pleasure. In short, it was great to be back home and, rather against the odds and public expectation, Manchester was cranking up to deliver an absolutely superb Games with the entire city buying into the experience. The buzz was amazing and as we head towards London 2012, British sport should not forget the Manchester Commonwealth Games and the Mancunians who made it special. They played an enormous role in London getting the vote from the International Olympic Committee in 2005. The Manchester Commonwealth Games miraculously put Britain back on the map as a world-class sporting venue.

I quickly got back into decent form and started riding well, but 2002 was not destined to be my year. In the Individual Pursuit I was up against Australia's Brad McGee and didn't respond well to the pressure. In fact, I choked horribly. I qualified with a very decent 4 mins 19 secs in the semi-final and felt great, but McGee immediately bettered it with a comfortable 4 mins 18 secs and in the build-up to the final I just cracked mentally. Not only did I not feel capable of competing, I almost didn't want to ride at all. It was complicated but let me try and explain.

Brad was the star rider of my very own team, Française des Jeux – he was definitely the 'talent' and was treated accordingly. I should also add that he was a cracking rider and deserved to be treated as the star. The team accommodated and nurtured him, to a certain extent catered for his every need and, of course, he would have been on seriously good money. He had won a stage of the Tour de France that summer, won the prologue at the Dauphiné Libéré and also taken the green jersey there. This was the rider, more than any other team rider, who was earning the column inches and air time that justified the sponsors' investment in our team. Meanwhile, I was a minion, a cycling serf, stranded in a godforsaken basement flat out in Nantes, seemingly forgotten and unwanted. He was the master and I was the servant, despite the fact that barely a second separated us on the clock in qualifying. I went into the race feeling totally inferior to McGee, both as a person and a racer.

The race was lost before it even started. Mentally I could not get my head around competing against this guy, despite the fact that statistically, around 16 laps of the velodrome, I should have been able to give him a good race and maybe drag myself to a personal best time. Instead I froze, scarcely got up a head of steam and he easily caught me. It was a massive anti-climax and humiliation in front of the large home crowd and live on TV. It hurt badly and if one single thing drove me on to win the Olympics two years later it was my humiliation at the hands of Brad McGee in Manchester. The thought of it still makes me angry, although in many ways it was one of the best things ever to happen to me as a competitive cyclist. A much tougher competitor eventually emerged.

The Team Pursuit resulted in another silver medal for myself, which sounds fine on paper but we were disappointed. The Aussies, who we had beaten in Antwerp, were beginning to mould a fantastic quartet and broke the world record in the final, with England – basically the GB World Championship squad – taking silver but not really rising to the occasion and producing our best. We hadn't seen the Aussies coming really, mentally, before the Games, we had them beaten in our heads, but they had taken the event onto another level. We were chastened to say the least.

But at least the curve was upwards personally. During the first half of the year I had sunk as low as I had ever been and now I had two silver medals in my pocket and a stack of parties around the city to enjoy. The Commonwealth Games are known as the Friendly Games and that certainly proved the case for me. I was three parts drunk at one gathering, at a place called the Glasshouse I seem to recall, when I met Cath and we spent the rest of the evening talking together, although I am not sure I was making much sense. I remembered her well from back in 1997 when she was a member of the GB junior squad with me as a sprinter, and I had fallen for her then although of course I had somehow failed to get around to the asking her out part of the process. I bottled it again this time in Manchester but at least I did manage to get her mobile phone number and promised to phone again when I returned from a busy month's racing on the Continent.

Physically I was now in better shape after the Commonwealths and started to ride well again – I was going great guns at the Tour de l'Avenir – and arrived at the Worlds in Copenhagen a stronger rider than a couple of months earlier in Manchester. But not wiser. Again I got psyched by the presence of McGee in the field and disappointed myself by only finishing fifth in the Individual

Pursuit, although objectively that represented progress of sorts, my best ever finish and nudging towards the podium. I was bloody angry though and got up the next morning and rode like ten men to help our under-strength Pursuit Team to a bronze medal.

It was there, I had it in me to do something special and lasting, but it just wasn't happening. And I was totally disillusioned with life on the road in France with a team that barely acknowledged my existence. Back in Manchester, I phoned Cath and we were together as a couple within weeks and living together soon after. I had been due to move to Nice in France but decided to stay with Cath in Manchester while she finished her degree. It just felt right, my first serious relationship and, by chance or fate, I had found my perfect partner at the first attempt. No more facing the world on my own. At a deep personal level I was now very happy but I was worried about my cycling career. McGee had got into my head on the track and I was hating – absolutely bloody hating – life with Française de Jeux.

The GB management had picked up on this and a conference of war to discuss 'the problem with Brad' was called in Manchester. Peter Keen, Dave Brailsford and Simon Jones sat there and didn't pull any punches. What was wrong with me? Why was I bottling it at the big championships in the Individual Pursuit and riding like a loser whenever McGee was in the field? Did I want a career in cycling or not?

Of course I went all defensive initially and went off on one. I was still young and hadn't exactly been a failure, I protested. I had endured a rubbish first half of the year in France but had still pulled it together at the end and won two silver medals in Manchester and a bronze at the Worlds. How many British competitors in any sport had managed that, eh? Tell me that. If you don't want me around I will happily bugger off to Australia and ride for them, or even Belgium. I am qualified for them as well you know. They would love me back in Belgium, riding out of Ghent and winning big medals on the track for them. I would be a local hero and feted around the place.

Even as I shouted those words I didn't believe them for one second. Despite my cosmopolitan background I feel British through and through; my mum is English, I was brought up a Londoner and the GB team has always been my home from home. I couldn't contemplate ever competing for another nation. I was just bloody narked, with myself as much as anything.

There was an embarrassing and slightly shocked silence. Were things really that bad? Nobody wanted that, not that a switch of countries was remotely feasible anyway. The sport doesn't allow you just to switch like that. These people in front of me had been brilliant and they had every right to find out what was going on in my life. And there were still those who believed in my ability utterly, without question. Shane Sutton always insisted that I was one of the most talented riders he had ever seen and that I was a nailed-on Olympic gold medallist in Athens if we got the preparation right. His word has always carried a lot of weight since he became involved, Dave Brailsford trusts his judgement on a cyclist implicitly.

After my explosion – and I probably needed to get it out of my system – we proceeded much more calmly. Operation Bradley had to be carefully thought out – how to get the best out of me and win a gold medal in the Individual Pursuit in Athens. Everybody wanted the same thing. There was no conflict of interest.

We talked everything through and hatched a plan which involved introducing Chris Boardman – not long retired and looking for a project to throw himself into – as my personal mentor for want of a better word. This is the same Chris

Boardman who, exactly ten years earlier, I had been called in from the street by Mum to watch winning his Olympic title.

Life was about to change, ultimately very much for the better, but it would be untrue to claim there weren't considerable teething problems in my relationship with Chris, who is very organised and disciplined and has an objective and remorseless approach to dealing with a problem. We met for the first time and he surprised me by getting out a pen and notebook and making endless notes as we spoke. He was going to minute every meeting we had and he would email those minutes to me the very next day. What was said at the meeting and – more importantly – what was agreed as the way forward and the training regime for the next couple of weeks was to become a matter of historical fact and not open to interpretation by me.

Chris simply was not going to allow me the luxury of pretending I didn't know what had been said and putting my own slant on the meeting. It was going to be there in black and white, no sliding away from the facts and blurring the issue if I hadn't done the correct training. Everything was accountable. Bloody hell, this was different. Chris was very harsh with me at this stage, a bit of a bastard really, that was the word I used with Cath on more than one occasion. Even then, though, I sensed he was doing it for the best. He had always been hard on himself as a competitor as well – a complete perfectionist – and I suspect the GB management think tank had decided that I needed a more disciplined approach in my life.

Looking back, I did need a massive kick up the arse and Chris, such an illustrious Olympic champion, was one of the few people I would have been willing to take it from. He would email me regularly, almost every night in the early stages, and Cath could hardly believe how seemingly aggressive he was. She started to get angry but I was determined to persist with Chris in my corner.

At one stage we sat down and set an interim goal on the road to the Athens Olympics which, logically, had to be the 2003 World Championships – scheduled for China but which, as it happens, were eventually switched to Stuttgart following the SARS crisis. Chris was in a rather irritating schoolmasterly mood and set me some homework. I had to draft an action plan to account for every day of my training, preparation and rest between now and the World Championships, a period of just under a year.

It was a daunting task for a confirmed non-academic but, with Cath's considerable help, I sat down, worked out exactly how I wanted to approach the Worlds and prepare for them, roughed out my precise schedule with comments and observations and then painstakingly tapped it out on the computer and emailed it to Chris. Week by week, session by session. Suggested races and recovery periods. A plan B with an alternative racing schedule if he didn't like plan A. Venues, times, targets. The entire process, in between training, took the best part of the week, and when I pushed the send button there was a real sense of pride in the end product. Without doubt the finest piece of written work I had ever produced.

The reply winged its way back in very short order. He had virtually red-inked the bloody lot. There was almost nothing he agreed with. It was rubbish, my ideas and plans were rubbish. At one point I remember he had written: 'This looks like the work of somebody who is very good at telling somebody what they want to hear.'

That hurt badly, basically because it was true. I was so in awe of Chris Boardman Olympic gold medallist, three times Tour de France Prologue winner and World hour record holder that I was doing precisely that. Telling Chris what he wanted to hear to get him off my case and give me some peace.

No chance. He was a man on a mission. He stayed on my case

and from my point of view was a bit of a sod, I used to curse him constantly at home with Cath. He was putting all that energy and drive from his racing days into 'Project Bradley' and there were times when it made me uncomfortable. It's not really me. I work hard and am dedicated in my own way but this full-on almost military approach was like taking a cold shower every morning.

But gradually he got me organised. We would have regular meetings and all the time he would take those minutes like a company secretary. He would take no excuses from me, if I started to contradict myself or backtrack on something he would dig out the minutes from a couple of months before and point out what we had agreed back then. 'Where are we in the programme?' he would constantly ask. 'What were the numbers last week? Aren't they a little down on what we wanted at this stage? Is there a problem? Why aren't you making the numbers? Let's have a look this. We are not leaving this room until we have got this sorted.' This was radical new stuff for me and it took a time to get used to.

It was a tough winter of training and consolidation, with the occasional excursion such as getting second place with Matt Gilmore in the Ghent Sixes, which I really enjoyed. Matt was basically an Aussie, like my dad, but he moved to Belgium and took out nationality in 1998 and went on to win a silver medal for the Belgians in the Sydney Olympic Madison with Etienne de Wilde when I finished fourth with Rob Hayles.

The whole Sixes circuit is a world of its own. The racing can be demanding at that stage of the season, although I suspect it's not quite so flat out and cut-throat now as in the old days. I doff my hat to the older brigade, including Garry, who were sometimes required to put in a three-hour afternoon session – the matinee if you like – before the main event every night, which started at about 6.30 p.m. and could go on until 4 a.m. or even later. These are totally inhumane working hours – and cycling wonders why the sport developed a drug culture?

There is a fantastic atmosphere at the Sixes though, with just about everybody totally bladdered by the middle of the evening, with the disco music rocking throughout. All the side rooms and nooks and crannies in the stadium are converted into nightclubs and restaurants and it is the social event of the year in whatever city the Sixes are passing through. Certainly it is the place to strut your stuff in Ghent. There are some fans out there who don't see daylight for a week and scarcely draw a sober breath in that time, but what a way to get through the dark winter months.

Meanwhile, I continued my fractious relationship with Française de Jeux, although by now I was based at home with Cath and would commute in and out of Europe for races. Not ideal, but much better for my morale. There were early encouraging signs when I managed to score a minor victory over McGee in a ten-minute roadman's pursuit to celebrate the centenary of Herne Hill, and I put in a couple of pretty solid rides in the Tour of Flanders and the famous Paris–Roubaix one-day Classic, when I got to Arenburg in the front group before crashing out.

Undoubtedly the main event of my road season was getting through the Giro D'Italia, which was bloody tough – the mountains on the Giro are every bit as hard as on the Tour de France and often ridden in colder and nastier conditions – but a necessary evil because I needed those long road miles in my legs for my assault on the World Championships in Stuttgart.

It was part of Chris Boardman's master plan, and the race went smoothly enough although it ended slightly controversially when I was in a group of 44 that got eliminated at the end of stage 18, a vicious day in the mountains in appalling weather when we were fractionally outside the time limit. It caused uproar in the Italian press – normally when you get that close to the finish in Milan and simply survive and get around such an evil stage in such exceptionally bad weather the race organisers would show mercy. And, of course, by culling the peloton they affected the dynamic and spectacle of the race in the final days.

After the Giro I was soon back in the comforting bubble that is the GB team environment and six or seven weeks of excellent training. I travelled to Stuttgart absolutely ready for it and for once there was no McGee to mess with my head. He had won the Prologue at the Tour de France, beating Dave Millar, and had looked in good form, but had experienced some sickness and eventually dropped out of the Worlds.

I was absolutely in the zone and my first senior World Championship gold medal, when it came, was almost routine. I posted a 4.17 to qualify in first place and although Australia's Luke Roberts didn't roll over and die in the final – Aussies just don't do that – I won by a second in 4 mins 18.570 secs. I was champion of the world and it felt great. A phone call even came through from Garry. It was the last time we spoke. His life was completely out of control by now. He had been banned from driving for driving over the limit while already banned and, following a third drink-drive offence, he did a runner to Tasmania to avoid arrest and a much longer sentence. Communication was non-existent between us and I heard all sorts on the grapevine, including that he had served a prison sentence for one of his drink-drive offences. There were also persistent second-hand reports of a bar-room brawl which resulted in a death, but this was being mixed up with an earlier incident when he first returned to Australia from Europe. Apparently, after a long night at the bar, he and a few others spilled out into the road and one of the guys involved stumbled, smashed his head on the pavement and died. I am happy to report that Garry was exonerated – a terrible accident was the verdict – but I pondered that it was no way to be spending what should be the best years of your life. It was nice that he phoned – clearly he was still following the racing and I know now that he was collecting the paper cuttings – but that was the sum of it. There was no great making up or promises about staying in touch. After that we drifted apart for ever, not that you could really say we were ever together.

After the excitement of winning the Individual Pursuit – and it really was a buzz because a dream coming true is so rare – I came down to earth a little the following day when the Australian quartet of Roberts, Graeme Brown, Peter Dawson and Brett Lancaster absolutely hammered us in the Team Pursuit when they set a world record of 3 mins 57.260 secs. They were class. We took silver but, following on from their Commonwealth title – when we had gone into the Games believing we could beat them – it was a bitter defeat to take. The gap was widening and there didn't seem much we could do about it.

Personally, though, I was on a high – a world champion at 23 in the Blue Riband event of track cycling, I could finally wear the rainbow jersey, which has a colour from every flag in the world on it. As we climbed aboard the plane home I took my seat next to Chris and assumed we would be cracking open the bubbly and enjoying the moment after a long slog. But he was straight on my case again; he could see that I thought I had cracked the event now and already had one hand on the Olympic gold medal – I was getting cocky.

'The World Championships are fine but it's not the Olympics and McGee wasn't here. But he will be in Athens,' said Chris. 'How are you going to beat McGee in Athens? You have never beaten him anywhere else except in a jolly at Herne Hill, so how are you going to beat him in Athens?'

'That's a very good question,' I said lamely, as I pushed

thoughts of champagne and a pat on the back to one side. Chris's comments – to the point as ever – sparked off a good discussion which lasted the length of the flight and by the time we had landed it had been decided that I simply had to get myself away from Française de Jeux, which I saw very much as being Bradley McGee's team. It was all set up to promote and assist him and all the time I stayed with Française des Jeux I would be treated as a second-class citizen and carry around this strange inferiority complex about Brad McGee, who is, incidentally, a bloody good bloke and a very talented, honest, hard-riding Aussie.

It wasn't Brad McGee the bloke I had a problem with, it was the master–servant relationship that Française des Jeux had established between us. That and the fact that I had grown to despise the management and the way they treated me, although I enjoyed the company of the team, especially the three Aussies. Ironically, I produced my best ride for the team right at the death when I took the prologue of the Tour de l'Avenir by a whopping 14 seconds and held on to the yellow jersey for two days before falling ill and having to bale out on the first big mountains day.

It was time for another move and Chris listened carefully and understood where I was coming from. He said he would make discreet enquiries at Credit Agricole, where he enjoyed near legendary status after his Tour de France exploits for them, and see if there was an opening for the 2004 season. And, fair play to Chris, that's exactly what he did. Pulling a few strings here and there no doubt, he got me the offer of a contract with one of the biggest teams on the Continent. Everything would be fine now. Wouldn't it?

—

Chapter Nine

2004: the worst of times, the best of times

And so the Olympic crusade began in earnest, and the most eventful year of my life. You might assume, looking back on the success I enjoyed, that it was all plain sailing, but you would be so way off the mark as to make it laughable. The year 2004 included some of the most difficult times I have known and saw me at my best and worst. Thankfully, for one relatively brief period in the summer, I pulled everything together. Cath was always there in the background; without her it would almost certainly have ended in tears. She put up with a seriously bad-tempered, confused and at times depressed partner for most of a year that, to the general sporting public, had looked golden and trouble free.

Mentally I was still too full of myself after Stuttgart. It had been a bloody good ride and gold medal and I was entitled to take much confidence from it, but it made me difficult to work with. 'Don't worry, I'm the World champion, I want Athens badly and everything will be all right on the night' was my attitude. Chris wasn't happy with this at all and got back on my case in a big way. His message was always the same. Athens was going to be twice as hard as Stuttgart, McGee will be planning and plotting and is capable of going under 4.15. You need to match that. You need to take a big step forward. Out he came with the detailed training programmes at our meetings as he busily red-inked my contributions. He was coming back to haunt me with a vengeance but his ruthlessly realistic approach ultimately helped save the day.

I let it all hang out a bit during the first part of the winter. I was a reigning World champion and was inclined to 'large it up' a bit. I rode five Six Dayers that winter and went at it hard on and off the track, drinking heavily in between the racing and getting to know many of Garry's old racing and supping colleagues. It was actually a very enjoyable period and I was still in cracking form – it all culminated with me winning the Ghent Sixes in my 'home' town which was a big thing for me – but this, combined with an extremely festive Christmas period, meant I entered the most important year of my sporting life a bit ragged to say the least.

The early part of the year was an unmitigated disaster. First, I became ill and run-down training in the British winter and missed stacks of conditioning work which needed to be done. This coincided with my joining up with Crédit Agricole, to whom I took an instant dislike, and I suspect the feeling was mutual. I was all over the place and in bad form and I can imagine the phones were buzzing between their headquarters and Chris up on Merseyside. 'What have you sent us, Chris? You promised us that Bradley was quality and dedicated to racing hard for the first half of the season before the Olympics. He is so unfit and shows no form. *C'est une catastrophe!*'

On top of all this myself and Cath had decided, for reasons that I now forget, to buy a house together in Chapel-Le-Frith in Derbyshire. The commitment that such a move implies was fine – I realised from the moment that we first got together that Cath was the one for me – it was just the practicalities and logistics that proved a nightmare. Your first house together is always a big step but, alas, as soon as we moved in, we realised we didn't really like the place or the house and didn't feel at home. It was a bit late, but we were young and stubborn and wanted to make it work.

The weather was rubbish but that was hardly unexpected – you don't move to the Peak District for the weather, do you – and I wasn't feeling 100 per cent. After my miserable experience living in Toulouse and Nantes I was trying to do the bulk of my training at home and commute to and from the Continent for Crédit Agricole team training and racing commitments. As well as it being chaos at home I was dashing around more than ever. Ironically, if you look back, this was probably the year when we could have usefully lived in France. As a couple we might have thrived; Cath would have made a home for us and I could have enjoyed the lifestyle and the early spring sunshine and put in some quality training. They always say hindsight is 20–20. Anyway, memo to any Olympic hopefuls out there: do not wait until Olympic year to buy a new house, move in and change teams and racing habits!

Olympic year needs to be routine. All the great Olympians – Redgrave and Pinsent, Michael Johnson, the Cuban boxers – glory in routine. Repeating the tried and tested formula, same locations, same regimes. Arriving at each new Olympics in the same mental and physical shape as four years earlier and taking strength from that. You've done well before, why change a winning formula?

Meanwhile, I was riding like a dog and hating every moment. Chris was on to me most days. I understood exactly what he was saying and felt guilty about letting him down with Crédit Agricole, but it is natural to be defensive and fight your corner. I was World champion, a pursuit rider through and through, and don't worry, Chris, I will be all right in Athens, was the mantra I used to try and fob him off.

I did a 4 mins 25 secs at a Revolution meeting in Manchester and Paul Manning beat me easily. Paul is one of the great Team Pursuiters in the business – he would be one of my first choices in an all-time line-up – but Paul simply should not have been beating me in the Individual Pursuit in Olympic year. Chris was mad as hell and called a council of war. 'We are on the verge of bloody well cocking this bloody thing up, what's the matter with you, Brad?' he exploded. He was not a happy camper and nor was I.

It went from bad to worse. While I was hitting the bottom of a slump McGee was in ominous early season form, posting a comfortable 4.19 in a World Cup meet in Manchester in April. I was diplomatically rested for the World Championships down in Melbourne – Rob Hayles was second fastest in the world thus far and had earned the right to race, producing a fine silver medal behind Sergi Escobar but in front of Robert Bartko. Paul Manning was an excellent fifth and together they anchored the Team Pursuit squad to a fine silver medal. The boys didn't seem to have missed me too much.

It was crisis time and coach Simon Jones was pulling his hair out. Rob Hayles had clearly earned the right for one of the two automatic places in Athens that the team had qualified for and now Paul Manning, in the form of his life and with his own Olympic dreams, was making a very strong case for the second discretionary place. Meanwhile I was riding like a bag of shit, while McGee had found the form of his life and had just finished an amazing 8th in the Giro. He was on fire. Simon phoned: 'Brad, you have got to get down the track and post a bloody good time by the end of May or else you are going to box the selectors into an impossible corner. You have got to get off your backside and get down the velodrome and give us a 4.22 or better.'

Just to complicate matters further Dave Millar – relatively untried as a track ride but clearly with the style and class to be a fine pursuiter – had put his hand up for Olympic inclusion as well, both in the Individual Pursuit and Team Pursuit. He was in the process of being integrated into the GB squad and, after his victory in the World Time Trial Championship in Canada the previous autumn, the GB coaching staff were seriously excited at the prospect of working with Dave.

This wasn't looking good. I got myself down to the Velodrome in Manchester and we set everything up for my 'trial ride'. It was a complete disaster. It was cold, I felt unwell and unmotivated, couldn't get the pedals moving at all and abandoned it after just six laps. As a trial ride to win an Olympic place, let alone a gold medal, it bordered on the verge of pathetic. As I came off the track that day I felt my Olympic place had gone, and along with it all dreams of a gold medal.

I prepared myself for the worst. What a comedown, the reigning Individual Pursuit World champion who couldn't even earn a place at the Olympics in his specialist event. There was just a glimmer of hope though, when I learned that my name was at least going to be put forward to the selection panel and I now know there was at least one very important voice – Shane Sutton – fighting my corner with the same tenacity with which he tackles everything in cycling. Shane never deviated from the view that I was the rider with the most potential in the entire GB squad and I was the rider most likely to win an Olympic gold. I had given Shane no evidence to support his view in 2004 but he was not going to be swayed and thank God for that.

Right at the death somebody else also went into bat for me and offered the supreme sacrifice. Paul Manning – fifth in the world a month earlier and with every chance of nicking say a bronze in Athens – contacted the selection panel and said he was going to withdraw from consideration for the Individual event because he felt I was the better rider and that if I would pull things together

I could win gold, something he realistically believed was beyond him. It was a massive shout from Paul, a man of high integrity and intelligence and a trusted colleague for well over a decade, now in the Team Pursuit. He certainly saved my bacon in 2004. A heartfelt 'thank you', Paul.

I was back in the frame but still had to get the nod over Dave Millar, who had a growing band of supporters and had been looking very good in training. Shane again voiced his strong opinion that I was our strongest gold medal contender with Chris Hoy, although God only knows where he was getting his confidence in me from – and Shane, as he usually does, eventually won the day. That decision looked even wiser a couple of weeks later as Dave encountered his 'difficulties' down in France, when the police found the syringes he had used the previous year to administer EPO illegally in his house in Biarritz. Dave didn't prolong the agony, admitted all, was stripped of his World title from the previous year, banned for two years from road cycling and banned from the Olympics indefinitely by the BOA. Suddenly he was no longer part of the equation anyway.

All this uncertainty had been making me even more depressed and the eventual resolution of the situation was a massive boost. I went off to the Tour of Switzerland with Crédit Agricole and got around okay – as you would expect there were plenty of mountains, but I began to drum up a little form and fitness – and joined up with Team GB in much better shape mentally and physically. I had despaired of ever feeling right in this most important of years but suddenly I was okay. Not great, but okay. There were 11 weeks left to the finals night in Athens. Could we pull something from the fire?

Training was full on and fun. Every week saw a small but definite improvement and I was coming to the boil nicely. An interim fitness test midway through this period showed I was back hitting the numbers I had achieved at a similar stage the year before in the build-up to the World Championships. I was delighted because I still felt a way short of full racing fitness, there was definitely more to come. We went off for a high-intensity training camp in Belgium – track and road work –and suddenly I felt on it. My form had returned.

Confirmation immediately came from the fact that Chris was no longer on my case. He just watched me ride, looked at the numbers, checked his notebook, looked at the numbers one more time and nodded his head slowly and said: 'You're on it, Brad, you're in the form to win the gold medal.'

Coming from Chris that was massive. Although he had been incredibly hard and critical he was also always consistent and fair. He was always objective, analytical and realistic. He told the story exactly as it was, even when I didn't want to hear it. He just looked at the facts, the figures and what he saw me doing on the track and compared them with the figures he knew I would be required to beat McGee and win an Olympic gold medal. He was remorseless in the way he never deviated from what needed to be examined, he never went down unnecessary avenues. The flip side of that was that when he stopped complaining, when he said I was doing okay, in fact better than okay, it had to be true. Believe me, he wouldn't say it otherwise. So five weeks out, Chris was nodding his quiet approval and I had turned a vital corner. The Olympic bid was back on track.

We became obsessive in our attention to detail; nothing was too small not to warrant our attention and my time was agreeably full as I concentrated on my own individual event and the demanding Team Pursuit drills. To a certain extent, the Madison was going to have to take care of itself, although myself and Rob Hayles had laid a good foundation of competitive riding together over the years. Throughout June and much of July we sweated away at Manchester and DaveB and co. decided to take us to the new velodrome down in Newport in South Wales to finish the job. The thinking was logical and typical of the way Dave and his team thought things through. Manchester was brilliant, everything we could possibly want was there, the velodrome was our 'manor' and many of us lived close by. It was a home from home and had become the powerhouse of British track cycling. But we weren't going to be competing at Manchester, we were going to be on the road in the strange and very different environment of Athens.

As a curious sort of halfway house, DaveB wanted to get us out of Manchester altogether for the final stages and down to Newport, training and racing on an entirely new track in strange surroundings. Different changing rooms, different feel to the track, slightly different corners, no easy familiarity, and no living at home but staying in a hotel nearby – albeit a beautifully luxurious one in the Celtic Manor, where they are basing the 2010 Ryder Cup.

Essentially it was all designed to shake us out of our Manchester routine and it worked well. We were beginning our taper already but the training we did was all high quality. Dave also asked for – and paid for – the heating to be turned up full blast with all the doors and windows firmly closed to build up the temperature and to recreate, in part, the conditions of Athens. We got up to 32 degrees one afternoon – the Athens high was about 36 – and he also installed a couple of sweat rooms where we could go and do some roller work in even hotter conditions.

The preparation was nigh on faultless, it was bang on. As our eyes turned to Athens itself, I had clocked the fact that Brad McGee's hot streak had also come to an end; he had endured a rough time in the Tour de France, having to abandon fairly early on. Obviously that would give him more time to prepare specifically for Athens, but at the same time it was a chink in his mental armour. Something had clearly gone wrong in France, his team would have wanted him riding for as long as possible, he was their marquee rider.

We left it pretty late to jet off to Athens, just four hours' flight away. Jet lag was never going to be a problem, we just needed a few days to adjust to the extra heat and we were ready. We got accredited and went straight into the village. I knew what to expect this time, there was no star spotting. Excited to be there? Yes, of course, but not overawed, just anxious to get on with the battles ahead. Two days out and I had a final tactical discussion with Chris and Shane and we decided to ride on a 4.17 schedule in qualification, enough we felt to make a statement of intent and ensure top seeding but not quite eyeballs out, there would be a bit left for the medal rounds.

That was the day Cath phoned me. Nothing unusual there but this time she had some major news. She was pregnant, we were expecting our first child. I was totally bowled over in a good way. This was brilliant. I couldn't have been happier but Cath was in tears at the other end. She had kept the news to herself for a while, she didn't want to interrupt my preparations for a start and had also wondered how I might react. We were both young and initially finding it all a bit daunting. 'I've wrecked it for you, I've wrecked it for you,' she kept saying.

She hadn't wrecked anything, I was thrilled and soon managed to convince her that everything was okay, that it was exactly what I wanted and had dreamed about. I was on cloud nine and experienced all the same emotions that most dads-to-be go through. I was very proud and walked around with the paternal feeling that whatever I was doing here in Athens would be for Cath and the child, and that if I could make a name for myself here and get that gold medal and make some money, it could change the little one's life. I could be a proper provider.

Mostly it was a great positive buzz, but there is so much waiting around at a big event like the Olympics that there were also negative moments. What if I wasn't good enough and McGee was on fire again and beat me? Nobody remembers who comes second, that wouldn't pay the bills and secure the future for our new baby.

At this stage of my career I hadn't really allowed Steve Peters – the brilliant forensic psychiatrist who works extensively with the Great Britain cycling squad – into my life. In retrospect, his input would have been invaluable, but, perversely, I only felt strong enough to allow somebody to delve into my mind and my intimate self once I had the self-confidence that comes from being an Olympic winner, having proved to myself, at least once, that I could conquer all on my own. Since Athens I have wised up and, on occasions, worked very closely with Steve, who is one of the most exceptional individuals in the sport. As he jokes now, you used to be considered odd and slightly suspect if you went to see the sports shrink, now you are odd and slightly suspect if you don't.

Back to Athens and the build-up to the Individual Pursuit with Bradley Wiggins, newly informed father-to-be, all keyed up and ready to go. One of the consequences of not going to the Worlds in Melbourne and competing in the World Cup series is that I was not seeded and rode fairly early in the qualification. That wasn't great; it is always easier going off late and knowing more or less exactly what you have to do, but what did work in my favour is that before I rode a little-known Ukrainian, Volodymyr Dyadya, raced around in 4 mins 18.169, which immediately got the adrenaline pumping. Welcome back to the Olympics. Everybody raises their game like never before and it's best not to make too many plans as you have to adapt to what is going on around you. A 4.17 might not be fast enough to guarantee a favourable draw.

The pressure was on and as I walked out to the bike and put chalk on my hands, unusually for me in the seconds just before a race I got very pumped up and aggressive, smacked my hands together and nearly choked on the cloud of chalk. I felt great from the start and was soon well up on my notional 4.17 schedule. No problem. I wanted to lay down the gauntlet; I had no intention of allowing some guy from Ukraine that nobody had heard of to lead me in qualification. This was the Olympics and he wasn't the only guy who was going to raise his game. I felt great, strong and in control and I absolutely hammered around in 4 mins 15.165 secs, a personal best, an Olympic record and the fastest time of the modern era since the banning of Superman bikes. My ride produced an average speed of 56.434 km per hour from a standing start.

You can't ride a 4.15 without it hurting badly; you are on the edge of what the body can do and cope with. But as I rolled around afterwards I wasn't going to let anybody know exactly how much that hurt. On the contrary, I was going to 'showboat' a bit and let them think that was just a stroll in the park. I pointed rather animatedly to the warm-up pens inside the track in the hope that McGee, Escobar and Bartko, and anybody else who fancied their chances, were there on the rollers feeling a tad worried at this turn of events. 'Take that – 4.15, guys, and there is plenty more where that came from. I'm hardly breathing!'

I cruised around smiling, without a care in the world, fighting the desire to collapse in a heap and vomit. When it finally hit me I disappeared down to our team cabin, where I stretched out, completely knackered for a minute or so. I recovered quickly though – I was supremely fit after my intensive 11 weeks' preparation

With Dad on the settee. Domestic bliss? Garry shows every sign of being a doting dad at our flat in Ghent from where he based his assault on the European Six Day circuit. Alas, it didn't last long.

Calm before the storm. We feed the ducks together at a pond near our flats in Ghent.

Grandad and Nan have always been great stabilising influences in my life.

Christmas, and Garry has long gone so it's me and Mum against the world. Linda never complained at the hand she was dealt but you can see the strain in the pic.

A sign of things to come. My first bike. Note the superb style already!

If you are a tyro cyclist you've just got to have the gear, and then the bottle to wear it!

(*left*) Garry ready to do battle in another Six Day Race on the Continent. I love the retro leather cycling hat.

Walking wounded – recuperating after my nasty accident. The compensation helped pay for my first proper bike. Note the cycling posters. Girl bands didn't get a look in.

Practising in the living room, as Olympic wannabes do. Hope there was nothing you fancied watching on the box, Mum.

Looking the part. Celebrating my gold medal in the World Junior Pursuit Championships in Cuba. On my right is national coach Marshall Thomas; my personal coach Sean Bannister is on my left.

A rare grown-up picture of me and Garry during one of our brief reconciliations.

(*opposite*) That's my boy! Giving Ben a big hug. He doesn't look too impressed with his slobbering father (*Getty*). (*inset*) Isabella, with her dad behind her on TV.

Athens. Three medals to celebrate, and did I ever celebrate? I hardly drew a sober breath for nine months (*Action Images*).

Bradley Wiggins OBE. A rare picture of sobriety and serenity post Athens (*Action Images*).

with the team – and was soon on the rollers getting the lactic acid out of my system, a necessary process if you are to compete again that day. If you don't get rid of the lactic you have no chance in subsequent races.

You invariably have to back up your qualification ride with a ride of almost equal calibre a few hours later and this is one of the great arts of pursuit riding. There are one or two riders who can produce a scintillating one-off, but in the Olympics you have to produce three world-class rides in 24 hours and not everybody can do that, not by a long chalk. You've got absolutely no chance unless you take care of your body correctly in the hours in between rides. You might want to sit around and chat with family or press, or watch the rest of the day's cycling, but the GB coaches literally frog-march you to the turbo machines or drag you away from press interviews to get you on the massage table. These are the vital hours when medals can be won and lost.

I put my headphones on and disappeared into my own little world on the rollers, although coach Simon Jones would pop over periodically with updates on the other qualifying rides – Sergi Escobar from Spain had zipped around in a very swift 4 mins 16.862 secs, McGee had done a solid 4 mins 17.510, Rob Hayles a cracking 4 mins 17.930 and Bartko 4 mins 18.991. It was absolutely as expected. No alarms – the only thing unusual in qualification had been me riding so quick so early.

By qualifying fastest I had earned the right to go last, in the fourth heat of the next round that evening, when the four qualifiers for the medal ride-offs are decided, and this was the ideal position to be in. As the former World champion who had failed to earn a seeding, I had been the rogue, maverick rider in the first round, but as you approached the business end of the competition it was much more preferable to control it as the last starter. The top riders went off and predictably it was McGee, the last to go before me, who set the standard with a 4 mins 17.978 in winning his heat.

That's pretty fast after a similar ride just a few hours earlier, but I was so super-confident at this stage and so in the zone that we simply worked out a schedule to do what was necessary, a 4.17.500. No need to do more work than was strictly necessary and what a strong message that would send out if I was so in control that I could actually decide by how much I was going to beat the great McGee.

And that, glorious to relate, is exactly how it happened. I felt in absolutely perfect shape and control throughout, Simon Jones scarcely moved as he 'walked the line' to denote whether I was up or down on the schedule and if I hadn't just upped it a bit in the final lap – human nature I suppose – I would have come home right on the button. As it was I was a tad faster than planned, 4 mins 17.215. I was in the Olympic final and there was finally chance of redemption – sporting and personal – against Brad McGee.

It was a long 24 hours before the final, the longest of my life to be honest. There is so much time on your own thinking about everything and nothing. How many gold medals have been won and lost during periods of waiting like that? The majority probably. Nowadays I would just knock on Steve Peters's door and have a chat, but at this stage I was still ploughing my own furrow. All the GB management were there for me, of course; they were constantly encouraging and instantly came up with anything I wanted, but essentially you have to get through those 24 hours on your own and it is a constant fight to stop your mind wandering off into the strangest directions.

I won the first mental battle straight after that second ride which saw me through to the final. I was required at dope control that evening and sat around with Chris Hoy, waiting for nature to take its course to produce a specimen. Chris had just ridden magnificently that night to win the Kilo event. The number one seed, he had sat on the sidelines while the three riders ahead of him all successively posted world record times at sea level. To keep your cool and poise in those circumstances takes some doing and, understandably, everybody in the team and all his family were delighted. He sat there tired, knackered but very happy as well-wishers came over to offer their congratulations. Happy days.

I would have nothing to do with it. I couldn't even bring myself to look at his gold medal, let alone touch it and feel it and read the inscription. Mentally I knew I must not have anything to do with Chris's superbly won gold medal. It was his, won entirely by his own efforts and the celebrations were for him and his camp followers. I knew, sitting there, that I couldn't let my guard down. His gold medal was no part of my gold medal. His was now an historical fact, mine was still in the lap of the gods. I still had to produce the ride of my life to earn mine and had to stay concentrating on the job.

That was my approach then, anyway, so there I sat with Chris on a hot Athens night in a slightly subdued and furtive mood, taking great care to shift in my seat to avoid looking directly at his glistening gold medal.

Back at the athletes' village I had a massage and some food but it was a tough night, tossing and turning until about 3 a.m. when I finally grabbed a few fitful hours sleep. All kinds of thoughts came crashing in, interrupting my peace of mind. It had been such a rotten bloody year, it had so nearly gone pear-shaped. Why did we move house when we did? Why had I lost the plot in the early part of the season? Why was I so unhappy at Crédit Agricole? Thank God I got it back together just in time and now, finally, here was a chance to salvage everything and win a gold medal for Cath and our little one. What a journey it had been. All this flashed through my mind in my half-asleep state. I tried to consciously stop this day-dreaming and nostalgia in its tracks and concentrate on the job in hand. But that would make me nervous and anxious and I wanted to save that for the immediate pre-race hours – so I let my mind off the leash again.

Morning came. I tried to sleep in later than normal, grabbed some breakfast, spoke to Cath on the phone, read a few papers that were lying around, had a little work-out on the rollers, had another short sleep, watched some of the action on the TV, had a light lunch, dozed some more, listened to some music, picked away at my guitar and eventually, after what had seemed an eternity, my date with destiny was upon me. Frankly, I don't ever want to experience anything like that again. I couldn't settle to anything. The day was never-ending, it went on for months.

We went down to the track about two hours before the 'off' and started my pre-race preparations and warm-up. I was really nervous now. Of course I was bloody nervous, it was the Olympic final and for just over four minutes the eyes of the world were going to be on me. I was more nervous than I had ever been in my life but I knew deep down that I was also in control. My legs felt good and I just wanted to get on with it.

Possibly I didn't look as confident as I felt. Chris Boardman kept on looking me in the eye and asking: 'Are you coping, Brad, are you coping?'

'Yes, Chris, I am coping, of course I'm coping. Please can we just get on with this so I can win the bloody race.'

Eventually we got to the bronze medal ride-off – my room-mate Rob Hayles just got pipped for the bronze – and then, after all the waiting, everything moved at a thousand miles an hour and it was a bit of a mad rush. I was on. I was about to ride in an Olympic final.

The bikes were slotted into the gates, I climbed on board mine and they started the 50-second countdown. The atmosphere was amazing, packed house, emotional shrieks of 'Come on, Brad' from all corners. I still get goose pimples thinking about it. I often run the Hugh Porter commentary from the BBC through my mind; as you can imagine, I've watched the tape a few times over the years: 'So this is the one we have all been waiting for. The Battle of the Brads. Wiggins, the 2003 World champion, McGee, the 2002 World champion.'

I shook my head and got all thoughts of the crowd and my family out of my mind. Time to get really serious. I was on a 4.15 schedule. We didn't think McGee was in 4.15 shape after his two qualifying rides and, if I delivered again, I would be the Olympic champion in just over four minutes. That was our stark logic. Now it was time, execute, Brad. Execute. I rehearsed the race one final time in my mind. Do it like you've dreamed of doing, Brad. Strong smooth start, like you have done thousands of times in training. That's it nice, really nice. Get up to speed and then relax. No glancing over the track to McGee, no glimpsing the TV screen, you will lose concentration. Don't do that, Brad, don't look at the screen. And don't overcook it too early. He will probably be with you at 2 km, you are not going to bust him in the first 2 km, he is the reigning champion and an Aussie, he will hang on to you no matter how fast you ride for the first 2 km. It is the second half of the race that will see him drop off. You are in better shape, he hasn't got the condition to live with you after halfway. Squeeze it out in the third km. I love that, going beautifully now, Brad, really smooth, perfect position, no looking at the screen. Nearly there. He's dropping off, he can't live with you now. Bring it home, Brad, bring it home. Smooth as you like, no looking up, keep concentrating all the way. It's your night, Brad.

12, 11, 10 ... the countdown clock was continuing. The crowd was hushing and I was ready. 9, 8 … suddenly on 8 there was a loud shriek from Chris Boardman which so surprised me I nearly fell off. Mr Cool, Calm and Collected – Mr Objective and Unemotional – had completely lost the plot: 'Go on, Brad, get him, get him!' he bellowed at the top of his Liverpudlian voice.

On any other occasion I would probably have laughed aloud at the incongruity of Chris morphing into a football supporter on the terraces, but I was deep into the concentration and his emotion added a final surge of adrenaline to the equation. If Chris was this excited, it had to be for real.

Where were we? 7, 6, 5, 4, 3, 2, 1 – off. I was away in the Olympic final and living the dream. My very own life-long dream, ever since I had watched Chris in Barcelona in '92, was coming true and, as I pushed down on the pedals, all the tension and anxiety drained away. Nothing was going to stop me. All the nerves of the previous 24 hours vanished. Suddenly I didn't feel sick, I felt invincible. Suddenly there was no other place on this earth I wanted to be. Three hours earlier I would happily have caught the next flight to Manchester that evening. Seriously. But now I was in my element.

Remarkably – or perhaps not – everything went exactly as planned and as I had rehearsed mentally before the race. McGee was still level pegging after 2 km – I was just shading it by 0.3 sec., but in the lap after the halfway point there was a huge roar as it went out to 0.7 sec. Then 0.8, 1.0, 1.4, 1.6. The great McGee was cracking. I was on a charge. The Olympic gold medal was mine. I was bringing it home, and in great style as well, and I eased off the pace a little with the race well won. I went through the line in 4.16.304 secs and my head just dropped as I rolled around. Olympic champion.

Initially I didn't salute anybody or celebrate but just enjoyed a quiet moment to myself. The burden of the last four years –

self-imposed initially and then the burden of expectation – had suddenly been lifted and my overwhelming emotion was of pure relief. I rolled around, taking it all in and trying to catch my breath, and eventually pulled up by Brad McGee, who was sportingly waiting on the fence.

He told me to enjoy the moment. I told him that he was the reason I was here. 'You don't know how much you have inspired me and pushed me on.' And I meant it. Without the harsh lessons Brad McGee had taught me in 2002 at the Commonwealths and Worlds, and without him to chase, I would never have won an Olympic title. Of that I am absolutely sure.

Then it was over to Cath and the family – my mum and brother and Cath's parents – and of course there were tears everywhere. I couldn't really think what to say other than our baby wasn't going to want for anything now. I was an Olympic champion and I was going to make sure he or she never wanted for anything. Then it was back down to the team and big hugs for everybody, Chris Hoy, Chris Boardman, Simon Jones, DaveB, Shane who had fought my corner so hard when I was riding like a drain, all the mechanics and backroom boys who do such a great job and live every minute of racing with us. For an hour or so it was everything I had imagined, the world seemed to be bowing to my command and to revolve around me. It's a special feeling and, as we all know, those moments don't last for long. I would be ushered here and there, people rushed around making sure I had got everything I wanted. The medal ceremony was special and emotional, and there was a riot of press interviews before a longer piece with the BBC.

I got back to our apartment and, optimistically, tried to sleep, putting the gold medal on the bedside table after taking a long look at it, the inspection I had deliberately denied myself the evening before, sitting with Chris Hoy. But I was way too excited to drop off and wandered around our block a bit and down to the physio room so as not to disturb Rob Hayles. Rob was disappointed to just miss out on bronze but delighted for me. We both had the Team Pursuit the next morning and I didn't want to keep him up.

Eventually I did settle down and grabbed a couple of hours' kip before getting up and trying to put my Team Pursuit head on. It was so difficult and, again, in retrospect this was where I probably needed to go to Steve Peters and sort out all the conflicting emotions going on in my head. Physically I felt rubbish and tired after three world-class rides in 24 hours, but I have ridden well when tired before, it comes with the territory on the road. It was mentally that I was shot to pieces. I had won an Olympic medal 12 hours earlier, I had climbed Everest and now I was being asked to start at the bottom and climb Everest again, the very next day. It can be done, but I needed to get myself sorted mentally to ride at my strongest for the team.

I shouldn't have ridden in the match round that night, I was awful and all over the place. I knew it and the boys knew it, even though they were so strong we got safely through to the final by catching the French. It was a tough call. The Team Pursuit boasted a fantastic field and we needed to be at full throttle from the off to fulfil our hopes of a big medal; if you were selecting our strongest quartet I was definitely part of that line-up – but not the day after I had won the Individual Pursuit.

But I rode that night and we got away with it. I rode partly out of duty – I was part of the team and didn't want to let the boys down – and partly because I am selfish enough to want to be an integral part of another gold-medal-winning outfit. Who wouldn't?

Earlier in the day we had finished second in the first qualifying round, three seconds behind the Australians, and I entered the fray in the match round that evening against the French.

The Aussies, meanwhile, put a huge dent in that ambition by recording a sensational world record of 3 mins 56.610 secs against Lithuania in the match round, which put a damper on the rest of the field. This was new territory and only a couple of teams – Great Britain would be one of them – could ever contemplate getting near to that. But frankly we were pretty overwhelmed by it all.

In the final, they were worthy winners and, disappointingly, we didn't manage to duck under four minutes, in fact we only just broke 4.02. Watching a recording of the Beeb interviews afterwards is instructive. The boys were very down, their one shot at a gold had been blown away by an outstanding Australian quartet and I am the only one who seems happy enough and philosophical about it all. Which tells its own tale really. I had already enjoyed my golden ride, my moment in the sun, and now had a silver to add to the collection, which was all very nice, thank you. It wasn't hurting me to come second anywhere near as much as it should have done, and since that day I have tried to remember that when doubling up and tripling up at major championships. Your next race is always your most important. Elementary stuff, but easy to forget.

By the end of the Team Pursuit I wanted to go home. Enough was enough. I wanted to celebrate my gold – my life-long ambition – and the silver was a nice bonus. How many British competitors in any sport get a gold and silver at the same Olympics? I was dangerously demob happy, and I headed into Athens with Cath for a long relaxing lunch and quite a few beers the following day. I told Cath I just didn't want to ride the Madison and, before I got too far gone at lunch, I would phone the management and tell them just that. I had done my bit for the team, nobody would mind. Cath immediately talked me out of such nonsense. 'You have been selected to represent Great Britain in the Madison and that's exactly what you are going to do,' she told me. 'You might not be feeling great but you will go out there and do your best and look everybody in the eye at the end of it. You've got a duty to Rob, if nothing else, and who knows, you might even get a second gold.'

I wasn't being very 'professional' but I had been on a tight rein for months and needed a little break-out. If nothing else, our long lunch relaxed me, and when I returned to the athletes' village that night I made a big effort to get my head around the fact that I was racing again tomorrow in the Madison. I couldn't change my mindset totally so I opted for the 'relax, enjoy and give it your best shot' philosophy.

Cath was right, we did have a very decent medal shout and it was also an important race for Rob, who had just missed out on an individual medal in the Individual Pursuit. For him the Games were far from over.

Luckily I woke up without any ill effects after my day AWOL and my legs were good. There was still plenty of juice left in the tank. Though we never really threatened for gold we were involved in the sharp end of the race all the way and were rewarded with a bronze. Not a bad reward considering that less than 24 hours before I wasn't going to ride. Three medals at the same Olympics, the first Brit to do that since Mary Rand in Tokyo in 1964. Not a bad week's work, I told myself with some satisfaction.

—

Chapter Ten

Brad Wiggins 'superstar'

That's when the madness started and for a while my life threatened to spiral out of control. For four years nothing other than winning an Olympic gold medal had really mattered and now, with that achieved – and a couple of other medals besides – it was like popping the cork of a champagne bottle. There was a lot of pressure to let off. I was ready to make up for lost time. The last year in particular had been the pits, a bitch of a first six months anyway, and then, when I had finally pulled myself together, I had trained and lived like a monk for 11 weeks. And by nature I am not a monk.

Apparently it's a well-known phenomenon, but Olympic gold medallists usually only lose the plot for a month or so ... My bender after the Olympics lasted a good eight or nine months and I wasn't quite right for at least a year. I wasn't just drinking for England during this period, I wasn't quite at the races mentally either.

To recap, a lot was going on in my life. I was just 24 and had won three Olympic medals including a gold in the Individual Pursuit, my main event. On the road I was stuck in a French team that I absolutely hated, and I was living in a new house and village where Cath and I were not happy. On top of that, Cath had told me 48 hours before the Olympics had started that I was to be a father and – because I loved her and wanted to be with her – in November we were finally going to get married after planning the ceremony for a couple of years. New house, wedding, Olympic gold medal, new baby on the way, French team I loathed, periods of depression, the occasional massive high. Apart from that it had been a pretty uneventful year.

Initially it was just full-on party madness, media appearances and general celebration. Bloody exhausting but fun. It started straight after the Madison. All of the GB team had planned a big night on the piss in Athens the moment Rob Hayles and I could get out of dope control, but the BBC wanted us at their rooftop studio somewhere in Athens for an interview with Sue Barker and Craig Doyle at about 1.30 a.m., presumably with a feed into their late highlights show that night. I always try to help the Beeb and, yes, like anybody else, I love the buzz of doing a live broadcast, but I was desperate to call time on the Olympics and get the party started.

I was getting a bit agitated at this stage – I wanted to get on it with the lads and, even though Cath was obviously on the orange juice in her condition, she wanted to spend the first part of the celebrations with us. It had been a very special week, she had been living every moment up in the stands and now she wanted to spend some downtime with us. DaveB – with a typically thoughtful gesture – had also booked myself and Cath into a luxurious hotel next to the airport for a bit of TLC before Cath flew home the following afternoon.

I reluctantly agreed to trek off to the BBC interview – we had already done loads of trackside stuff – but only if Cath could come along, not an unreasonable request. She was with me now, the cycling was over. Of course, she had none of the relevant accreditation to get her anywhere, and there are as many jobsworths in Athens as most big cities, but a combination of menacing language by my good self and our medals hanging around our necks eventually got us through to the makeshift studio where Rob and I immediately set about the task of emptying the minibar in the green room. Rehydrating is a serious business when your participation in the Olympics is over. The interview went okay. I'm normally only too happy to oblige; it was just the timing on this occasion that wasn't great – we had done the trackside stuff and were booked in for another big hit the next morning, frankly this seemed one interview too far. After we had finished it was late, the celebratory moment had gone, a night on the town no longer seemed so enticing and Cath was tired, so we headed back to the hotel DaveB had arranged.

We enjoyed a bit of a lie-in and a leisurely breakfast before she flew back to London and a BBC car arrived to pick me up to take me back into the village for another big interview session, this time in tandem with Chris Hoy, to wrap up what had been a great week at the velodrome for Great Britain. Then, finally, we really did get on it, Rob, Steve Cummings and myself tipping beer down our throats until the early hours. Cyclists so rarely get let off the leash that when we are the results can be quite spectacular.

I wasn't a well man the next day but somehow I got myself back to London where Cath and my mum picked me up and, feeling a little better, I suggested we adjourn to a hostelry on Hampstead Heath, where I could continue the party with the two women in my life. I was getting used to this. No rest for the wicked, though. The next day, a Saturday, I flew to Brussels for a strange two-man time-trial on the Sunday. I was competing for Crédit Agricole with Christophe Moreau, a top bloke who, alas, I hadn't seen enough of during my season with them, and Christophe was in sparkling form. He had finished eighth in the Tour de France just before the Olympics started and really for him the season was over. Nothing else mattered. He had covered himself in glory for

Crédit Agricole and guaranteed a stack of useful money-making personal appearances at Criterium races until the end of the autumn. He was ready to party, I was already partying and we hit the town big time.

All things considered – i.e. collective hangovers that would have stopped an elephant in its tracks – we conjured up a miraculous performance the following day to finish a creditable fifth and earn much needed – for me – brownie points with Crédit Agricole. Straight after the finish and a final two or three beers with Christophe, I dashed for the airport and flew back to Manchester where Cath picked me up and we went straight off to her mum and dad's for another never-ending night of celebrations. This was the life.

I was still feeling great and it seemed no inconvenience at all when Cath had to drive me and my latest hangover down to London the following evening in preparation for an appearance on GMTV early on Tuesday morning. Dawn start or not, I was still out that evening with some of my London mates, but it hit me like a ton of bricks after we had finished in the studios and were tucking into some breakfast. We were meant to be at a big press conference back in Manchester at 1 p.m. to help promote the Tour of Britain, which was starting the following day and which, I belatedly remembered, I was meant to be riding in.

Needless to say we didn't even leave for Manchester until gone 11. It would be fair to say that the gathered press and camera crews were getting a little disgruntled by the time I shambled in, well after 4 p.m., looking – well, looking like a man who had been on the batter for the last four or five days, a man who had barely slept during that time and had somehow fitted a bike race over in Brussels midway during the piss-up. Apart from specific questions on Athens, which I managed to get my head around, I was all over the place. To be honest I could hardly remember what day of the week it was let alone answer deep meaningful questions about the future. Was it the end of my track career? Was it the Tour de France now for me? At various times I answered differently to every question – the questions come around more than once – so the press cuttings for that press conference are 'interesting', with many seeming to contradict each other. Luckily, there was a great sense of goodwill and celebration still around and nobody got hot and bothered about it. All the journalists knew more or less exactly what had been going on since Athens ended and sympathised with a smile. Everything will soon settle down and then we can get some sense out of Brad.

No chance. The Tour of Britain was upon us and it quickly developed into a gloriously liquid nationwide lap of honour. I was introduced and feted wherever I went – and I am as prone to enjoying a little flattery as the next man – while all the racing was great fun against many old mates. We went hard all day on the road and then gave it another thrashing most nights as well, a scenario many club cyclists might recognise. It is the exception among the professional ranks, however, despite what some people may think, but there was a real end-of-term feeling to the race and a determination for those involved in the sport to celebrate Britain's success in Athens.

I remember, vaguely, at least one big night with DaveB during the tour, and he doesn't hold back when he is in party mode. Eventually the entire circus moved to London for its big finish and we had the mother of end-of-Tour parties with all my family and cycling friends. Absolutely epic. We should have struck medals for the survivors of that session.

The next afternoon I groggily got myself across London to record an episode of BBC's *Question of Sport* – I was in Ally McCoist's team with Gordon Strachan, and Shane Warne was also there in Matt Dawson's team. I was hungover to hell but I think we won. It was good fun, but the pace of life was now relentless. That evening we drove back north for a quick pitstop before flying out to Spain the next day to record the relaunch of *Superstars* at the La Manga Golf Club down in the sunny south of Spain, near Murcia.

We arrived in the afternoon and they put us up in a luxurious apartment with an impressive health spa next door, but I wasn't interested in any of that. I was thirsty and looking for drinking partners, despite the fact that Cath was understandably not feeling so great in the early months of pregnancy and wanted to go to sleep.

No matter, I was Olympic champion and deserved my fun time, at least that's what I told myself as I headed down to the main resort hotel, the Hyatt, and its famous Lorca Bar, which seems to be where everybody meets. I left telling Cath I would only be a couple of hours but she knew different and resigned herself to not seeing me much before breakfast. That's how it was at the time. I was a bit of a bastard to her, not intentionally, just in an unthinking away. I was proud and excited at the prospect of impending fatherhood but the reality hadn't sunk in yet. And I was pretty oblivious to how Cath must have been feeling at the time – apprehensive as well as tired and occasionally sick. I simply went my own selfish way.

The first people I bumped into at La Manga were Brendan's five brothers, who, by complete coincidence, were down there on a golfing jolly. The first drink didn't touch the sides, nor the second or the third, and I was off again on a four-day session, interrupted occasionally by the need to compete in some of the *Superstar* events. I wasn't the only one, mind. Not many of us took the competition that seriously; after Athens loads of us were on the razzle, not least the rowers and in particular Alex

Partridge, who had unluckily missed out on a place in the 'famous four' with a lung problem. Steve Williams had done the decent thing and invited him along as his 'partner' for a week's drinking, a small consolation prize for missing out on Athens. The rowers – normally so dedicated and monastic like the cyclists – set a fierce pace in the bar. They started quickly and then accelerated into the distance. Impressive stuff.

The show ended with a marathon – drinking that is – with an all-nighter at Spikes – the disco/bar at the hotel – when we paid the staff to stay on and keep the place open until breakfast. A few hurried farewells and it was back to Manchester and the briefest of stopovers before heading out to the Continent again for the Grand Prix of Nations, the prestigious end-of-season 50-mile time-trial at which Crédit Agricole had hoped I might make a decent showing. After all, I was the Olympic pursuit champion.

It was a forlorn hope. I hadn't been on a bike for two weeks and the first person I bumped into at the team hotel was Christophe Moreau. A few pecks on the cheek French-style and Christophe insisted that we had unfinished business and that he had been saving a particularly fine bottle of red so that we could celebrate my Olympic title one more time. I couldn't tell you when that particular session ended but I do know I finished last the following day, some six minutes behind Michael Rogers.

That was it, I'd had enough with bikes for the time being. After I got home the following day I didn't touch my bike for two months. Didn't do a bloody thing. Instead I threw myself full time into the social circuit – Olympic parades, the BOA Gold Ball, celebration dinners, cycling club dinners and presentations, meeting the Queen. It was never ending and not really me but I got sucked into it. I had enjoyed my massive celebratory blast in the first three or four weeks and that should have been it, but now I was beginning to lose control. After being so disciplined for the last ten years, with just the occasional very brief break-out, I had lost all control and, of course, the invitations kept rolling in.

I remember with shame one particular evening being invited to dine with the Princess Royal at a small gathering of the chairman and chief executives of all Team GB's major sponsors and a cross-section of our gold medallists – Matt Pinsent was there, Dame Kelly and Jason Gardner from the sprint relay team. As usual, I had a hangover, but I tried to keep my end up and give the impression of being a serious sportsman and answer the fairly detailed questions of our generous benefactors. Hopefully I got away with it but, at one point, I distinctly remember looking around the great and good and wondering if any of them had any idea I had been blind drunk the night before and had been throwing up on Hampstead Heath. I shook my head and smiled to myself. Probably not.

—

Chapter Eleven

The wheels fall off

What was happening? I had no self-control any more and it was scary. I would turn up to some club function where I was meant to say a few words and present a few prizes and I would be too drunk to complete those simple formalities. I was drinking to get drunk and ending up unconscious. Luckily, I am quite a pleasant drunk and don't go around trying to start fights, but I was becoming a drunkard nonetheless. I wasn't comfortable being considered a 'hero' and role model. Steve Redgrave, Matt Pinsent, Kelly Holmes and the likes of Seb Coe, Steve Ovett and Daley Thompson from the old days – they were British heroes and worthy of acclaim. I was only Brad Wiggins.

That was the weekends, but it wasn't any better at home either. Cath had decided to work through her pregnancy for as long as possible and was leaving the house early every morning to get into the hospital and not getting back until well after six in the evening. What could I possibly do to occupy myself for the rest of the day?

Not a problem: 11 a.m. on the dot I would be outside the front door of my local in Chapel, waiting impatiently for the landlord to open up. I wouldn't move for the next seven hours as I steadily sipped my way through 12 or 13 pints. I would fit in the odd game of pool or darts, read the newspapers, treat myself to a spot of lunch, make a few calls, watch the sport on the TV – it was everything you dream of doing when you are putting in long hours of training. At least in that environment the drinking wasn't a manic race, I would steadily pour the pints down my gullet at the rate of about two an hour. Remarkable to relate, I was rarely in a bad state when I headed for home to start cooking Cath her dinner for when she got back.

Cath knew where I had been and what I had been doing – though hopefully not quite how much I had been necking the beers – but I wasn't roaring drunk and, being very wise and knowing me better than anybody, she sensed it was a phase I had to go through. If she started making an issue out of it, the problem and the arguments might escalate. For the time being she played it very cool and we would even crack open a bottle of wine, perhaps two, as we discussed her day and she started to wind down in front of the TV after another stressful day at work. Normally she would go up early, ahead of her early start the following day. I hadn't finished yet, no way. I had my cellar to explore yet.

Let me explain. One of my personality traits – and probably one Steve Peters could offer a cogent explanation for – is that I have mad passionate periods discovering something and have to become the world expert on that particular hobby or interest. Perhaps I am trying to build permanence when previously it had been lacking in my life. Perhaps, like many cyclists, I am just over the top and have to max out on whatever I'm doing.

Although we train bloody hard, possibly I have got too much time on my hands, but I am, naturally, a collector and hoarder. That first came to the fore when I became totally obsessed with accumulating boxing memorabilia, spending a small fortune in the process at auction houses or the occasional Sky sport auctions. Signed posters of Ali and Frazier – I've got one in my broom cupboard I paid £800 for years ago, Foreman, Spinks, Sugar Ray Leonard and all the great British boxers over the years. Gloves, boots, headguards, programmes, cuttings – I had to have the lot. I've still got most of the stuff stashed away, although I woke up one morning and suddenly wasn't interested any more. The only hobby or passion that has stood the test of time is my love of music and my guitar collection.

The guitar mania started about 2000, basically arising from my love of the Jam and Oasis and the need to fill my many hours of free time. Playing, and learning to get better, is therapy, complete relaxation. At home I can't put the guitar down and I will normally pack one when I go away. Even if I don't have a guitar around I will occupy myself playing the chords in my mind. I've got eight or nine guitars I really cherish and have collected over the years. There is my Fender Stratocaster, a beautiful pale white with gold pick-ups, which I suppose you would classify as the classic Hendrix guitar. Then there is my Epiphone Casino, Gibson ES335, Gibson SG, Rickenbacker 360, Gibson Firebird, Fender Telecaster, Epiphone Sheraton and Guild 12-string.

They are my pride and joy and I store them all away very carefully when I am not playing them around the house. A little jamming session in the sunroom is a perfect way of relaxing after a tough day's training.

So the writing was on the wall when I decided that Belgian beer was going to be the latest grand passion in my life, alongside Cath and my guitars that is. This was not going to be a half-hearted affair. Originally, after listening to wine buff Rob Hayes, I started collecting fine wines, but soon got bored with that. If you were collecting the real quality stuff it was quite expensive and took a while to build up a cellar and I quickly lost patience.

So then I turned to Belgian beers, which are universally

considered the best and strongest in the world, although some of our brews in Britain and the Czech Republic run them close. Traditionally, there are meant to be 365 different types of beer in Belgium, one for every day of the year, but this is a massive underestimate if you ask me. If you include the different varieties of the same brand it is closer to 800 and I set about collecting as many as possible.

Where do you start? They are all gorgeous and hit the spot. Piraat, Pater Lieven, St Bernardus, Trappiste Rochefort, La Chouffe, Boon, Saison Dupont, De Dolle, Triple Moine, Ramee, Tappiste Achel, Westmalle, Witcap, Abbeye de Malonne, Brugs, Satan, Bonsecours, St Paul, St Louis and many others.

After dabbling for a while I had started collecting them seriously during my adventures on the Six Day circuit, and then went into overdrive when GB staged their pre-Olympic training camp in Belgium earlier in 2004. I took full advantage of our off-duty hours to put together an impressively varied selection and finally returned to the UK with a van laden with the stuff. Each and every bottle was lovingly stored in my cellar at Chapel.

But not for long. In my post-Athens binge I would sit around the house for a few hours after Cath had gone up to bed, mulling it all over and, of course, started reaching for my Belgian friends. They slipped down beautifully but after a couple of months I started noticing that there weren't many left!

My all-day sessions at home pretty much lasted all the way through to Christmas 2004. The bottom line was that I was inexplicably depressed and was struggling to shake myself out of that mood. The immediate months after winning an Olympic gold medal are always going to be an anti-climax after the initial partying and back-slapping, but this was much deeper and more severe than I had ever anticipated. I had invested so much emotional energy in cycling and getting the gold medal that I was completely drained and empty when it was over.

I was 24 and had achieved my lifetime's ambition. What on earth comes next? I had absolutely no idea, I had always assumed that the lifetime ambition came towards the end of your career, and then you ride off into the sunset and live happily ever after. Here I was, with potentially ten years left as a professional and I had already achieved exactly what I set out to do.

Also there was a sense of being hugely undervalued. I had assumed that the Olympics would change my life and that, along with the party and dinner invites, there would be copper-bottomed commercial offers, endorsements, opportunities to earn real cash and secure my family's future. They just didn't come.

I was so confused by everything and disappointed that my Olympic achievements had not altered my financial situation one jot. I wasn't expecting a pot of gold but just assumed somehow that things would change. If I was such a big 'celebrity' that I was required every week to present prizes and make presentations, and dine with captains of industry, I somehow assumed this would translate into concrete earnings. Wrong. It has only been in the last couple of years, since my road career took off, that our situation has become very comfortable.

One drunken evening during the Tour of Britain I even agreed to a contract extension with Crédit Agricole, the team I loathed and despised. I had been earning a modest £30,000 a year basic and, as Olympic champion, should have asked for five times that, but in my confusion and urgent need to at least raise some money to pay the mortgage, I signed for £45,000, a 50 per cent increase but a pitifully low figure for an Olympic gold medallist. I got 'done' good and proper by Crédit Agricole and one particular businessman in their management team. It still hurts. As for the £45,000 – that's a week's wages for most average Premiership footballers. I don't like to think about that too often.

The alarm bells rang again at the BBC *Sports Personality of the Year* show in the December when initially Cath and I were sat down the front with the other gold medallists for all the cameras to concentrate on during the evening, to get the close-ups and conduct the interviews. As the first Brit to get three medals at the same Games for 40 years I was nervous but looking forward to my interview and five minutes of fame. Half an hour before we went on air a rather self-important producer came up and said I wasn't needed down the front any more and I would have to move to a seat at the back, away from the cameras, and there would be no room for Cath at all.

Come the actual show itself and I – comfortably the most successful of Britain's Olympians in 2004 – scarcely got a mention, and there was absolutely no chance of an interview or set-piece item. Not for the first or last time at that particular show, British cyclists had been sidelined and put in their place. I was not at all happy – for myself, Cath and the sport itself. The BBC's attitude is curious – their actual coverage of our major championships is excellent. Hugh Porter has forgotten more about the sport than most people know, Gary Sutton is the perfect sidekick and Jill Douglas is very good post-race interviewer who has taken the effort to understand the sport and to get to know everybody concerned within track cycling.

But when it comes to the wider sporting world, the BBC suddenly panics, perhaps mixing track and road in their minds and not wanting to be seen to take 'drug-tainted' road racing seriously. Which would be ridiculous. Surely they wouldn't cover athletics at all if drugs was the issue? Adrian Chiles's, 'interview' with Nicole Cooke in 2006, a year in which she had won everything going, was condescending and just plain embarrassing, while how Team GB could not be given the team prize for their seven gold medals at the World Championship in 2007 is beyond me.

One happy interlude during this difficult time was our wedding on 5 November. It was a very happy day and I was definitely pledging to spend my life with the woman I loved; but, true to form, I was absolutely bladdered for most of the day. I hadn't got things organised properly so we ended up having my stag night – that autumn was just one long stag night really – the night before and, with swimmer James Hickman and my brother Ryan leading the way, we were in no mood to be sensible and eventually retired hurt at 6 a.m. By 11 a.m. I was down in the hotel bar to greet all my family travelling up to Manchester for the wedding and, of course, we were soon having a few sharpeners and toasting the day.

The service itself was brilliant – I felt clear-headed and very emotional – but at the reception afterwards I was soon back on it and up to my normal tricks and got absolutely plastered. When I was invited to lead the bride in the traditional dance I, for some reason, thought it would be amusing to do a break dance in the middle of the floor. I don't think Cath, five months pregnant, was wonderfully happy about this, but she was well used to me by now and handled the situation with as much style and dignity as you can when your husband of a few hours is being a prat. By the end of the night I was certainly in no state to carry her to the bedroom as protocol demands, in fact I rather suspect it was me who was carried to the bridal suite and laid out on the matrimonial bed like a corpse.

There was a much-needed period of relative peace and calm during our honeymoon – spent just relaxing in the Lake District, which we both loved. We had moved to a nice house in Rufford near Cath's parents by now, and I began to think seriously about the ramifications of becoming a father. Cath always knew exactly how it would change our lives. With me being away racing so much she would need all the support she could get. I reintroduced myself to my bike – you know, that thing in the garage with two wheels and a saddle.

Grossly unfit and a stone overweight despite my fast metabolism and lean build, I started the long process of regaining some condition and shedding the pounds. I was a professional cyclist after all. Cath had stopped work by now so there was somebody at home all day. That calmed me down a bit in the week, although the weekends were still a minefield of invitations and drinking opportunities. Although I was still drinking way too much for an elite sportsman I was beginning to get some control back. Gradually the muscles started working again and I started to feel better about myself, which cleared the brain a little and we had a wonderful family Christmas.

There was still no purpose or intent in my training though. In my befuddled state on the Tour of Britain I had re-signed for Crédit Agricole but I didn't want to be there. I bitterly resented them for getting me cheap – in truth I was the only one to blame for that, I should have been much more on the ball – and I had no clear objectives for the coming seasons. I had this romantic notion about riding in the Tour de France but hadn't done the correct preparation and wasn't working towards it as a specific goal. It would be something great if it came along, but I wasn't making it happen. I would be off training and racing fairly regularly but nothing lit my fire and by now there were also complications at home, with Cath suffering from pre-eclampsia and really not well at all on occasions.

Most of the time I was a good diligent husband and a couple of times abandoned races abroad to come to her, but I was still well capable of losing the plot. Occasionally, possibly feeling guilty at my lack of dedication to Crédit Agricole, I would veer radically the other way and race for them when really I should have been at home with my wife in her hour of need. That's how, to my eternal annoyance and frustration, I managed to miss the birth of our gorgeous son Ben. I was off racing for a team I despised when I should have been at her side. I rushed home, but too late, I had missed one of those great milestone moments that mark a couple's life.

What a day that was all round. As young Ben Wiggins was entering the world, 6000 miles away in Los Angeles Mark Cavendish and Rob Hayles were winning the World Madison title for Great Britain, and a day earlier Great Britain had taken the Team Pursuit. For some reason, I always make the association when celebrating Ben's birth.

The arrival of Ben was a huge jolt to the system and sobered me up, literally and metaphorically, for the first time since the Olympics. Suddenly, apart from feeling extremely happy and proud, everything made sense. Everything going forward had to be about Cath and Ben, looking after them and soldiering on, and doing the best job I could until I got a break in my professional career. It was also the final, defining moment in my relationship – or should I say my non-relationship – with Garry. I had got a message from him after the Olympics and, during my drinking marathons in the autumn, I had been brooding about him. Bloody hell, there were some drunken days when I even wondered if I was becoming like him, that I had inherited his wild drinking genes as well as his cycling DNA. I had been pondering if there was any way we could be reconciled or if that was even desirable, but the birth of Ben immediately put everything into perspective.

How could any father abandon his children? Relationships go wrong and couples split up – there is little point getting hot and bothered about that, sometimes it seems that half the world comes from a split family – but a father should never walk away from his responsibilities to his children. How could he have done that, not once but three times? He always has a responsibility to them. As a proud new father myself, I started to get really angry thinking about how Garry had walked out first on Shannon, then me and now Madison. It crystallised and hardened my thoughts perfectly. I didn't like this bloke anyway, although I admired his class and guts as a rider. But now, as a father myself, I had a real insight to his actions all those years ago. NO, I didn't want him in my life, or Ben's for that matter. End of story.

I had finally put the brakes on and virtually stopped drinking altogether now and, after three weeks learning to become a dad and fitting in training rides, I was off to the Giro d'Italia for another three-week slog around one of the planet's most beautiful countries. I should have been excited and highly motivated about that but, because I had no objectives in my cycling life any more other than to earn the money to support my family, it passed me by. It started spectacularly with a night-time prologue, a ridiculously short course of just over 1 km along the sea front up the famous Reggio Calabria – you could see Mount Etna across the straights of Messina – and I took 11th in that, two seconds behind the Australian winner Brett Lancaster. After that, it was soon a matter of survival on a brutally hard Tour and working for our GC contender Pietro Caucchioli, who eventually finished eighth overall, nearly 12 minutes behind the popular Italian winner Paolo Savoldelli.

The best thing that can be said is that I got around, finishing 123rd of the 197 starters, some three and half hours behind Savoldelli. Nothing spectacular other than that I had proved to myself again that I can get around one of the biggest Tours – as ever the mountains on the Giro were brutal – and I had also got a stack of miles in my legs which was to have a beneficial effect later in the season.

To the surprise of nobody Crédit Agricole didn't select me for the Tour de France, which was nonetheless a bit of a slap in the face, although I wasn't in the mood to be bothered. The opening 12-mile time-trial in Noirmoutier should have suited me well and I had been pencilled in to play a big role on stage four, a 42-mile team time-trial between Tours and Blois, but I didn't make the cut and that was that. Instead I had June and July virtually free and was able to spend most of that time at home experiencing all the joys of fatherhood.

Soon after the Tour de France squads were announced my long-serving coach Simon Jones rang and suggested a meeting. Simon wasn't critical but he stated the bald truth – i.e. that it was nearly a year since the Olympics, I seemed to be all over the place and what were my plans? He had a project for me if I was interested. Why not have a crack at the time-trial at the World Championships in Madrid in September?

Why not indeed? It was a great little self-contained project that could salvage something from a rotten season. I had never entered a World time-trial before and it was essentially a new event for me but I had a pile of endurance in my legs after the Giro, now I needed to knuckle down and do some speed and technical work. It was a long tough course and it wasn't absolutely ideal for me but I should nonetheless be able to go well. We had 15 weeks left and it was definitely better than running up the white flag for the season. I started training exceptionally well and fell in love with cycling again – we had been estranged for too long, we had been going through the motions. I even managed a nice stage win on the Tour de l'Avenir and coming into Madrid I rode one of the best races of my life to finish seventh in a race that wasn't really suited to me. You will excuse me if I disregard the results of three of the riders above me – Andrei Kashechkin, Alexander Vinokourov and Ruben Plaza – because all three have subsequently been banned for doping, so in my mind I was fourth and just missed out on bronze medal, one of the very best rides of my career.

It was incredibly hot that day and the course, 40 minutes outside of Madrid, was basically horrible. It was long, included a fair number of harsh, barren climbs exposed to the elements. After a pre-race discussion we decided to cut the arms off my skin suit but I felt good from the moment I pushed off and went out very hard, perhaps too hard. I began to 'blow' about a third of the way around and thought, that's it, just bring it home as best you can and enjoy the day. But then I came good again and started to really fly before blowing again just before the end. I was totally knackered but delighted, it had been a really competitive eyeballs-out effort and, as one of the early starters, I had to spend a very long afternoon sitting in the Tissot seats – the current top three have to sit there so the cameras can capture all the emotion as their times are beaten and they fall off the medal podium. Only right at the death did I begin to move back in the pecking order. Michael Rogers from Australia took it with a brilliant ride, Spain's José Iván Gutiérrez and Fabian Cancellara from Switzerland were both 24 seconds behind, and then came the trio of Plaza, Vinokourov and Kashechkin just ahead of me.

Definitely one of the highlights of my career and a feel-good week – Cath, Ben and my in-laws were all over, lending support and making it a family occasion – was completed when I signed a new contract to join Cofidis, who, despite my distinctly average year in the saddle, were keen to sign me for well over double what Crédit Agricole were paying their Olympic pursuit champion. In short they believed in me. Things were to eventually turn a little sour with them two years later at the Tour de France, when emotions ran very high, but generally they were a superbly run and supportive team and I enjoyed many happy days proudly wearing their colours. They backed me to the hilt in what I wanted to do, were sympathetic and understanding bosses, and they employ some of the very best backroom staff in the business.

They were, and remain, a top team, and for the majority of my time with them I could not have been happier. The first thing they said was: Brad, you are a reigning Olympic champion, you are pre-selected for the 2006 Tour de France. End of discussion. A new and painful chapter in my life was about to start.

Chapter Twelve

—

The Tour de France at last

The approach from Cofidis and their offer of a contract helped redefine my career. I was going to be a road rat for the next season or two. All thoughts of track competition were put to one side, or at least relegated to a distant second place. Of course I had 'clocked' Great Britain's excellent results in the 2005 World Championships in Los Angeles – four gold medals to celebrate and particularly the Madison on little Ben's birthday – but was a little alarmed to find I didn't miss being there and didn't really feel associated with the results, despite the fact that I knew everybody involved and they had been my close friends and colleagues for much of the previous year.

After Cofidis came in for me I also decided to shelve any thoughts of the Commonwealth Games in Melbourne in March 2006, which would have featured a fiery head to head with the best Australian riders who had dominated in Athens. That was a little bit of a wrench; I hadn't won a Commonwealth Gold yet and racing the Aussies on their own patch would have been fun, but with thoughts of the Tour de France filling my head it was a decision that had to be made. And, having dropped out of the Commonwealth, I also effectively dropped out of the Worlds, which were being held in Bordeaux about ten days later, a crazy turnaround but one which our team seemed to handle with their usual professionalism.

For much of that winter I became a Tour de France bore; it was the only thing I could think about. The race, in fact, provided my very first sporting memory because I distinctly remember sitting at home watching some of the duels between Greg Lemond and Laurent Fignon in the dramatic 1989 Tour, which Greg won by the ridiculously small margin of eight seconds. It wasn't quite a Damascus moment like Chris Boardman in 1992, but it had made me sit up, and a desire to ride in it was there, bubbling away in the background, for many years.

Miguel Indurain – Big Mig – was the Tour de France rider I identified with; I just loved his power and style and the inscrutable way he had about him – you never really knew whether he was struggling or not and whether he was stressed or not. I also pestered Mum and Brendan to buy the tapes of old Tours so I could soak myself in the history. I can be a bit of a cycling anorak given half a chance, and soon there was little I didn't know about the Tour and its lore.

I started training well and, with the Tour in mind and anxious to impress my new employers, I overcooked it again. I really should have learned my lesson by this stage but I was overkeen. The result was not catastrophic but I was only 90 per cent all season, which meant that although I was competent and there were no particularly bad lows, there were no great highs either.

I grabbed a pleasing seventh in the Prologue of Paris–Nice – just five seconds behind the winner Bobby Julich – and overall finished in the bunch in a race won impressively by Floyd Landis, who was displaying outstanding form. For the first time, I finished in the second group in the annual Paris–Roubaix, a brute of an early season Classic, and it was with modest hopes that I embarked on my first Tour de France and set out for Strasbourg for the *Départ*.

Wow. It was about ten times bigger than I ever thought

possible and I knew it would be big. And that was just the *Départ*. When you are right in the middle of the Tour de France the world outside ceases to exist. You move in a massive self-contained bubble for the best part of a month and eat, drink and sleep the Tour. It is madness of a high degree but that is half the appeal.

It starts right at the beginning with the *Départ*, which is three days of festivities, meetings, interviews, sponsors' events, corporate hospitality and mounting excitement before the prologue – a time-trial of varying length but, when short, one of my strong suits – and then the start of the first stage proper. It is cycling's biggest talking shop of the year and a huge happening in its own right, with rival cities outbidding each other financially for the right to host the *Départ*. Hotels are booked out from the moment the destination is announced a couple of years earlier.

Everything is on such a huge scale. Before the Tour I was used to chaotic impromptu press conferences with perhaps 15–20 journalists thrusting their microphones in your face and jostling with camera crews for the best position. At the *Départ*, massive conference halls and cinema-style rooms seating 300 or 400 are hired out for the press conferences and it is nothing to have 200 media in attendance for one of the team press conferences or big names. Different league.

It becomes the melting pot of our sport. Because the sport's media are gathered from around the world, people tend to hang on to stories and release them in the week of the *Départ*. Teams and sponsors make all their big announcements. It all becomes a bit frenzied.

And of course Strasbourg developed into the most sensational *Départ* of all. It had started with a blindingly honest press conference from Dave Millar, who sat there on the top table and was reduced to tears at one stage as he talked about his drug use and return to the peloton after a two-year ban. That was interesting enough. Those receiving bans have, in the past, never openly admitted the problem, a sort of *omertà* exists which ensures that the integrity of the peloton itself is not challenged but here was Dave speaking about it openly.

The fact that he was returning in reasonable nick, although with no competitive miles in his legs, was interesting. Dave had a well-established performance pattern over the years and it would be interesting to compare his performances against riders he had been competing against for a long period now he was drug-free. Not everybody welcomed him back with open arms.

But Dave Millar was just the warm-up. Later that day the entire Tour was torn asunder by the eviction from the race of a number of riders whose names had been connected with Operation Puerto, the undercover police investigation in Spain aimed at exposing a blood-doping ring centred on Dr Fuentes and allegedly involving many top footballers, athletes, tennis players and Continental basketball stars as well as cyclists.

The UCI had been provided with a list of the riders involved and was determined not be seen sitting on such a list of shame on the eve of the sport's showcase event, putting the Tour de France organisers under enormous pressure to act before any of those riders had been formally charged or implicated by the Spanish authorities. A meeting of the 21 team managers was held and they were told that their riders on the list had to be withdrawn and those riders could not be replaced. People who constantly criticise cycling should remember that. The Football World Cup was going on at this stage and I don't remember FIFA even acknowledging the existence of their list of shame in Spain, let alone acting and disciplining those on it. That would, of course, have been terrible publicity for football at such a time.

Meanwhile, back in Strasbourg, Jan Ullrich, Ivan Basso, who had won the recent Tour of Italy at a canter and looked unbelievably strong in the mountains, and Francisco Mancebo were, in one fell swoop, thrown out of the race – i.e. the three favourites to win in the absence of Lance Armstrong, who had finally retired after seven successive wins. Ten other riders were also barred from the race. The Tour de France was in uproar, the sport was in uproar. This even more dramatic than the Festina scandal in 1998.

The rows and debates raged all night and it seemed the very future of the sport was at stake. I never accepted that it was that serious – cycling will always be a major sport – it's just how well it is policed that matters. Trying to concentrate on my first ever Tour and the Prologue – on paper I should go reasonably well – was difficult, and it was about this time also that I began to be 'pigeon-holed' as the unofficial spokesman for the clean brigade. I've never made any secret of my abhorrence of the use of drugs in cycling and sport in general, but equally I am not a preacher – I didn't seek the role.

What happened, I believe, is this. First, as a high-profile member of the GB track squad, who have made a virtue of their ethical stance and challenge anybody to test any of their riders at any time, I was someone whose view was possibly worth quoting. And, second, in purely practical terms there are only so many English-speaking riders on the Tour – certainly you wouldn't need the fingers of one hand to count the Brits on the 2006 Tour.

Dave Millar, although an eloquent talker and a reformed druggie, was still tainted to a certain extent so soon after ending his ban, so I became the obvious bloke to seek out among some of the English-speaking press. To the world at large it must have looked as if I was standing on my soapbox at Hyde Park corner, denouncing all those who take drugs and putting myself forward as some saintly figure, but I can assure you that this was not the case. I just became the 'best quote' and, once that label stuck, I was the first person the journalists phoned when any drug issue arose. None of this went down too well with well-established members of the peloton, who were left wondering why this debutant appeared to be doing all the talking, having yet to ride a single kilometre of the Tour de France. They had a point.

The Prologue itself was like my season, middling. It was a short, fast, 7 km route and to my liking, but the build-up had got to me and I was too slow in the early stages which cost me the top ten place I had secretly hoped for. In the end I came home 16th – far from disgraceful, one place behind my old drinking partner Christophe Moreau – both of us were entirely sober this time – and one ahead of Dave Millar on his much heralded return. There were a few classy time-triallists behind us – Andreas Kloden and Bobby Julich – so it was a decent ride without setting the world on fire.

A shower, massage and a decent meal and I was ready to start the Tour in earnest the next day. Little did I know that the controversies were far from over.

My immediate concern was to keep my head down, do my job for the team and get around. Strip away the emotions of the ride and its later controversies and that's what happened. I got in a break during the first week which always pleases the team sponsors, acted as a bottle carrier during the long days, got through the mountains in the Groupetto and showed at the front of the race for a while on the final day hurtling down the Champs Elysées. My ambition was no higher than that.

At the start of a race there are 21 team leaders of whom, let us say, ten have a realistic chance of making the podium for GC in Paris. Another small group of riders have a chance of taking the points and mountain jerseys but that's it. There are only so many riders who can challenge for honours in the Tour de France and they are very much reliant on the efforts of their team. Everybody has a well-defined role. Very few riders have realistic chances of winning a stage when they get up every morning, although if the chance ever offers itself you have to grab it with both hands.

Initially, just coping with the sheer scale of the event is the biggest challenge. Every day can seem like an Olympic final so you must just immerse yourself in routine and simply 'doing the job' or become completely overwhelmed. It looks so glamorous but is anything but. Let me try and give you an idea of a typical day in the life of Brad Wiggins, Tour de France rider.

8 a.m. The alarm goes off, hopefully after eight or nine hours' uninterrupted sleep, and there is a knock on the door just to make sure from one of the *soigneurs*. You slowly regain consciousness, and then it hits you like a ton of bricks. You are on the Tour de France and before the day is over you have got ride 140 miles in 32 degrees of heat with four Category 1 climbs and a mountain-top finish. Just like yesterday in fact. Ever so gently you ease your way out of bed. It's amazing how often you can twang a muscle or feel something give first thing in the morning after a night in an unfamiliar bed with stressed muscles pulling every which way. You successfully manoeuvre yourself into the standing position and immediately log how your legs feel. Heavy, light, strong, weak. Good legs or bad legs. Most of the time you can tell there and then whether you are going to have an okay day or whether you are in for another day of pain and suffering. Having assessed you legs you grunt a good morning to your 'roomie' and head to the bathroom before slipping into tracksuit and T-shirt.

Next comes possibly the highlight of the day – breakfast. This will be the 'Full Monty' starting with a big bowl of porridge with chocolate cereal, followed by a bowl of pasta, a couple of chocolate croissants, orange juice, *café noir* and perhaps a piece of fruit. You then pick up your kit which has been washed the night before from a big basket by the table and head for your room where, despite the groaning breakfast, it is time for a stretch, usually by yourself but with one of the *soigneurs* or physios if you have a specific problem that needs working on. After that, it is on with the race gear before packing your case – by midway through the Tour you can do it in your sleep. As you close the door on a hotel room that you will never seen again but for 12 hours was home and a refuge from the madness, you leave your case outside the door for picking up and then head down to the team bus.

9.30 a.m. Two hours before the peloton rolls out and you get onto the team bus, for, hopefully, a shortish trip down to the start. If I am travelling with my guitar I will carefully load it onto the coach myself – it would be unfair to ask a *soigneur* to do that. If it gets damaged that has to be down to me. I will often have another quick stretch as we wait around. It is gloriously sunny and the mountain air is crisp but it's going to be very hot. A cruel day in prospect.

Aboard the bus we all have our 'claimed seats' and mine, naturally, is on the back row. Somebody will put some music on and I will usually try to phone Cath, just to touch base and make sure everything is all right. She normally has her hands full with the kids at that time of the morning – an hour earlier back home – so I keep it brief. As we approach our allocated parking slot at the start the nerves kick in slightly as you see the fans on the road and there is a flurry of activity. On with your cycling shoes and sunblock, check you've got your favourite shades and your food sack for the start. The Directeur Sportif will say a few words, briefly outline the route for those who haven't studied it too closely, explaining our objectives for the day, going into a bit more detail about some of the climbs – these are the places to either attack or expect an attack for those in contention and this the likely cut-off time for those in the Groupetto.

And then it's out into the bright sunlight, the temperature rapidly rising, and the first media scrum of the day around the coach as the immediate questions of the day have to be negotiated. As soon as I can reasonably slope off without being rude I hop on my bike, sign on and head off towards the Tour village.

This is one of the traditions of the Tour and for some of us represents the nearest thing to a social life we will get for three weeks. The Tour village is an enclosed area where the tour organisation and all the sponsors literally set up a village overnight so they can entertain their guests and promote their products. The local town or even village out in the middle of France will also promote its local products – mainly food and wine – and there are also a few home comforts like a hairdresser, a postal service, money-dispensing machines and suchlike. It is a place to see and be seen, but also very relaxing, and I always make a point of popping in every morning.

First call was the Orange marquee, where they offer free international calls and I phone home for a longer chat with Cath, and then it was straight off to the Crédit Lyonnais tent and a part of a foreign field that is forever England, well at least Britain. There I will scrounge a final coffee and croissant and settle down for half an hour or so to read that morning's English papers which miraculously appear courtesy of the bank. Strange to behold, I usually find the British press availing themselves in exactly the same way, and Dave Millar as well, with occasional guest appearances from Geraint Thomas on his debut year in 2007. It is all very congenial and relaxing as we put the world to rights, discuss the football and cricket scores and swap a bit of race gossip. Occasionally I have been known to lose track of time and one of the team *soigneurs* will be dispatched – they always know where I am – to rush me off to the start line. It's just a mental process really, delaying the final moment when you have to commit your body and soul to the race and those agonising miles ahead. Only one person can get you to the end and that is your good self.

11.30 a.m. We roll out from the start for a couple of miles in the neutral zone – no racing is allowed as we will often be going through narrow village streets and there may still be a few stragglers in the race caravan ahead, getting themselves organised and ahead of the race. And then we are off. Sometimes it's a sluggish start and you can spend an hour moving through the peloton having a chat, other days it is eyeballs-out from the start and you are fighting for your life not to be spat out the back. Even a slow day on the Tour de France is considerably quicker than the norm in other races. Everybody is raising their game, these are cycling's Olympics and everybody is a star in their own right. Most days somebody in the peloton is having the ride of their life and that means everybody has to try and match it or just survive. It is bloody tough.

On a long mountain day the Groupetto will get organised about mid-race and by the third week a good spirit will have built up and we will help and encourage each other. But on a hard racing tactical day there is little time for niceties as you ride to protect your GC contender, shielding him from the wind, chasing down breaks or dropping back to the cars to collect more water or food. No matter what kind of a day it is, there will be moments when you wouldn't be doing anything else for a living and other moments when you seriously question your sanity and promise yourself never, ever, again.

5.30–6 p.m. Finish. If it is a mountain stage the Groupetto will be anything from 30–40 minutes behind the winner and, even though you have been trying to pace yourself, you will be on your knees on the final climb. God knows how we get through some of those days. It is so hot on the road and the mountains just go on for ever, there is no relief. And the descents are just as hard in their own way, you have to ride right on the edge to try to make up time and stay with the Groupetto. Although you might be at the back of the Tour de France you are still riding at a level beyond most riders in the world. Sometimes I run my favourite music through my head trying to wish the hours away, sometimes I let the scenery into my consciousness and try to become inspired by it, and other days I just count the kilometres down one by one and tell myself it is good for the soul and, if nothing else, all these hard yards have to make me a better pursuiter on the track.

You flop over the line into the arms of your *soigneur* who, as long as you haven't been selected for a random dope test, leads you to the bus where the first thing is to stand or slump under the shower for ten minutes, the bus having managed to plug into the mains and provide running hot and cold water. Fantastic, almost the best moment of the day. On with your tracksuit, a couple of milkshakes and a sandwich and you begin to feel vaguely human again. You kick around the bus discussing the day with your colleagues as the bus makes its way to the hotel, probably an hour or so away. I will ring Cath again, just a check call really as she is busy with feed time and baths back home, just to say that I'm okay, I haven't crashed and I will live to fight another day. Eventually you get to the hotel; you are already checked in so you pick up your key card, throw away the key card from the previous night's hotel and go straight up to the room, unpack your bag and immediately look for the massage list posted on the door. Hopefully you are first up at 7, which gives you time to shower the oil off afterwards and get downstairs for the team dinner at 8.30 p.m.

After that you might kick around in the lobby for half an hour – maybe a couple of friends or somebody from Team GB will have arranged to drop by for a coffee – or occasionally you might even have the energy for a stroll and a stretch outside for ten minutes, which I always try to do up in the mountains, enjoying the cool of the evening before heading for my cot. It is a totally full-on day and there is time for nothing else. You might take your sound system, or a book and DVD player, but in the end you invariably end up crashing out. I will probably pick away at my guitar for 15–20 minutes but that is the limit of my ambition. You don't have the energy for anything else. Killing time is not a problem on the Tour de France, believe me. Sleep comes instantly, like having an anaesthetic needle inserted and, luckily, I sleep like a baby. I can't imagine how anybody gets through the Tour if they can't sleep properly.

The body is infinitely versatile and as long as you are basically fit and healthy you can get into a rhythm, so much so that when one of the two days off comes along you would rather not stop. The body starts to recover and stiffens up, that's why you have to go for a two-hour spin anyway to stop your muscles seizing up. Because you are in a set pattern the body doesn't want to use those extra hours sleeping and in any case the one thing you must not disturb is your sound sleep pattern. Rest days, frankly, are a pain and more for the benefit of the race organisation and media to catch up. I'm always glad when they are over, especially if a big day is looming the day after.

Chapter Thirteen

The Landis affair

So that's how I spent my days on my first Tour de France, although my simple itinerary gives no impression of the sheer physical effort, or of the grandeur and the beauty of the surroundings. Even when the going is tough I love the setting and I am enough of a cycling historian to know the significance of most of the major climbs we fight our way up. For me, it helps. I was enjoying it in a low-key, gritted-teeth sort of way, the crowds were extraordinary and the racing post-Armstrong was open and unpredictable, although to my eyes – and in fairness I viewed the race very much from the rear – Floyd Landis looked the class act and likely winner from a fair way out. Then the race was blown apart in two extraordinary days and the ramifications are still being felt.

Stage 15 finished with a fine win for Frank Schleck at the top of Alpe d'Huez, while a rock-solid day in the mountains saw Landis finish fourth and take the yellow jersey from Oscar Pereiro, with the likelihood of much more time to come the following day because Landis, a former world mountain bike champion, is extremely consistent in the high mountains and Stage 16 was the stage from hell, possibly the Queen Stage of the tour, being relatively late on during the final week. Along the way we had to climb the mighty Col du Galibier (42.8 km at 4.5 per cent), Col de la Croix de Fer (22.7 km at 7 per cent), Col du Mooard (5.8 km at

7 per cent) and finally the long hot climb into the ski resort of La Toussuir, listed as 18.4 km at 6 per cent although it seemed longer and harder to me

It was a sweltering day and the story of the race at the front was that Michael Rasmussen, a natural-born climber, had a day of days and spent 173 km and over five hours at the front, dictating events, eventually breaking clear to secure a superb stage win. Everybody else had to hang tough and 5 km up the final climb the group *maillot jaune* – the peloton gathered around Landis – was holding steady at just over five minutes behind when Landis suddenly and unexpectedly went out the back, obviously suffering like hell.

It was a desperate struggle up that final climb and Landis eventually trailed home 23rd, 10 minutes and 4 seconds behind Rasmussen, and 8 minutes and 9 seconds behind Pereiro. On that final climb the yellow jersey had dropped from first to 11th overall, the most dramatic, non-injury or non-crash-related collapse of the yellow jersey in Tour history. Incidentally, I came in 44 minutes after the winner and 34 minutes behind Landis in a huge Groupetto that tested the judges' patience as to whether we had officially made the time limit. Luckily there was safety in numbers and we were allowed to continue.

So what had happened to Landis? To these eyes and from what I heard on the grapevine it was a pretty classic case of straight-forward hunger knock, just not getting enough fuel on board during a stressful day defending your position and blowing up spectacularly at the death. It has happened many times before and no matter how experienced you are and no matter how strong the team around you, it can catch anybody out.

It was an especially hot day and hydration and heat exhaustion may have been a problem for Landis. Certainly the following day, on the now infamous Morzine stage, if you watch the DVD you can see Landis constantly pouring water over himself on his solo break, as if overcompensating for an oversight the previous day. He went through gallons and gallons of the stuff.

Landis himself says he didn't feel great from the moment he got up that morning, and that his Phonak team had done a great job nursing him to the foot of that final climb before his body could take no more. Whatever, it was a terrible day at the office but an experience that most top riders have endured at some stage, although probably not when wearing the yellow jersey in the Tour de France.

So, at the start of the Morzine stage the following day, what was the scenario? Well, up to the previous stage, Landis had been the class act and, although he had blown up in the final half-hour the previous day, I certainly hadn't discounted him from the race altogether, although obviously he had a huge mountain to climb so to speak. He had nothing to lose now and, at the very least, it was certain he and his team would try something – everything – to salvage his reputation. To repeat, the one thing absolutely certain that morning was that Landis would come out guns blazing. And sometimes you can wake up and just feel great – it has happened to me. Riders talk about having 'good legs' and you can wake up after a bitch of a day and just feel okay.

What I am saying is that it was no surprise to me that Phonak went crazy just after the first feed station before the first climb of the Morzine stage – it was going to be a real grippy day, two Category 1 climbs and another couple of sharp ascents and tough riding from the gun. The perfect day for a long break, that's for sure. Phonak hit the turbo and suddenly we were all strung out in a line doing 60 kph, discarding feed bags and bottles as we rushed to get down into the racing almost time-trial position. This was bloody suicidal this early in the day – a brave do-or-die effort by Landis and his team was my immediate reaction, and well timed because most people assumed he was dead and buried – but, whatever, the race was soon split every which way. By the time we got to the top of the first climb – the Col des Saises – Landis was away and had stolen four minutes on the field with 180 km to go.

There must have been 80 or 90 of us left as we crested that first climb; we had been riding virtually flat out and already we had been reduced to the day's Groupetto. It was bizarre. Landis was gone and gradually his lead built – 6, 7 and then 8 minutes, and just as gradually his team-mates faded back into the group, absolutely spent – they had put every last ounce into getting their team leader away. Something pretty extraordinary was happening that was for sure. At one stage, before the final climb of the day, Stuart Grady and CSC were in a break trying to finally drag Landis back and must have been hitting 60 kph on the flats but were making no impression. It was like trying to catch a motorbike.

We crawled into Morzine that night scarcely able to take in what had happened. Landis had won the stage from Carlos Sastre by 5 mins 42 secs, and taken 7 mins 8 secs out of Pereiro's yellow jersey. He was now only 30 seconds behind the Spaniard with a big time-trail to come at which he was a specialist. If it was genuine, it would have to rate as one of the greatest solo rides in Tour history, if not the greatest, given the dramas of the previous day.

At the time, as opposed to looking back now, I was pretty amazed but not totally sceptical as I am when riders I know to be average time-trialists and certainly inferior to me suddenly cane me by three or four minutes. On those occasions you just know instantly. This time around I was, initially, prepared to give Landis the benefit of the doubt, and despite what many journalists will tell you that was the universal reaction in the press as well. Look at the reports of his ride the following day. The cycling romantic in me wanted to believe in this incredible ride. Landis is an extremely classy rider who had been my tip for the Tour until he had one horrible day, which was probably self-induced by not feeding properly. He then stormed back with a seemingly heroic all-day break over a tough stage and won by five minutes to put himself right back in contention. It was unusual and exceptional but not unprecedented – Tour history is scattered with instances of amazing one-off rides. Charlie Gaul's solo charge in 1958 would be of the same ilk.

For a while I thought nothing more of it. The Tour rumbled on, the press the next day was full of Landis's heroics, but for me getting to Paris was the only thing that mattered. He occupied another world entirely, a team leader and contender for GC. I really wasn't too bothered about Floyd Landis. Survival was the name of the game and getting through the following day from Morzine to Macon, which was horribly hot – 100 degrees plus – from start to finish. And then came the final decisive time-trial, when Landis, as expected, put in a powerful ride to finish third, 91 seconds quicker than Pereiro, a ride which sealed his overall Tour win. I rode simply to get around, finishing over seven minutes behind the winner, Sergei Gonchar, in 56th, but as far as I was concerned it was job done.

With the final day promenade into Paris and a quick burn-up around the Champs Elysées I was sure to finish my first Tour de France and it was a nice moment. I certainly hadn't set the world alight but that wasn't my aim or indeed my designated job. I did what I was capable of at that stage of my career.

A massive celebratory bash in Paris awaited. Cath was coming over and she had struck up a good friendship with the girlfriend of a racing colleague of mine at Cofidis, Cristian Moreni, and was enjoying a few glasses of champagne and bit of shopping as we closed in on Paris on the Sunday. I found enough energy to give it a quick burst down the Champs Elysées at the head of the peloton to catch the photographers' attention and then, before we knew it, the race was over and Floyd Landis was up on the podium in yellow and the Stars and Stripes was again belted out to acclaim the winner of the Tour de France. As for me, I was busy looking for Cath and planning a big night out after an official team dinner. It was one of the happier days in my racing career. A Tour that had started so disastrously back in Strasbourg had finished on a relative high.

It was two days later that the cycling world came crashing down again. First came the leaked news that a rider – unnamed – had tested positive for testosterone at the end of the Morzine stage and then, the following day, came confirmation that it was the Tour winner Floyd Landis after his epic solo break that day. Turmoil. After the B sample proved positive the Tour had no option but to ban its own winner and declare Pereiro the champion, but what a shocking indictment of the sport and a terrible message to send out to the world. I felt physically sick when I heard the news.

My first reaction was purely selfish and related to only to me. 'You bastard Landis', I thought. 'You have completely ruined my own small achievement of getting around the Tour de France and being a small part of cycling history. You and guys like you are pissing on my sport and my dreams. Why do guys like you keep cheating? How many of you are out there, taking the piss and getting away with it? There is me trailing home 131st and, for all I know, I might be a top 50 rider if we all started on a level playing field. Sod you all. You are a bunch of cheating bastards and I hope one day they catch the lot of you and ban you all for life. You can keep doing it your way and I will keep doing it mine. You won't ever change me, you sods. Bollocks to you all. At least I can look myself in the mirror.'

As happened at Strasbourg, the phone started ringing because I am English-speaking and generally an amenable chap and I let rip in trademark fashion with a huge number of expletives having to be deleted from my quotes. Loads of peloton riders felt exactly the same but either kept their heads down or were not approached for quotes, so again it appeared as if I had somehow become an unofficial spokesman and keeper of cycling's moral keys, so to speak. Far from it, but I have got my own standards and opinions and, if asked, I will occasionally shoot from the hip.

Briefly I spoke about giving the sport up, but that was never really a serious option – that was just me trying to express my anger. I will still be cycling in some shape or form until the day I drop. As I calmed down I started putting things in perspective. Landis, meanwhile, was angrily protesting his innocence and started to fight everything through the courts, a process which ended this summer when his final appeal was dismissed. I ran the entire day over in my mind again and none of it makes much sense.

Testosterone. Why testosterone? Nobody in the sport can understand that one because if you were looking for a quick short-term boost to try and salvage your race and career after a bad day, testosterone is not your poison of choice. I am told it can help with improving muscle strength over a given period of time, during a particularly heavy period of pre-season training, but something with much more immediate and dramatic effect would have been required for the Morzine stage.

High levels of testosterone can be recorded naturally with alcohol consumption and sex raising the levels above the accepted norm. All this is well established and known by the medics, and many competitors testing positive, from all sports, have been declared innocent using that defence. Indeed, from what I can judge the majority of testosterone cases get thrown out.

But the big difference with the Landis case is that the tests demonstrated clearly – although Landis has always contested this – that the testosterone was synthetic, i.e. not naturally occurring and had been introduced to the system at some stage.

So this is getting complicated, but one scenario, considered the most likely but vigorously denied by Landis, is that he was using testosterone during an intensive training period much earlier in the season and had some blood drawn off at that stage and this blood was mistakenly used in a transfusion – doping – the night before the Morzine stage, i.e. the evening immediately after his collapse going up the final hill in La Toussir.

That makes some sense but not a lot. It certainly provides an explanation, but would Landis, or people involved with him, be so stupid as to make such an elementary doping mistake? It's an interesting point. You wouldn't expect a habitual doper to make such a cock-up, although it might be the sort of mistake made by somebody experimenting with using performance-enhancing drugs for the first time. The bottom line is that we will probably never know. One thing never changes: athletes *in extremis* do strange things and lose the plot in all sorts of ways.

I'm interested and I'm not. This is my sport and my profession and I want it to be clean, and in that respect there is an urgent need to understand why these people need to cheat and how it works. Some of them are guys I consider to be decent human beings who obviously, in some way, have a serious flaw in their make-up. That doesn't necessarily make them bad people, just imperfect humans. At the same time I abhor what they do, their actions make my life as a cyclist infinitely more difficult, and want absolutely no part of it. It's a dilemma. Sometimes I care deeply about it and them, and sometimes I go into denial and can't be bothered to even acknowledge it goes on – I just want to get on with my life and make sure these cheating maggots don't impinge on my life one jot. Ultimately, there are cheats in every

walk of life and everybody must do their own thing and live with
their conscience.

When the dust had settled, the major consequence of the
entire Landis saga for me was to reignite my desire to get back
onto the track. I could never desert the road racing entirely, I love
it too much, but suddenly I urgently needed to be back on the
track, racing with and against people I had no doubts over and
where everything is genuine. My thoughts turned immediately to
the World Championships in Palma, Majorca, the following
March and I got down to some serious work at home with at least
three visits to the track every week. In fairness to Cofidis they
continued to support me all the way. The team has a close affinity
with track riders. Arnaud Tournant – a key member of France's
team sprint squad over the years and a great rival of Chris Hoy –
was a team member for a number of years. Cofidis financed his
successful attempt on the World Kilo record at altitude in La Paz
in 2001, when he set a scarily fast time which even Chris couldn't
beat six years later.

The Cofidis management also sensed just what a huge upset
the Landis thing had been – to the entire sport, not just me – and
were more than happy for me to concentrate on the pure world
of track and earn them much positive publicity in that way. Their
support never wavered and a contingent turned up in Palma to
cheer me on and generally enjoy the sight of one of their boys
racing for gold, albeit in GB colours.

It soon became a very happy and fulfilling time. Ben was a
toddler and Cath was preparing to have our second child,
Isabella, in November, so I was based at home training locally
and at the Manchester velodrome. We flew out to Majorca early
in 2007 for an endurance training camp, then it was back to
Manchester for more speed work and a concerted effort by me to
break back into the Team Pursuit squad for the first time since

2004. Nothing could be taken for granted; the event had moved on and our squad was getting stronger every year, with exciting new talent coming through from the various development programmes.

By way of a dress rehearsal, Manchester staged a round of the annual World Cup series and I came back firing on all cylinders in the Individual Pursuit and Team Pursuit, while the GB team generally went off the Richter scale and won gold in eight of the events. The public was possibly a bit disbelieving, it was only a dress rehearsal for the Worlds after all, and in Palma all the nations would be at full strength and flat out.

We begged to differ, the team was totally confident in its preparation and our talent. We were very much on track and everything was building towards a special time in Palma, where it may have rained for five days solid outside but inside the spanking new Palma arena everything was bright and sunny for British track cycling as we powered our way to an incredible seven World Championship gold medals.

My mindset had changed significantly and I was now devoting an equal amount of my emotional energy and time to the Team Pursuit, alongside my own individual event. The ageless Paul Manning was still around as the squad captain, but two young hot shots, Geraint Thomas and Ed Clancy, had forced their way into the squad and it was clear the GB quartet was going places and was on the verge of making the big breakthrough at World and Olympic Championships. To be a member of this squad – and I badly wanted to be part of the action – there could be no compromising on training and turning up as and when your individual training schedule permitted. And there could be no going AWOL mentally after finishing my individual event. They were strong enough to win major medals without me, so I needed to show more focus on the event to earn my starting place. Although I had always given the Team Pursuit the very best I could on the day, I hadn't always given it my full attention. That was changing and indeed had to change if I was ever to fulfil my dream of winning two, let alone three gold medals at one Olympics.

It was great to be back and I was determined to lay down a marker with my first Championship ride since 2004 in the qualifying of the Individual Pursuit. Having only one World Cup result, albeit a good one, behind me I was again unseeded so had to establish my mark early on. We scheduled a 4.16 and that is what I delivered – 4 mins 15.976 secs, the fastest time in the world since my Olympic victory. I started off with my usual 69-second opening Kilo from the standing start and then simply reeled off three 62-second laps. Again I rolled around trying to look easy and stress-free, which wasn't difficult because actually I felt as okay as you can when delivering a time like that. Nothing was going to stop me in the final – I reckoned I still had a bit to come if required and nobody in Palma that year was remotely in the form to challenge. Germany's Robert Bartko was second fastest in 4.19 something but I fancied he had dug deep to get that and would fail to back it up.

So it proved. I went out on a 4.15 pace and was moving just as smoothly as during qualifying, better even, and caught him with five laps to go. Perhaps I should have gone on to clock something really special – I was flying – but it's not really the done thing in a final and within seconds of catching Bartko I had my race head on again and was thinking of the Team Pursuit the next day. I enjoyed the moment – I have rarely produced two such high-quality rides in a day – but the job was only half done and there was a tough day ahead tomorrow. No need to go mad. I was definitely growing up and maturing as a competitor.

The field in the Team Pursuit the following day was not the strongest either, a number of opposition squads were under-strength and having a quiet year before gathering themselves for the Olympics, but we decided that we were going to make it as hard a day as possible and replicate some of the pressure we might experience at Beijing. So the quartet of Ed, Paul, myself and Geraint didn't hang around in qualifying that morning, dipping under four minutes with a 3 mins 59.579 secs, a full five seconds quicker than second-placed Ukraine. The gold medal was clearly there for the taking, with something to spare, but we wanted to make a statement to the Aussies that night so gave it everything we had to smash the British record with 3 mins 57.468 secs, then the third fastest time ever, which earned a standing ovation from the Majorcan crowd. I was really pumped up by the occasion and the time, and the excitement of achieving something so good with these guys who I had been training with all winter. It was every bit as thrilling for me as the Individual Pursuit and a special moment.

The rest of the week was a total pleasure. There were three golds from Vicky Pendleton to enjoy, two from Chris Hoy was signed off with his last Kilo gold – the IOC have inexplicably dropped the event from the Olympics – but then proved that he was going to be a force to reckon with in the Keirin with an impressive win. Chris is a powerhouse cyclist and supreme athlete who sets out to master everything he does and that was just the latest example. And then, after the Union Jack was run up the flagpole for the last time, the sun made a belated appearance and I stayed on in Majorca for a holiday with Cath and the kids. I was rested and relaxed but even then beginning to look towards Beijing. I wanted it as badly as ever. It was the perfect start to a tumultuous year that was to bring many more satisfying highs and, just in case I was beginning to get complacent, one abysmal low that was as depressing as any event in my cycling career.

Chapter Fourteen

London calling

Not only had the World Championships in Palma reignited my love of the sport, they had also demonstrated that I was in exceptional shape and the challenge now was to try and preserve some of that form for the Tour de France, and particularly the prologue which was going to be the centre piece of the *Grand Départ* from my home city, London. This had been looming on the horizon for a long while but in a positive way. The British public understand and 'get' sport more than almost any other nation on earth and this was a great chance for them to get a proper insight into the madness and the great appeal of the Tour de France. The circus would be in town for three or four days: Saturday would be given over to the prologue and then Stage 1 was going to take us down to Canterbury before we finally hopped over the Channel – in fact under it on Eurostar – and arrived back in France. It was the biggest and most ambitious *Départ* in Tour history. The organisers were hoping it would generate loads of positive PR after the traumas of the previous year, while it was good news all the way for London. A big earner with the circus in town and over a million fans on the streets for the prologue, and a brilliant toe in the water exercise with regards to staging such a huge event before London 2012, not least in all the security issues.

Ultimately it was a staggering success and I have rarely felt more proud of this country and the way we made it work. For weeks after cycling fans in Europe would congratulate me on the wonderful *Départ* as if I was personally responsible! That was totally down to the London authorities and the fans – with a bit of help from the weather gods – but let's not get ahead of ourselves. Post-Palma, and although I am racing, and racing well for Cofidis on the Continent, thoughts of Prologue were beginning to fill my head.

It was a fast 7.9 km route and I had an outside chance, although I certainly wasn't the favourite. The British media wanted to build me up as a potential winner and I went along with it a bit because I wanted London to be a success and was happy to do some promotional work and talk about the chances of winning, but it was always unlikely. The course had Fabian Cancellara written all over it, that vicious stamping pedal action can really build the speed on the road and he is such a talented bike handler that he gains even more time on the technical sections. Andreas Kloden was another the course could have been built for, but, what the hell, I was going to give it my very best shot and I should certainly be in the mix.

My early season form was excellent, if anything too good. I posted a second behind Kloden on the time-trial on the Circuit de la Sauf and then got very close to him – just two seconds behind – in the prologue in the Four Days of Dunkirk. I was flying and, just before the Tour, produced one of the best performances of my life, winning the prologue in the prestigious Dauphiné Libéré – well established as the final and best warm-up for the Tour de France – defeating a clutch of time-trial specialists such as Dave Millar, George Hincapie, Levi Leipheimer and David Zabriske.

By London, I had just fallen off that form a little – trying to 'sit on your form' is one of the most difficult aspects of cycling and a real art. It is such a tough sport you just cannot – at least naturally – be firing on all four cylinders all season long, and trying to get your peaking just right can be a nightmare, especially for riders like me who are in the minority and combine their road racing with a winter on the tracks. I got it marginally wrong for London but I was still in very good shape and had the home crowd behind me.

I grinned my way through the whole London thing. I had a smile on my face from the moment we arrived and got organised, setting up camp with our team bus down at the Excel Centre in the East End. We stayed in a hotel locally. It was all superbly organised and although the weather had been rubbish all summer, come the Friday, the day before the race started, and the sun and the heat arrived and London looked sensational. The butterflies arrived that Friday night when the roads around Trafalgar Square were closed and we rode around waving to everybody before the official presentation of all the teams – going out live on TV – on a big stage right in the middle of Trafalgar Square. This was unbelievable stuff for Britain. It might have been the norm abroad but this was new territory for us. After having my Tour de France the previous year tarnished by all the controversy about Landis, this was the perfect antidote. Here we were, stopping the traffic and holding centre stage in the middle of London's most historic square on a gorgeous Friday night with Hugh Porter announcing us all as we went up on stage. This was a venue reserved for the nation's heroes – soldiers, politicians, the World Cup rugby team from 2003 and the 2004 Olympic parade of champions – and now cycling, very much against the odds, had been both honoured and offered a chance to showcase itself.

We had been riding around a bit, under Admiralty Arch and down the Mall, all closed off, and it felt like London was mine for the weekend. One sight I will never forget was Horse Guards Parade in Whitehall – where they hold the Queen's Birthday celebrations and parade every summer – transformed into an authentic tented Tour village, with the smell of French coffee and croissants, the popping of champagne corks and all the colourful nonsense we normally see at the start in some sun-drenched French town. It was very evocative and seems to have set a trend for staging the unexpected there. Apparently they are going to stage the women's beach volleyball there in 2012.

The Prologue was everything I had hoped. Well over a million people encamped en route – a fast 5-mile route taking in Whitehall, the Houses of Parliament, Buckingham Palace, Green Park, Hyde Park, the Serpentine, Constitution Hill and the Mall – and a hot sunny day for everybody to enjoy the build-up, the caravan and then four hours of racing. I was in the last bunch to go, just before six o'clock and was delighted with my ride, but nobody was ever going to beat Cancellara on the day. He deservedly finished a full 13 seconds ahead of Kloden, with George Hincapie a further 10 seconds adrift and myself in fourth, just two seconds behind George. I rode my best race on the day and was content with fourth.

The Sunday was sheer pleasure. I was pleased and proud of my ride on the Prologue, I hadn't let anybody down and could now just enjoy a ride down to Canterbury and soak it all up. I might have to work a bit for Cofidis at the end if we had a sprinter involved but this was going to be a day for the scrapbook.

Sunday morning and we were gathering on the Mall again for the start and roll out. It felt like France, with the blaring loudspeakers in French, French TV and radio journalists stuffing their microphones under their noses, the smells lifting over from the village and the hot sun, but I turned around and looked down the Mall and saw Buckingham Palace with the Union Jack fluttering on the ramparts and gave myself a little clenched fist of satisfaction. I remember in the warm-up just gliding down to Buckingham Palace, with the road closed and rolling around that big roundabout outside Buckingham Palace three or four times on my own – just because I could and wanted to enjoy the moment – before gently making my way back up to the start. I am sure all the other British riders involved felt the same. Everybody in the peloton were pleased for us and pushed us forward at all times to have our pictures taken and allowed us to lead the race out under Admiralty Arch around the bottom of Trafalgar Square and down a very quiet and shady Northumberland Avenue as we headed for the Embankment. The madness was surely over. Saturday had been tremendous fun and the public knew I had an outside sniff in the Prologue and had turned up to support me and Dave and the other lads. In the prologue there is a guaranteed four or five hours of action as all the riders go off and if you get bored you can nip into a café or pub and generally have a day out.

But now it was down to the serious business of the race itself and the peloton passes through in just a minute and then it's gone for ever. And it might just be that nothing much is happening at that particular time and the peloton is just rolling through, gossiping and yawning their way into the day. Would the public buy into this? Would they understand that the caravan – distributing freebies for the kids and whipping up the atmosphere – goes through about an hour and half ahead of us, and that's part of the scene as well, along with the press cars driving like lunatics under the mistaken impression they are rally drivers.

As we cruised down Northumberland Avenue bang on the stroke of 11 a.m., with church bells ringing all around London, I thought probably not, but as we swung right onto the

Embankment I nearly fell off my bike. There, on this beautiful sunny morning it seemed like half of London was gathered on the route, 15 deep both sides of the road for the first 40 or 50 km as we made our way down to Gillingham and on into Kent – Maidstone, Teston, Matfield, Tenterden, Ashford and finally Canterbury. It was absolutely incredible, a staggering demonstration of Britain's passion for sport and determination to support one of the world's great events as it made a rare visit to these shores. If nothing else it was confirmation, if any confirmation was needed, that 2012 will be an absolutely stunning success, because nobody in the world cares about sport – all sport and all the competitors, not just the winner – more than us British. I had a lump in my throat for most of that first hour and a huge smile, if such a combination is possible, as I abandoned racing protocol and tried to wave to the fans as often as possible.

Dave Millar, with a splendid sense of timing, got involved in the break and gave all the British fans something to cheer for most of the day – he even won himself an unlikely King of the Mountains jersey for his efforts on the three 'mighty' Category 4 climbs at Southborough, Goudhurst and Farthing Common – and actually it developed into a really decent hard day's cycling. The only disappointment, from a partisan's point of view, was that Mark Cavendish, who arrived on the Tour in red-hot form, crashed at a bad time on the approach to Canterbury and couldn't get back on terms to contest the sprint.

Robbie McEwen also crashed, but earlier in the proceedings, and had managed to get back on terms before taking it in exciting style. As the rest of us crossed the line, I gave a little sigh of relief. The entire British leg of the Tour had been an absolute bloody triumph. No drug scandal in the build-up, cracking weather, two days of excellent races and huge crowds, exceptional organisation

and policing, loads of good humour and willingness to understand what was going on, and a phenomenal turn-out even by
the standards of the Tour de France.

The French media was staggered and spent the next two or
three days praising *les Anglais* and commenting how the London
Départ had breathed life back into the Tour with its enthusiasm,
honesty and integrity. There were calls to include Britain more
often on the Tour itinerary and generally it was a very good time
to be a Brit racing on the Tour. Our stock was high and, by virtue
of London's efforts and our improving performances on the road,
you could feel many involved with the sport treating us with a
new respect.

The Monday morning in Dunkirk was very much the Monday
after the weekend before. You could sense the hangover even if
you didn't have the headache. The weather had turned drizzly
and grey and the crowd on that first day back in France was
virtually non-existent by Tour standards. Anti-climax hardly does
it justice and I wasn't alone in struggling to get the pedals
moving. The party was over, there was still the best part of three
weeks to go and endless hours of climbing and pain. It was a
head-down, get-the-stage-over sort of day.

Things picked up pretty quickly, however, once we got into
Belgium. Their fanatical love of this sport is infectious and the
stage was finishing in Ghent, my home town in many ways and
certainly a place I have grown to love with my forays on the Six
Day circuit. The Ghent Sixes always tops the list of events I enjoy.
By the Tuesday of the Tour I was back on good form and in good
spirits and there then followed one of the best fortnights of my
life before it all came tumbling down.

People will always try and rewrite history but, for much of the
2007 Tour, there was a huge feel-good factor, which clearly
started with the triumphant London *Départ*. Once we re-entered

France from Belgium the crowds finally flocked back – it was their national institution and they didn't want Britain and Belgium hogging all the limelight – and the Tour was full of challenging open racing, the kind of shifts in fortune you would normally associate with a pretty 'clean' race, with riders making a huge effort one day and being unable to back it up the next. For the first couple of weeks that is how it felt.

I was in goodish form myself and along with Dave Millar we were also enjoying the company of a couple of British newcomers – Mark Cavendish and Geraint Thomas – who I took under my wing a little although of course they were not in my team. Geraint was a member of our GB gold-medal-winning Team Pursuit squad in Palma and a rider I had spent endless hours of training with. We are firm mates and it was thrilling to see him get a Tour ride so early – in fact, at 21 he was the 'Benjamin' of the Tour, the youngest rider and so called because in the Bible Benjamin was the 12th and youngest son of Jacob, the baby of the peloton so to speak. 'Cav' is my 'roomie' with the Great Britain team, an irrepressible and amazingly talented sprinter, full of confidence shall we say, but a great upbeat character who I am very fond of. I can say, hand on heart, that I knew from the moment Cav started racing professionally on the Continent that he was a going to be a sensation.

On this occasion Cav was always going to drop out before the big mountains and I thought Geraint might blow once we arrived in the Alps but he is a suicidally brave rider and was having none of it. Somehow he dragged his arse around the Tour, which is incredibly tough when you are spending your day looking after your star riders, getting them back in contact after a crash, leading out your sprinters and making little effort to conserve energy for yourself. When I see G putting it all on the line to get around and then think of some of the chemically assisted riders cruising around barely breaking sweat, that's when I really do begin to lose it.

We often found ourselves in the Groupetto at the end of a long mountain day and occasionally I felt strong enough to give him a bit of a push. He might be in an opposing team Tour but above all he is my mate and colleague with GB, and that counts for everything. And there is a certain honour in the peloton, certainly among those who really care about the sport. I've been helped along the way during my time as well, had a bottle of water and an energy bar passed to me when I was gasping by an opposition rider.

Towards the end of the first week I was feeling really good again, although the Tour had begun to encounter a few local difficulties with a positive drugs test for testosterone predating the Tour from T-Mobile's Patrick Sinkewitz coming to light. He was booted out and with him went most of the German TV and radio stations, for whom it was the final straw after a rash of admissions from former T-Mobile riders that they had used drugs throughout the 1990s and the continuing linking of Jan Ullrich with the Fuentes affair. The Sinkewitz affair may have been big news in Germany but it didn't affect the Tour itself – it had not occurred during the race and had little impact on the peloton.

The excitement and adrenaline surge of London had receded, the anti-climax that followed was past, the race had settled down except for the departing German media, the weather was nice … and suddenly it was Friday 13 July, which is Cath's birthday. She always has the race on the TV – Eurosport and ITV 4 were providing extensive coverage – and I was definitely in the mood to try and celebrate her birthday with something special. If I could get in the break I would be on TV all day and that would be a nice way of spending the day together – me at the front on TV and her at home drinking coffee and doing the ironing.

En route to my Olympic record in the qualifying of the 4 km Individual Pursuit. It really hurt but I rolled around without a care in the world afterwards to try to psyche the opposition (*Rex*).

(*overleaf*) Bringing that gold medal home! Just over four minutes of inspiration and a cycling lifetime of perspiration. The Wiggins family are out of their seats, en masse (*Colorsport*).

Brad McGee had been a great champion and driven me on to gold but I had to settle for bronze with Rob Hayles in the Madison (*Getty; PA*).

(*above*) Tour de France rider at last. Note the typically understated and tasteful gear again (*Getty*).

(*below*) 'So, Dave, this Tour de France lark, what's it all about, mate?' Dave Millar looks at me askance. 'Brad, you've got absolutely no idea, it's madness, complete madness' (*Getty*).

(*overleaf*) Onwards ever upwards. Fighting my way up the mighty Galibier in the Alps on the Tour De France. The Tour has to be the hardest sporting event in the world (*Graham Watson*).

London Calling. The 2007 Tour de France started brilliantly but ended in farce and tears thanks to Cristian Moreni (*Getty*; *PA*).

Despite what many people thought at the time, I was not aware that Friday 13 July was the 40th anniversary of Tom Simpson's death, high on the slopes of Mount Ventoux in Provence. Of course I was very aware of the Tom Simpson story generally, and his massive reputation within the sport and cult status among British riders. I have read and reread his biography and seen the agonising footage from the 1967 Tour, when Britain's finest ever all-round road cyclist collapsed in the furnace-like heat and died less than a mile from the top. He was clearly badly dehydrated but the post-mortem later indicated that he also had amphetamines in his system and there were traces of alcohol – probably the result of a café raid at the foot of the mountain as the riders went in desperate search of liquids. In those days, remarkably, the Tour regulations restricted them to just four bidons a day and, after a long stage, most of the riders were probably already riding on empty as they approached the mountain, which is known for its stifling heat in the summer and extraordinary gusts of wind in the winter. World record blasts of well over 200 mph have been recorded.

All this I knew. Tom Simpson, who won the World Championship in pouring rain in San Sebastian in 1965 and took great classics such as the Tour of Lombardy, Milan–San Remo and also won the prestigious early season Paris–Nice stage race, was and is the benchmark for all British road racers. But I was racing during the summer of 2007 with thoughts full of the Tour *Départ*, my Prologue and trying to make a bit of a mark on the race rather than just get around, as was the case the previous summer. The exact significance of the date had passed me by totally.

We started the stage in Semur-en-Auxois, a delightful little village where the visit of Le Tour will be talked about for decades to come and, in a positive frame of mind, I positioned myself at the front and was perfectly placed when the break went after a couple of miles. There were five of us and we went reasonably hard but without any real conviction. Only CSC responded and, after giving chase for a bit, they thought better of it and lost interest. There was nobody in the break who was seriously going to affect any of the jerseys and it was bloody hot. The day before had also seen a frantic flat-out last hour after Alexander Vinokourov had crashed and fallen – he suffered a small fracture to his coccyx and cut his knees nastily – and his Astana team had worked like dervishes to get him back in touch with the peloton to preserve his chances. The peloton, in turn, had upped the pace to try and take advantage and there were some sore legs that needed nursing the following day. The peloton waved us goodbye, at least temporarily. They would stir themselves later but for the time being they were content to slumber.

Back in the front my four companions caught the mood and decided to drop back, so ten minutes into the race I found myself on my own. My lead increased slowly but steadily. First 200 m, then 300. Suddenly I was 40 seconds then 50 seconds, and finally a minute ahead. The minute mark is a big one mentally. If the peloton haven't given chase and closed you down by then they aren't interested and it was time just to squeeze it a bit more. Two minutes, three minutes. Bloody hell, I was out on my own. I was away on a solo break in the Tour de France, something that every cyclist in the world of whatever ability has at some stage dreamed about.

I took stock. There was over 200 km still left – in fact I was away on my own for a total of 199.5 km, which has been calculated as the eighth longest break in Tour de France history – and it was well over five hours to the finish. The sensible thing would be to drop back myself, work at the front of the race and wait for a second, more decisive group, to break and make sure I went with that.

But, what the hell, I was feeling good and enjoying myself and it was Cath's birthday. Let's have some fun. Also, as the money men will tell you, a long solo break is often worth more in advertising air time for the team than even a stage win. For five and half hours the TV cameras had to concentrate on me, they had no choice, I was the leader, *tête de la course* as they say, in fact I got so far ahead that after I had put 5 minutes 40 seconds into the field I was *maillot jaune virtuel*, which means that if the organisers, hypothetically, stopped the race at that precise moment in time I would be the leader, the virtual yellow jersey.

For most of the day the TV camera bikes, and occasionally my team car, were the only company I had, although in my mind Cath and the kids were with me for the entire day. For one day at least the Tour de France was all about Brad Wiggins and Cofidis, and among the many thoughts that long hot afternoon was that at least I was paying Cofidis back big time for their support of my track ambitions over the last year. I felt good about that. Every rider, at some stage, enjoys their 15 minutes of fame on the Tour; I was to gorge myself for well over five hours.

How to play this? Like an opening batsman setting his store at the crease for a long couple of days, aiming for a double hundred to save the game, I decided to give myself little targets and landmarks. First I would count the kilometres gone – 30, 40, 50 – then I would tick off the small climbs on that day and finally I would start counting down the distance to go – 90, 80, 70. Mentally I am suited to long breaks. Pursuiting is all about a fine balance between optimising speed and conserving energy, never going too far into oxygen debt or overcooking the pace. It's about riding to a schedule and concentrating totally on what you are doing and giving little or no heed to the other guy. Ninety-nine days out of a hundred you can't do that on the Tour, it's all about tactics within the peloton and sudden killing bursts of energy and activity. This was my chance.

So off I set. The villages and small climbs clicked by – St Sabina, Bligny-sur-Ouche, Grandmont, which was a gentle 2 km climb, Bel Air ridge, the high point of the stage, Chegny, Fontains, St Boil, Cormatin, the col de Brancion, Pont de Vaux, Montreval en Bresse. These small outposts, unknown to me that morning, suddenly became the centre of my universe.

It was a hard day but it didn't drag. I felt strong and within myself and there was an infectious supportive mood among the crowd. Spectators love a long early break away, it sets the drama of the day and lengthens the period of time the race takes to move through their patch but, looking back, I now appreciate that they were very aware of the Simpson anniversary, even if I wasn't. He was a great favourite in France during his career for his daring and aggressive riding style and that morning *L'Equipe* newspaper, France's national sports paper, had unknown to me published a nice appreciation and retrospective on Tom Simpson. *L'Equipe* is effectively the *Daily Tour* newspaper and probably two in three fans en route will have digested every word in it as they sit in the sun enjoying a picnic lunch waiting for the race to reach their village. When the lone 'brave Brit' appeared before them on the anniversary of Simpson's death trying to flee the peloton it appealed to their sense of history and occasion. '*Formidable! L'esprit de Simpson.*'

Onwards ever onwards. I started thinking I had no chance and now there was just a glimmer. Riding strongly and smoothly with an economy of effort my lead went up to 20 minutes – if the peloton lost concentration now I really would be away. If the communications broke down for five minutes, or if there was a crash in the peloton on a narrow road which took a while to sort out and for the bunch to regather, I could make it. But there were no mishaps and the peloton was alive and alert. Over years of experience at chasing breaks they instinctively know when they have to start working and very rarely do they get the maths wrong. Gradually, with about two and half hours left, they began to reel me in.

But even then I nearly made it. Going into the final 25 km a strong late afternoon wind blew up and veered around to batter me head on. If it had been behind me I would have sailed home, no problems, but it was a brutal headwind and it felt like I was riding with my brakes on. In the peloton you can get out of the wind for long periods while others do a turn up front, but on your own you suffer badly in the elements and eventually, with just 5 km left, the peloton gobbled me up and my day in the sun was virtually over.

I had earned respect among my peers and felt a genuine pride in what I had done. Many of the gnarled old veterans in the peloton gave me a pat on the back as they passed or muttered congratulations or 'Bravo' out of the side of their mouths as they started to breathe hard as the race quickened further. Kim Kirchen came over and gave me one of his full water bottles by way of a reviver, and Jens Voight moved alongside and paused for a chat. He told me I was his hero and that he had hoped I could scrape home. A nice touch that, Jens is famed for his exciting breaks and is a rider I admire.

I got spat out pretty quickly as the race moved into sprint mode – that invariably happens after a long break – and finished a couple of minutes behind winner Tom Boonen, back in 133rd position as I recall. I crossed the line and thought 'Well, that was nice while it lasted' and started looking for my *soigneur*, anticipating a shower in the team bus and three or four cold milkshakes, and that would just be for starters.

Wrong. I was immediately besieged by a scrum of journalists and seven or eight TV crews. It was complete bedlam. Much to my embarrassment, halfway through the interviews big Tom

Boonen, who actually won the stage, went quietly past, virtually unnoticed. The world's media – and to be fair they normally have a good handle on what the story of the day is – had chosen pretty much to ignore the stage winner and made a beeline straight for me. I still hadn't made the Tom Simpson connection.

Only when the impromptu press conference was under way, and the questioners seemed to assume the entire day was a personal tribute to Tom Simpson, did the poignancy of the day hit home. Once I had digested that, it made me feel even prouder. The day, for me, was primarily a birthday present for Cath, but it was extremely pleasing also that it put British cycling in a good light on such a poignant date. The only downside of the entire sweltering afternoon came when I handed over the combativity trophy, which they give after every stage, to a member of the Cofidis staff for safety and never saw it again. Not to worry, the memory of that day will never dim and I've got the DVD as well somewhere.

The feel-good factor continued into the second week. The day after my solo break, the first mountain stage, I went out the back early on, but my legs felt surprisingly good and I got round with few difficulties and even the day after that, a big mountain stage that ended in Tignes, I was in good shape and relishing every single moment of the Tour. Talk about living the dream.

Away from my personal little bubble, things were beginning to happen, with a growing rumpus over Denmark's Michael Rasmussen, who first stood accused of missing not one but four out-of-competition tests from the pre-season and then seemed a little confused as to exactly which Continent he was on at a given date when those tests were missed. I didn't pay an awful lot of attention, I was enjoying myself and finally getting to grips with the world's greatest cycle race, but the story was gaining momentum and was threatening to dampen what had been a bloody good Tour.

The Rasmussen affair would return to haunt us, but initially it was Alexander Vinokourov from Kazakhstan who torpedoed proceedings and left me feeling very angry and cheated. Vinokourov had been a bit of darling of the crowds for years, given to spectacular dashing efforts that left you wondering if you quite believed what you had seen, while on other occasions he didn't feature and looked average. Getting towards the end of his career, 'Vino' had seemed to discover some consistency with his new team, Astana, and had been touted as a favourite for the 2007 Tour, but that bad crash in the first week had almost seen him go out and he was crawling along with a bad knee and sore backside and was generally nursed through the race by his team. The knee was interesting: because it had to bend countless thousands of times a day on the bike the wound had to be very loosely stitched and bandaged so that the cut and the kneecap were still open so that it didn't rip to shreds every time he applied pressure. I will give him one thing, it took guts to ride on.

So we came to the long time-trial in Albi on the penultimate Saturday of the Tour, a stage that earlier in the Tour I had looked at and thought was probably not my sort of course. Also, everything seemed to have caught up with me and I was completely knackered the night before and felt very lethargic indeed walking around on the morning – on time-trial days you have a little more time to yourself and, as I pottered around, even walking seemed an effort. If I had been at home I would have been taking myself off to bed believing a dose of flu was imminent. It didn't augur well for the afternoon but I decided to just bite the bullet and somehow get round. I had been enjoying myself so much that I certainly wanted to get to Paris. I couldn't be bothered to reconnoitre the route in the team car, I just did a quick 10-minute warm-up and wandered over to the start, where I remember having a chat with Barry Broadbent, a Brit who has become one of the most important commissionaires on the Tour. I got comfortable on my bike and strangely didn't feel too bad – like settling down in the office – and composed myself on the ramps. The countdown began with the starter showing first his full outspread hand then four fingers, three, two, one, zero … I was off and, miracles never cease, suddenly feeling like a million dollars.

This is one of the great mysteries of cycling. Why you can have 'good legs' one day and 'rubbish' the next. I had been weak and tired since the previous evening and here I was feeling the best I had all Tour, it required no effort whatsoever to push the pedals. The transformation had occurred in a matter of moments. It's one of those factors that have to go into the equation when considering something like Landis's incredible ride in Morzine. Back in the 1958 Tour, Britain's Brian Robinson won a transition stage by over 20 minutes, just a couple of days after finishing outside the cut on a horrible stage in the Massif Central. He was only allowed to continue because an obscure rule that then existed stated that somebody starting the day in the top ten – Robinson was ninth – cannot be eliminated. Form can be very elusive and comes and goes, although you will never have it without being basically fit and having done the groundwork somewhere along the line.

So, miraculously, I was back on it and humming along with minimal effort in badly deteriorating conditions. It started raining very hard after 10 km so the majority of my ride was in very treacherous conditions and, because I hadn't looked at the route, I was very conservative during the technical phases. And because my mindset was initially just to get around I rode well within myself early on, scarcely believing how well I was going. If I had reacted a little quicker I would have finished with an even better time.

I finished in a cracking 1hr 8 mins 48 secs and, for a good while, that looked like a winning time to me, until the weather improved considerably and Vinokourov, a man barely alive for much of the previous weeks, charged around fully two minutes ahead of myself and a minute ahead of Cadel Evans, who was followed home by Kashechkin and Kloden.

My pleasure turned to real anger. Not for one second did I 'believe' in Vinokourov's ride, it was totally ludicrous and clearly drug-fuelled and I expressed 'extreme scepticism' at the time. Nothing that happened subsequently surprised me in the slightest. When Vinokourov's positive test for doping was announced two days later, during our rest day in Pau, nobody had any sympathy for him, he had taken the piss out of us once too often. Kashechkin's ride also seemed like an insult to our intelligence. I have ridden and trained with him many times and know him well as a rider – and his time-trial in Albi defied belief. He didn't fool me for a minute. Perhaps he didn't test positive on the 2007 Tour – although he had to leave when the Astana team were kicked off – but he got caught and banned for drugs a few weeks later. In real terms nobody will ever convince me that I didn't come third that day in Albi behind Cadel Evans – who was denied a worthy and thoroughly deserved victory on the day – and Andreas Kloden. The Tour was beginning to turn nasty, but the real nightmare was just about to begin.

—

Chapter Fifteen

'Come this way, Mr Wiggins, you are under arrest'

The rest day in Pau was far from restful, despite the glorious weather and an idyllic setting right at the foot of the Pyrenees. We had the usual spin to stop our legs seizing up and about teatime the news – not the most surprising I have ever heard – started coming through that Vinokourov had tested positive for doping and he and his team had been chucked off. Bloody good day's work by the Tour testers was my initial reaction, and I stand by it, although my second reaction was 'Here we go again.' The previous year the Tour had been marred for me by the Landis affair and now, after an absolutely belting fortnight or so, I had that horrible *déjà vu* feeling. I also caught a glimpse on TV of an extraordinary lunchtime press conference with Michael Rasmussen, who looked like a rabbit caught in the headlights as he was 'monstered' by the world's press in the City Hall. All was not well in the state of Denmark. He was a man under siege and his answers as to his whereabouts for the four tests he had missed in the months leading up to the Tour became less convincing by the day.

I was trying not to get too emotionally involved in any of this nonsense; I was still dead set on finishing the Tour and there was one last very promising time-trial on the horizon, between Cognac and Angoulême. With Astana on their way home, others caught up in the GC race and the kind of form I was in, this represented a real chance to get my first Tour stage win. With regards to Rasmussen, in as much as I thought about it all, I was trying to keep an open mind. He has always been a phenomenally talented climber ever since his days as world mountain bike champion and a considerable talent on the bike who was very fallible elsewhere in the Tour, notably time-trials and sometimes riding in the bunch. I had no particular feelings about his case except that when you are head down busting a gut trying to defend the yellow jersey it must be difficult suddenly to be confronted by 600 of the world's press and a conference hall full of cameras, trying to give a precise account of your actions, day by day, hour by hour, for the past six months or longer.

Whatever, I was concentrating on getting over the last mountain stage, a classic brute of a day culminating in a mountain top finish on the Aubisque, a famous mountain climb in Tour history, being the first to be successfully negotiated in 1910. The riders that day accused the race organiser of being a murderer, so inhumane was the task he set them. It is also famed for often being shrouded in mist and for the cattle that suddenly appear out of the gloom on the narrow road, which has steep drops on either side, but Wednesday 25 July dawned with perfect cobalt skies and at breakfast time it was already stinking hot. It was going to be a long day in the saddle; the 2008 Tour had a sting in its tail.

That's if we ever got started. When I got down to the village the word was that a lot of the riders were going to stage a sitdown strike or a ride slow – a protest at the 'druggies' in the sport. I was having none of it. I had ridden clean all my life and I will continue to ride clean whether I finish first or 187th – I was vaguely disgusted at some riders making this sudden bid for the moral high ground. That's where the entire bloody sport should be all the time. And I just knew how it would all be interpreted in the papers the next day if I joined in. 'There's Brad Wiggins sounding off again, does he never stop? What makes him so qualified to be the moral conscience of the peloton. What makes him so perfect?'

No, thank you, count me out, and I had a bit of a strop on as I managed to negotiate my way around the would-be protesters to the start line. My mood was darkening by the moment and generally there was a feeling of gloom and anxiety about what would happen next.

It was bloody awful from the moment we rolled out. Some riders were racing, some weren't and had decided to sit up for a promenade. Some were talking, some had suddenly become Trappist monks for the day. At one moment it felt like the race still counted, the next I couldn't be bothered and wanted to be on the next plane home. Eventually the mountain goats disappeared up the first hard climb – this was their terrain and they still wanted to race – and a massive Groupetto formed to go at our own pace. The organisers could do what they bloody well wanted, we were going to move through a bitch of a day at our own pace, time limit or no time limit. If they wanted to disqualify half the field, that would be absolutely fine and I could be home having a glass of wine with Cath by lunchtime the next day.

Even in the Groupetto it was a blisteringly hot and shitty day and I was in a foul mood by the time I finally crossed the line at the summit of the Aubisque – 1709 metres high, I remember – only to be confronted by one of our *soigneurs*, who seemed unusually agitated. He tried to put a jacket on me and rush me into a team car as he explained to me that my team-mate and sometime 'roomie' Cristian Moreni had tested positive from Stage 11, a stiflingly hot day between Marseille and Montpellier.

Bollocks to that. Hot sweaty and knackered, I wanted to towel off, get into some clean dry gear first and free-wheel down to the team bus at the foot of the final climb. I had absolutely no intention of being rushed off in a car with a blanket over my head looking like a criminal with something to hide. The photographers would love that. By now the press had gathered around and were shouting out questions in various languages. I wasn't in the mood and hit them with some good old Anglo-Saxon expletives, which I regret now but made me feel a whole load better at the time.

I rolled down the mountain to the bus, enjoying the cooling wind in my face, but as I pulled up was besieged by another media scrum and this time gave them what is politely known as a Churchillian salute, a picture of which featured prominently in *L'Equipe* the following day. Probably not one for Mum's scrapbook. What I was actually trying to say in my rather emotional state is 'F*** this sport, this is nothing to do with me and I am hating this.' It wasn't personal with the journalists, it was my personal comment on what I thought about this pile of a manure cycling was getting itself into. 'F*** cycling and f*** the Tour de France,' I raged to myself as I climbed into the relative sanctuary of the team bus. Or so I thought.

The police outriders were forming up around the team bus, a number of officers were on board and in charge and, as soon as all the riders were on board, they started up the blue lights and sirens and escorted us to Pau police station, not the easiest of tasks as most of the roads were still mobbed with spectators. A police officer on the coach explained that our hotel rooms were already being searched by other officers as he spoke, but perhaps something got lost in translation. Surely we have to be present when our rooms are being searched? Anything could be planted in our absence. This was getting very serious. I took the opportunity to quickly phone Cath and tell her what I knew – which wasn't much – and she immediately burst into tears. For a while I felt pretty scared. Everything was moving so fast and I had no control over anything. What if one of my colleagues had left something in my room? What if a French policemen decided to 'find' something there? We really were in the lap of the gods. My panic lasted about five minutes. Gradually I calmed myself down. I hadn't done anything wrong and there was nothing to fear.

The phone rang constantly and text messages were pouring in; mostly I ignored them as I tried to keep in control but I was delighted to pick up one call from William Fotheringham of the *Guardian*, who was in a car of British press along with Richard Moore of the *Scotsman* and Brendan Gallagher of the *Daily Telegraph*. They were stuck in a huge four-hour traffic jam coming off the mountain – they had tried a short cut and it backfired spectacularly – and were trying somehow to piece together the dramatic post-race events to file their copy. I think you can safely assume they were relieved when I noticed Will's call and answered. In fairness, I was very keen to get my version of the story out there in the public domain as soon as possible – the more people who knew of our predicament the better, was my reasoning – and it was one of those scenarios when you expected your mobiles to be confiscated at any time. So I chatted away quietly for ten minutes, trying not to attract too much attention, telling the British press exactly what I knew and that we seemed to be heading for the police cells. It was comforting to know that the 'home' media knew exactly what was going on and the wider world would soon be getting an accurate update before wild rumours started circulating.

We got to the police station and the team bus was parked in a courtyard out the back. The forensic guys immediately started going through it inch by inch. We were taken off to interview rooms and by now everything was a bit calmer. The officers dealing with us were polite – they were a specialist anti-doping squad and had been doing exactly the same with the Astana team the day before – and they quickly reassured us that no search of our rooms back at the hotel would be made until we were present. At which point they decided that we were all wasting our time at the police station and we should move en bloc to the hotel in Pau. A police car was whistled up and, along with my roomie Sylvain Chavanel, we were given the full treatment – flashing blue lights and outriders – as we were driven through the busy streets of Pau to the Novotel at 100 mph, which only seemed to add to the drama. We could have got there five minutes later and not risked life and limb of half the citizens of Pau but when in France …

A scrum of excited Continental journalists were there waiting and the picture of myself and Sylvain getting out of the car and being escorted into the lobby by two uniformed policemen was manna from heaven for them; the cameras whirred. It was the image that they all wanted and the image which dominated the news bulletins that night and the French press the following morning. Shit. How did I get into this? To this day I wish I had picked up my trolley bag, swung it round and caused as much damage as possible. If nothing else I would have felt better.

The two gendarmes – they told us later that usually they work in plain clothes but they were ordered to put on their uniforms that day for the arrests – escorted myself and Sylvain up to our room and for exactly an hour they went through everything quietly and methodically. Strangely, their efficiency and professionalism were reassuring; they knew exactly what they were doing but weren't over-the-top zealots or cowboys looking for a 'result' and a commendation. They were just doing their job properly and after an hour they were satisfied that our room was completely clean. We then had to sit down and complete a few formalities. We had to sign a paper saying the search had been conducted properly and that nothing had been found, and then each of us had to give a brief statement on what we knew about Cristian Moreni and what we had observed about his conduct during the race up to this point.

By then I was nearly passing out with hunger after a long trying day, and I was parched as well, so out of habit I went down for the team meal. The atmosphere among all the riders and back-up staff was horrendous. Emotions were very raw, accusatory and personal things were being said, 60–70 jobs within the team were possibly on the line and I didn't want to be there, so I wandered around aimlessly a bit and then found myself knocking on Dave Millar's door – his team were staying at the same hotel – and went in for a chat. Despite some press speculation to the contrary, Dave and I have become good friends and have a lot of mutual respect for each other. He is an extremely classy rider and, although he took the wrong path at a bad stage in his career, he has bounced back the right way. Above all else, he is totally in love with cycling, a passion I share.

So after this extraordinary day it was Dave I found myself with, offloading all my anger and frustration and – fair play – he sat there and listened, which was all I wanted. Given his well-documented troubles, Dave clearly had an intelligent insight into the entire scenario and I found it very reassuring when he said time and time again: 'Brad, you've done nothing wrong, everybody knows you always play by the book, hold your head high and don't get dragged down by this. It isn't your shit. You are no part of this.'

Feeling a little better, I headed for the bar – my Tour was over, my team had been split asunder – and I felt a sudden urgent need to shift a few beers after nearly three weeks full-on toil. As chance would have it, Geoff Thomas, the former England and Palace footballer, was there with Peter Slater, enjoying their rest day from their brilliant project in which they were basically shadowing the main Tour and riding the complete route a few days behind us to raise money for Geoff's leukaemia project.

They were very sympathetic and good listeners. Then Peter Dalter, a friend and colleague of Geoff's, suggested only half-jokingly that I join them to complete the Tour with the charity's amateur riders and enjoy a bit of craic over the last three or four days. I was very tempted indeed – what a great way to make my point, much more acceptable than a two-fingers sign to the cycling world – but after we kicked the idea around for a few minutes I realised the balloon had burst; I really did have to get out of Pau and France and get home to Cath.

Late on, just as I was heading for my cot, it all went off again, this time with the news that the yellow jersey, Michael Rasmussen, had been kicked off the Tour. Sensation upon sensation. The world as we knew it was collapsing, complete madness. The Tour had become a complete nuthouse. Technically Rasmussen was withdrawn by his own team, who were unhappy at his inability to explain his whereabouts during those periods of time he 'missed' tests, but clearly the team were coming under huge pressure from the Tour organisers to act. Their worst possible nightmare would have been for Rasmussen to get to Paris, take the GC and recoil in horror when some even more damning evidence came out to discredit him and, of course, the race. Frankly, I couldn't take it all in after the day I had endured.

A restless night followed. I don't feel like I slept at all really but must have done because suddenly I was coming to and Sylvain was in 'civvies' trying to quietly pack his bags without disturbing me. Briefly I wondered why he was in civvies and then the whole nightmare came crashing back. We said a fairly mournful farewell. He was as fed up with the bloody nonsense as I was.

Breakfast. Things are rarely so serious that a cyclist will miss breakfast, and as I walked past what had been Moreni's room I noticed his freshly laundered kit hanging on the door knob outside his room. I had no idea if he was inside – I strongly suspect not – but it struck me as totally incongruous. I remember stopping and looking at his bag a second time, wondering for some reason if I ought to remove it from public view. It seemed vaguely obscene and wrong. Hadn't anybody told the cleaners that Moreni was gone? The Tour had gone to hell, cycling had gone at all levels.

What the hell. It was still fairly early but it was time to get out of this madness. I sought out Dave Millar to say goodbye and the anger was rising again. I physically couldn't stand to be in Cofidis gear any more – I was disgusted, perhaps irrationally, with the management for allowing this to happen and wanted nothing to do with them as I made my escape from the Tour. Dave gave me one of his T-shirts and I hot-footed it for Pau airport, hoping against hope that nobody would recognise me. It seemed to work, the Rasmussen story was in any case taking over by now. When I got to Pau airport I stuffed all my remaining Cofidis gear in a waste bin in the departures lounge – I would have happily set fire to it – and gratefully checked in and headed for the café.

Home sweet home and, although the phone kept ringing – the press interest was still constant – I was among friends and normal people again. After being reunited with Cath we quickly decided on a two-part plan of action. I would call a press conference on the Friday in Manchester and keep everybody happy on that front, then I was going to turn the mobile off, Cath's parents were going to take the kids, and we were going to stay at a luxury hotel in Manchester and enjoy 48 hours on the town and catching up. It wasn't Paris, where we originally planned to have our reunion, but we were going to have a ball, which we did.

But first the press conference. Mentally I felt much calmer, but all the reports the following day talk about how angry and emotional I still was. They should have seen me on Big Wednesday when it all kicked off.

The best course of action was to simply have my say, and with the press conference going out live on all the big channels – just as well I didn't know that or else I would have been tongue-tied – I simply related my story as concisely and honestly as possible so that the facts were clear and everybody else could make up their own minds. Talking about Moreni himself was a bit difficult. I have to put my hand up and confess that I like the guy and, yes, Cath and his girlfriend had got on okay the year before and been planning to meet up again in Paris that very weekend, as the race closed in on the finish.

The Cristian Moreni I knew over a season and half of racing together irregularly was a particularly bright, intelligent rider, a very fiery Italian coming to the end of his career. He was good company – a very distinct character as opposed to some of the serious and inward-looking French guys – and among other things I seemed to have the ability to make him laugh. He thought I was hilarious for some reason, and we always shared plenty of light-hearted banter. His girlfriend was lovely, spoke perfect English and there was definitely a rapport between the four of us.

But if I am honest, I had him down as a 'possible' doper from early on but had been hoping I was wrong. He fitted the profile perfectly. Experienced rider very close to retirement seeking one final payday and afternoon of glory. Go out with a bang, sneak past the dopers, head for a final round of money races in the autumn and call it a day.

Ultimately he got caught and the one thing I will give Cristian credit for is that he didn't even ask for the B sample. He put his hand up, admitted he had cheated by using testosterone and didn't try and muddy the waters by implicating his team and others. He did wrong and he got caught but that doesn't make him a bad person. We haven't spoken and I haven't sought him out since that fateful day, but if I bumped into him tomorrow I wouldn't cold-shoulder him. I would go and have a chat. I would want a few answers to a few direct questions but I would also be interested to find out what's been happening in his life.

The sport of road cycling has been going through the most difficult and important phase of its history. This is the purge that we have all called for and it is a painful process. The testing – by the teams and UCI – is the most stringent in the world in any sport, and big names are being hit time and time again. Rather than lament that, I now see it as something the sport should be congratulated on. We are coming to the end of that era when riders consider some degree of drug usage if not the norm then certainly not strange. The younger generation of riders are much less tolerant of dopers as are the new sponsors. When a team like T-Mobile decides – hopefully only temporarily – to withdraw its scores of millions from the sport, the game is up. Change or die. They want a positive return on their outlay, not negative doping headlines. I firmly believe that within seven or eight years the Tour de France and the sport will be entirely clean, and I sincerely hope I will be just about clinging on and riding well enough to be part of that, perhaps riding in a GB national team and helping lead out Mark Cavendish or some other young British sprinter. The greatest irony of all is that a drug-free Tour de France will be an immeasurably better event to watch. The yellow jersey would change hands more often, more people would unexpectedly blow up or crack, more riders would challenge for stage wins and the air of unpredictability would encourage more aggressive riding from the teams.

Chapter Sixteen

—

Back in the groove

After the 2007 Tour it was a case of licking my wounds and getting my head together. Despite a very close and happy working relationship with Cofidis throughout most of my time there, it had turned extremely sour right at the end and I found it hard to forgive the backroom boys for letting Moreni through the net. A bit illogical, I know, because Cofidis worked hard at the blood tests and hair analysis, but I had to blame somebody for the mess and the team copped a lot of my anger for the humiliation they had heaped on me during Big Wednesday.

Anyway, the split wasn't very harmonious but was made easier by the immediate interest shown by T-Mobile, whose top man Bob Stapleton was waging war on the dopers, including those in his own team as it transpired. Nonetheless I liked their proactive approach and also relished the prospect of riding with Mark Cavendish, who I have got on with and admired from the moment we first encountered each other. Mark is an absolutely brilliant young sprinter who has been frightening the world's best and writing his name large during his first two seasons as a professional. We spark off each other – I enjoy his droll wit, he enjoys my mimicking, I love his cocky confidence, he professes to love my guitar playing when we room together. The prospect of leading Cav out on some of his sprint finishes and also of riding with Roger Hammond, another very fine British rider who specialises in the tough Spring Classics, was very tempting and guaranteed to bolster my belief in and appetite for the sport.

Bob was building an awesome squad that ticked all the boxes with GC candidates, sprint aces, climbers, time-triallists and all-rounders who could fit in wherever. I liked the sense that I would have a real role, helping to lead out the sprinters on their big days and nurse them through the mountains in the Groupetto, ride hard in all the time-trials – Individual or Team – and generally work my socks off. My one big complaint tactically at Cofidis is that many of us were too alike, opportunist riders who could challenge for stage wins on a good day, but we were lacking riders who would take the big jerseys. And that meant I was often unsure exactly what role I was expected to play.

The other soothing balm, of course, was my continued love of track racing and the feeling – give or take the occasional spats and frank discussion between friends – of being completely at home and valued at Team GB. I was beginning to think big. I wanted to travel to Beijing with realistic chances in three events – Individual Pursuit, Team Pursuit and Madison – and for that to be even remotely possible I clearly needed to make a strong showing at the World Championships the following March in Manchester. Although the schedule didn't exactly replicate Beijing, the cumulative challenge was similar and I wanted to get out of the mindset of relaxing and considering the job done after my own individual event. I had made a good start in Palma but trying seriously for three golds was going to require an extra special effort as well as a degree of luck.

Everybody at Team GB was 100 per cent on board with regard to me attempting the triple so the first thing we did was to make a conscious decision, however unpalatable to me, to prolong my road season so I could take some exceptional late season fitness into my heavy winter programme. So I bit the bullet and kept racing up to the World Championships in Stuttgart, where I came a very solid tenth in the time-trial on a testing course. I was happy enough with that – it had been a very long and arduous season, mentally and physically – but after a two-week family holiday I felt in surprisingly good nick and went to work that autumn with a vengeance. I have rarely trained better or felt more contented in my work.

My basic regime was disciplined and gave shape to the week. It certainly wouldn't suit everybody but it was perfect for me. For three mornings a week – Monday, Wednesday and Friday – I would get up at 5.30, have a quick coffee and drive straight to the velodrome so that I would be there, ready and waiting, when they opened it up at 6.30 every morning. It wasn't a deliberately masochistic move on my part, simply practical. With two very young children, if I didn't head out before they were up I would struggle to get in before mid-morning and would be left chasing my tail all day. And if you linger at home there is always something else to do. By rising before dawn and getting into the velodrome with the early staff, I was effectively clocking on at the office and that, I was beginning to realise, was quite important psychologically for me. I can't maintain that intensity of discipline all the time but at important phases of my career I have always been very strict myself.

Having greeted everybody with a yawn and grabbed another coffee, I would start with a constant and pretty intensive two hours on the rollers in the gym before a late breakfast, heating up my own food. Then I would kick back, do my emails, read the papers and have a chat with DaveB. Shane was away with the rest of the pursuit team, doing a big six-week training block in Australia but, with two toddlers, I decided I couldn't sign on for that and needed to be at home. Nothing heavy, just touching base really and making sure they are happy. After that I would go down to the physio's room, find a bed and curl up for 40 winks. I can sleep anywhere and it sets me up nicely for the afternoon track session. Quality rest is almost as important as quality training, in fact it's part of quality training. The afternoon would be a combination of basics – half a dozen race starts – followed by a fairly strenuous set of five or six rolling kilos with 20-minute breaks in between. That would just about complete the afternoon session and hopefully enabled me to miss the worst of the rush hour traffic as I headed for home, well exercised and happy, to catch up with the kids before bedtime.

Tuesday and Thursday were based at home. If the weather was dry I would be out on the bike for a steady three hours' endurance road work, if the weather was rubbish I would get on the Cateye training machine in the garage. Over the weekend, depending on what family commitments we had, I would try and take one day off and put in another road ride on the other.

Time flew by and before I knew it Mark and I were out in Ghent at the end of November, dipping our toes in the water as a team at the Sixes. I had tons of experience in the Sixes and just love the entire scene, Mark was a novice in comparison, but we thought it worthwhile simply putting in the racing time together with a view to getting a Madison partnership together for Beijing. It wasn't a stunning success but it served its purpose. I was in disgustingly good form for that time of year, whereas Mark was in pieces at the end of his stellar first season as a professional and wasn't very well either with a bad cold. Unfairly, he took a bit of stick from the press for our modest performances, but he could easily have taken the soft option and dropped out. He kept plugging away as we put in the hours together.

The World Cup season was suddenly upon us and we headed down to Sydney where the Madison was a bit of a disaster. The

Ghent Sixes are tough but fairly gentlemanly – you can't have all the teams knocking the hell out of each other on the first night, the promoter is relying on full houses for the next five nights as well – and the World Cup is a real shit fight in comparison, with teams laying down markers for Beijing.

Things weren't looking great and Mark was still struggling badly for form as we finished down the field – he probably just needed a complete rest – and we were a tad anxious as we headed off to Beijing for the next round. First, we badly needed somehow to conjure up a podium finish to secure a qualification for the Olympics in Beijing. DaveB, always looking to find an edge in performance, played a blinder at this stage by raiding his war kitty – he squirrels away some of our Lottery funding for emergencies – and decided to upgrade the entire squad from zoo class to business for the long haul from Sydney to Beijing. Many of the competitors from other countries were on the same flight as us and the look on their faces as we went through the door and turned left was extremely good for morale.

Come the Madison on the Olympic track and I think it would be fair to say I carried Mark a fair bit, but we managed to work well together to gain a vital lap and came home with a silver in second place. Job done, qualification secured, but much work still to do.

We were all home in plenty of time for Christmas, one of the happiest I can ever recall and I was completely focused in a relaxed kind of way. I was loving family life and being a father and husband but also enjoying my training – on the road if it was crisp and dry, in the garage when the weather was mucky. This was the sporting life I had always planned and plotted for and a much-needed drop in intensity before the long haul started in earnest.

The new year saw myself, Paul Manning, G and Ed Clancy

heading to Majorca for an epic block of training to help set ourselves up for the Worlds. We essentially repeated blocks of three days designed to test us to the limit and see exactly where we were.

On the opening day the four of us put in a straightforward five-hour ride on the island's testing roads at very nearly racing speed. Day Two was a complete swine. In the morning we were required to complete a two-hour ride at zone three on our time-trial bikes – at high intensity but not quite flat out – on our own, and that would be followed by an afternoon of torture on a particular short sharp hill we know. It is basically a seven-minute climb at normal racing speed and what we did was to put in four separate efforts of maximum effort of exactly five minutes to see how far we got up the climb before virtually collapsing and rolling back down the hill. There we would circle around the roundabout at the foot of the climb recovering slowly before we would go again. You would be entirely right in guessing that this was not the most popular day in the schedule.

Day Three and we were back clocking up the mileage – six hours a day on Majorca's rugged terrain, taking in a sprinkling of the island's top climbs. A day off – maybe just a light spin – and we would repeat the three-day cycle again. With the Worlds in March it was all essential miles in the legs. You cannot short-cut the 4 km pursuit – you need the endurance those six-hour rides can produce, as well as your natural speed and the speed you develop after years on the track.

There was more, at least for me. Team High Road – the T-Mobile team had been re-named when they quit and then later in the season we became Team Columbia – wanted to use Majorca for their main winter training block, so I stayed on and put another extremely intensive, high-mileage week with them. By the time I returned home I was exceptionally fit. You can never quite replicate the racing competitiveness of a Tour in training but that time in Majorca was a pretty epic training block – I had gone harder and faster earlier in the year than I can ever remember.

And that was the state of play when I took that fateful phone call from Shane Sutton telling me to phone Australia about my dad. I won't deny that the shock of Garry's death and the circumstances surrounding it didn't cause a bit of a wobble, but looking back I held it together well. The key decision was not to go down to Melbourne for the funeral. Not only did I contain the emotional impact by keeping my distance but, because I was feeling so good physically, I was able to lose myself in training. It was exactly what I needed. Routine, familiar surroundings, keeping busy. Training proved a great therapy in difficult circumstances and, because I had done so much high-quality work, I was feeling good about my cycling and life generally. That in turn gave me a feel-good factor that perhaps the circumstances didn't really warrant.

Then it was off to the United States for another block of training and the Tour of California. I had visions of sun-kissed rides down the Pacific Highway and up into the Sierras, but the weather was wet and cold and the racing pretty tough. I caught a cold as well, but a second place in the prologue, with only Cancellara ahead of me, was very pleasing and another indicator that everything was on track.

Suddenly it was early March and three weeks out I went into that bubble of preparation that has served me well in the past. The Great Britain team were beginning to gather and, for all sorts of reasons, I moved into our modest little hotel/headquarters near the velodrome, from which we have launched many of our campaigns.

The advantages outweighed the disadvantages. Team spirit

within the group is fantastic and I buy into that totally and feel we should all muck in together, with nobody being granted any special privileges, like nipping home to the wife and kids every night when that is an opportunity denied to many. Then there is the practical consideration of trying to avoid colds and viruses – as all parents will testify, toddlers can be bug factories and three weeks out I needed to keep that risk to a minimum. At the hotel I could eat, drink and sleep the Championships and, in many ways, I had the best of both worlds because DaveB still encouraged everybody to take time out at the weekends and I did nip home then.

Time went surprisingly quickly. Cyclists are creatures of routine and habit and days tick by. I had one of my guitars with me so I spent many an hour picking away, and had arrived armed with a stack of DVDs I wanted to catch up on. In the final week, Cav arrived from his busy racing schedule on the Continent – complete with a rather suspect and expensive-looking Gucci white leather man-bag – and the old firm were reunited. It was great to have him around. I seem to act as an older brother figure to Cav and G and it's a role I enjoy. Occasionally I pretend to be Mr Mature but it's not an act I can keep up for long.

—

Chapter Seventeen

The brain mechanic

A week out from the start – I was racing on the first day, 26 March – I suddenly started getting very nervous. Not panicky, just nervous. I was older and mature now, a different person from the guy who nearly blew it at Athens but clawed it back at the death and my early nerves surprised me. Perhaps it would have all worked itself out naturally – after all I did get through the pre-Athens nonsense and the games themselves pretty successfully in the end – but why go through all the agonies when expert advice is at hand? Since Athens I had allowed Steve Peters into my life, the GB brain mechanic, and my little pre-World Championship wobble was a classic case of how he helps me.

Steve is basically a very wise man indeed who understands sportsmen in the context of life generally. Rather late in life – around his 40th birthday I believe – he took up athletics and, in no time, he was winning World Masters Championships at distances between 100 m and 400 m, all on very limited training time because his every daylight hour seems to be spoken for, what with his duties with Team GB and his job as a forensic psychiatrist. He has worked at Rampton High Security hospital and is on call with police forces around the country for especially trying cases.

My inclination was always to give such mind boffins a wide berth but Steve is very different. He doesn't in any way preach or dictate. He has an office at the velodrome in Manchester and you can formally book in to see him but he operates in a very relaxed manner and is a master of just being around when you need him at a big championship or crucial training block. He will just sit you down quietly over a coffee or, if you mention you fancy a word, he will pop into your hotel room and have what has the appearance of being an everyday conversation. Except that when it is over you realise he has very cleverly sorted out whatever has been clogging up your mental process. He is a professor in common sense, as far as I am concerned, and the thing about common sense is that it isn't very common! Let me try to give you an insight to our conversation this time in Manchester, a week before the World Championships on my home track and with me feeling, unaccountably, a little edgy. Obviously I wasn't taking notes but it went very much like this:

'Evening, Brad, I thought I would drop in. How's it going? Are you prepared?'

'Hi, Steve. Yes, I think I am. My time in Majorca was quality all the way, I feel like I'm over Garry's death, I got a bit ill in California but feel fine now and all the numbers stack up. I'm in good shape. I'm well prepared.'

'Well there you go, Brad, that sounds good to me. All the coaching staff say you are absolutely on it. Flying. They are talking about a possible world record ride in the Team Pursuit, winning the IP with a bit to spare and frightening the life out of the Madison field with Cav.'

'Yes I know, Steve, but it's the World Championships in Manchester, my home track, it feels like I will know half the crowd personally. I feel like everybody is looking at me like never before this week. All my family and friends are going to be up for it. The Beeb are doing all our big sessions live in their entirety. It is a massive week for the sport in Britain. It all seems a bit daunting. Losing here will be ten times as bad as before if it happens. I don't want to mess up.'

'Forget Manchester and the velodrome for a minute, Brad. Are you in good shape and are you going to do the very best you can on the day?'

'Yes, of course I am, you know that.'

'In that case it really doesn't matter if you are riding in front of a full house in Manchester with a live TV audience of millions or in a deserted velodrome in Bognor Regis at midnight in front of the security man.

'Brad, if I told you now, this very minute, that I know for sure that you are going to finish fourth in the Individual Pursuit next Wednesday does that mean you would miserable for all this next week, knowing that you were only going to finish fourth?'

'No, Steve. It's the World Championships in Manchester. It's a massive week for track cycling in Great Britain. All the press and TV are here, every session is sold out, all my family are coming. It's Ben's birthday just before we start. I want to enjoy this gathering of the British cycling clan and be part of it. These are the weeks we live for.'

'Well, there you go. You have the power to relax and enjoy yourself whatever the result. It is your call. You have a choice, Brad. You can either enjoy this next week and the five days of competition, whatever results come your way, or you can get strung up with nerves and probably not ride to your full capacity.

'Do you know what, Brad. I have seen you in training, I've spoken to Shane and DaveB. I think I will put a million pounds on you winning the Individual Pursuit next Wednesday night. What do you reckon about that? Do you reckon you will win? Is that a good bet?'

'Yes. Something pretty strange would have to happen next week for me not to win the IP. The numbers all stack up and I am in bloody good shape. I haven't heard that any of the opposition are going particularly well.'

'But what if you came fourth, or something freakish happened to your bike and you had mechanical problems?'

'I would feel like I had let myself down, and my team and family. And wasted all your money.'

'But, Brad, do you seriously think the GB team or your family, or me, will think you have let us down if you finish fourth next week? You are the Olympic Champion, you won three medals for your country in Athens, you have won two World Individual Pursuit championships, you put some great rides together on the Tour de France last year, you helped make the London *Départ* a triumph we can all be proud of. You don't owe any of us anything. Do you seriously think we would forget all those achievements in an instant? Do you really think any of us would stop supporting you because you finished fourth or your bike played up? What do you think the fans would say if you came fourth?'

'Probably something like "Brad had a bad day at the office but he's saving it for Beijing. Peaking for Beijing is the main thing this year. He was all over the place before Athens, in fact do you remember at one stage he didn't look like he would make the IP, and look what he did." Or if my bike went tech it would be "Poor old Brad, that was bad luck on your own patch but better it happen now rather than in Beijing."'

'So what are you worried about?'

'Nothing.'

'Exactly. Enough. You know where my office is, Brad, and you've got my mobile. Phone any time, but you won't be needing me again this week.'

Steve has the great ability to take the emotion out of any

situation and just get you concentrating on the logic. As an Individual Pursuiter you can easily get caught up in stressing about the opposition. You probably recognise the scenario from other sports:

'I wonder how McGee or Escobar are doing in training? Word is they are absolutely flying. Escobar's got a new trainer, he's looking really fit. Who's this new Ukrainian who's knocking out 4.19s for fun?'

You can get wound up but a quick word with Steve does the trick. I can hear him now: 'We can sit here and get stressed about these guys for the next three hours and it will not do us an ounce of good, Brad. There is absolutely nothing on this earth you can do to alter or control how they go in training and, come competition time, they will ride what they ride. The only thing you can control is your training and your performance in competition. Get that right and you have done your job.'

It is stuff that of course you know deep down, but nerves can badly erode your confidence and occasionally you need the message to be hammered home. Since Athens I have learned to use Steve as and when I need somebody to run things past. We rarely have any sort of formal sit-down but he is always in the background at the big meets and now I am confident enough to make the first move and grab five minutes with him. Often it will be when I'm having a rub-down, or we've even been known to start up one of our chats in the lavatory! In Manchester, in addition to our longish – for us – session about a week out, I had a specific chat with Steve on the eve of the Individual Pursuit, and he popped his head around the corner after the qualifying round when I came second but had plenty in the tank. He just wanted to make sure I was confident about everything. He's just there constantly for a quick, on the road, mental MOT.

I remember he sat me down once and explained why it is,

sometimes, in the very last minutes of something you have dedicated the last six months of your life towards, that suddenly you don't want to be there. You would give your life savings to be anywhere else in the world. It is, apparently, completely normal in the natural world. When confronted by a massive challenge or threat the three fs take over and I am not talking about bad language. 'Fright, flight and fear' – they are completely normal in the natural world and, as long as you recognise that at some time they will try and kick in, you can be ready to fight them off.

Steve had a little device to be proactive in this respect as you enter competition mode, he calls it exercising the chimp.

The mental image you create is of this irritating chimp who is always close at hand, living in his little box. The chimp will constantly throw all sorts of rubbish and negative thoughts at you: 'Your family are coming tonight, wouldn't it be horrible to let them down, especially little Ben? It's his birthday today and he will be expecting you to win on Wednesday as a late present. The press say every session is sold out and the BBC are going live; bloody hell, this track cycling is catching on, it would terrible to mess up now, wouldn't it, Brad? You are one of the names now. If you mess up the public will soon lose interest again. McGee is back, Brad, it's Olympic year so you know he will be on business this year. You felt a bit muzzy-headed this morning, I wonder if you are going down with that flu that has been sweeping the country; Cath was feeling groggy with it the other day when you nipped home, I expect you are going down with something …' and so on.

If you let it, the bloody chimp can chirp away all day, under-mining your confidence. All those worries – or similar ones – are there all the time. So what Steve does is to make sure you confront them once a day, preferably at a set time, say for ten minutes in your room after breakfast.

So you let this irritating little chimp have his say, you allow all those worries and negative thoughts into your mind and deal with them. 'Won't it be great to have the family along and how big will be the smile on Ben's face when I show him the gold medal I have won for his birthday. What a brilliant week for the sport in Britain, the Beeb going live and every session sold out. What a great challenge it will be to have McGee back, you've beaten him before and he makes you raise your game. Having him back will make you even better. As for flu and illness, the medics took my blood yesterday and say I am A1, not a virus or bug to be seen. Nothing to worry about there.'

And having exercised the little bugger you then lock him away in his cage for the day. He is not allowed to utter another word until I choose to talk to him, same time, same place tomorrow, by which time I might have considerably fewer worries on my mind. If you exercise the chimp regularly he becomes less restless and agitated and gradually he will have less to nag you with. Eventually, by the morning of competition itself, you are not talking at all. He will be in his box sulking with nothing to throw at you.

As we moved towards Manchester I was also talking through with Steve the specific challenge of attempting to win three gold medals over four days and trying to replicate that, more or less, in Beijing when my programme would be spread over five. I badly wanted to perform at my very best in all three events, and needed to get my head around the challenge and address the fact that I went a little AWOL in Athens, even though I did pick up a silver and bronze after my Individual Pursuit.

Physically I knew I could cope, but that wasn't the problem. I needed Steve to help get down off the high of winning the Individual Pursuit and straight back to business for the Team Pursuit and then again straight into race mode for the Madison.

It was going to be a roller-coaster ride, that was for sure, and Manchester was going to be a brilliant dress rehearsal. What emerged was an approach, a bit of mental gymnastics, in which winning the three events comprised just one gold medal and therefore I hadn't 'won' until Cav and I brought the field home in the Madison. I am not saying it worked totally because, for example, our gold medal and world record in the Team Pursuit was an extraordinary achievement and ride, and it needed marking and celebrating briefly, but with my new approach in place I certainly came back to earth quicker.

Chapter Eighteen

'Madchester'

The World Championships in Manchester were always going to be a huge test, mental and physical, and I look back on those days with great pride, both personally and also because of being part of an amazing collective effort by the British team.

By the Tuesday night before my first race, the Individual Pursuit, I was in a good place, feeling just right as I sat down with Shane Sutton and Matt. The previous night I had nipped back for a few hours for Ben's birthday party and a quick meal with Cath before returning to the hotel. There was a real focus and businesslike atmosphere there and I felt comfortable. I did feel slightly anxious – or rather, in the old days I would have described it as anxiety – but since working with Steve I realise this is the body beginning to produce adrenaline as it prepares for supreme challenge. I have learned to enjoy and welcome that feeling now because I know things are on track when it comes.

The next morning I woke early, did some mandatory UCI blood tests and went down to the velodrome to do a bit on the rollers before returning to the hotel for an early lunch and a flop on the bed watching *Only Fools and Horses* DVDs. Shane phoned about midday: 'Brad, just to tell you Rob has just gone over the 50 per cent mark on his haematocrit levels – he recorded 50.3 – and has been withdrawn. Just thought you ought to know so it doesn't freak you out when you get down to the track and he's not there. Keep it to yourself for a while, it's not public knowledge yet, but we will be putting out a press release very soon.'

A haematocrit reading is actually a simple blood test that records the proportion of white blood cells to red cells. Anything above 50 per cent – Rob was 50.3 per cent – is considered abnormal and the rider has to be stood down for a fortnight pending further tests. It is in no way a 'positive' and can, as the scientists are finding with increasing regularity, occur naturally. Some riders have naturally occurring high readings and some are always very low, but the testers say that it can, in some cases, be indicative of possible drug use which requires further investigation. Fair enough; we are aiming for an ideal scenario of an entirely clean sport so we must let the testers do their thing even if it can lead to uncomfortable experiences for entirely clean and innocent riders.

Bloody hell. What a start to the meet. Rob's a good mate and long-time colleague. I knew without a moment's hesitation that he was clean but you can occasionally – in fact more than occasionally – get abnormally high readings on the haematocrit reading, especially at the end of a long taper after you have put in exceptionally heavy training blocks earlier in the year. He was meant to be racing the Individual Pursuit with me later that afternoon but now, clearly, had to be withdrawn. I knew that this would be causing a fuss and there would be a media flap on – DaveB would be in meltdown – but I couldn't allow it to distract me. Earlier in my career such news would have played on my mind but I could hear the voice of Steve Peters even if he wasn't in my room: 'Brad, is there a single thing you can do to change what is going on with Rob at the moment? No, well just get on with what you can control and that is banging out your qualifying ride on schedule.'

I went down to the track about 90 minutes before the qualifying and suddenly clicked into super-confident mode warming up and picked up as the crowd began to build. I went off like a rocket and after 2.5 km I was slightly up on schedule and flying, heading for a ridiculously fast – an unnecessarily fast – time given the opposition and the need to race again that night and then in two more events so I throttled right back. A little too much as it happened and, after losing concentration slightly, I finished second behind Holland's Jenning Huizenga who had taken eight seconds off his personal best, the first occasion I had failed to finish first in qualifying since 2001.

One or two people around me seemed a little spooked – this wasn't in the script – but I was okay. I found a seat at the back of the gym and said straight away to a slightly concerned-looking Shane that everything was all right. I recovered quickly and felt fine. I knew I had throttled right back and lost momentum but no harm had been done. Steve Peters called by quickly – he had seen exactly what happened and had nothing specific to say but just wanted to make sure I was mellow with everything. I was.

The final was satisfyingly straightforward, although there was another salutary reminder in the latter stages to always finish the job properly. I went out on a 4.15 schedule and was absolutely on the nose after 2.5 km with the race virtually won – Huizenga couldn't back up his earlier ride and was struggling. I then started to daydream and let my mind wander to Cath and the kids, who I knew were watching in the crowd. I also started to look up at the big screen and watch myself racing, which is totally bizarre and not to be recommended at all. Three laps out and I definitely had won it so I started to count them down and enjoy the moment, allowing the crowd noise to hit me and spent most of the last lap laughing and smiling. The release of tension was massive and as I hit the last straight I sat up and punched the air and celebrated in a fashion I hadn't felt able to in Athens. This was fun and I really enjoyed my couple of laps of honour before pulling up alongside Cath. I had delivered Ben's birthday present after all.

The next hour and half was fun in a mad kind of way – lots of backslapping, hurried press interviews, TV, the medal ceremony. I allowed myself to enjoy all that but then, as I had discussed with Steve, I deliberately broke away from the madness. I took my rainbow World champion's jersey straight off, stuffed it into my bag and headed back to the hotel at about 10 p.m. to get some dinner and go through some stretches with the physio.

Cav was fast asleep in the room and, although I felt myself coming down nicely, I was still 'wide eyes' and couldn't settle to an early night, so I went back to the physio's room and watched the highlights of the France/England football game in Paris and just chilled out there, smiling to myself. It had been a bloody good day. At about 2.30 a.m. I suddenly felt the need for sleep, slipped back into the room and was soon off.

The next morning I woke up with my Team Pursuit head on and, although there were still a few congrats at breakfast from people I hadn't seen the night before, I tried to politely brush them away and slip into my role for the day, being a member of the GB Team Pursuit squad. We had breakfast together. My Individual Pursuit gold was done and dusted and only to be mentioned again at the end of the week, when we kicked back with a few beers. Today was totally about us and nothing about me.

Perhaps now would be a good time to explain exactly what goes on in the Team Pursuit. It's an event that seems to fascinate spectators and there is no doubt that, when it is done well, it becomes a thing of beauty rather than just a sporting endeavour. I've heard so many people over the years describe a good Team

Pursuit ride as 'beautiful' or 'sporting perfection' that it is clear it strikes a chord – and not just with the cycling fanatics. It is the cycling event the general sporting public seems to 'get' first. As a rider there is certainly no better feeling in cycling than strapping in, being part of a 'train' that rattles around the track and covers 4 km in under four minutes. There is an extraordinary feeling of rhythm and, when everything goes well, hopefully, it looks effortless. But there are many pitfalls and hundreds – no thousands – of hours go into making sporting perfection look so natural.

Let's start at the beginning with a highly trained GB team taking their place on the start line and on world record schedule. The job of man one, aided by man two, is to get the team up to our optimum cruising speed of 66 kmph in the first 40 seconds or so. It is a huge task and sets the tone for the ride. We generally have Ed Clancy at one and he is a very special animal, if the Kilo was still around as an Olympic event he could seriously challenge in that. He has brilliant natural dynamic speed but also has enough endurance – and this is what makes him special – to hang on after his initial lung-busting effort and get the trip. He's a strange hybrid athlete but our times have improved markedly since we – in fact I believe it was Shane Sutton to be precise – had the idea of giving him his head at the start.

From a standing start Ed will take the first lap and a quarter flat out and generally swing up after about 25 seconds, at which point he will have got us up to approximately 64 kmph, then the number two man – normally Paul Manning – will come through. The number two man has been hanging on for dear life, getting a slight tow but nothing like the protection riders three and four have been receiving, and now he must somehow accelerate smoothly up to that optimum 66 kmph. The emphasis here is on smooth. You are so on the edge of what the body can do physically in a top-level Team Pursuit that you cannot afford dips and then power surges to correct those dips. They drain your body, put even more lactic into your body and you will always pay the price in the final 1.5 km, when you will hit the wall and lose great chunks of time. Unless you are totally in control you can set out riding for a world record of 3.56 and end up coming home in 4.03 if you blow. The Team Pursuit is one of the ultimate events in giving it everything, but in a controlled measured manner.

When the number two man swings up after two and a quarter laps, we should generally be at top speed, and if we have gone off too quick our captain Paul Manning will be calling for us to 'hold'. Paul has got a computer for a brain and judges these things to perfection; we always respond exactly to what Paul says.

I usually enter the fray at number three, having had a relatively protected ride so far although I have still had to work bloody hard to keep up with the hares. My job on my first stint is to bring everything under control and set the stride and cadence. It has to be absolutely bang on, with the throttle set at 66, not a fraction higher, not a fraction lower, and give riders number one and number two – who are blowing hard and struggling for breath at the back – a small window to settle down and concentrate on riding a perfect line 2 cm behind the man in front and generally work on their body position and technique. Ideally we would all be the same height so there would be a consistent airflow over us, but at 6 ft 3 inches I immediately mess that theory up so all we can do is concentrate on keeping perfect form and, when I am in the middle, I have to be aware to keep as low as possible without compromising my speed.

I will do a full lap and then the number four man, normally Geraint Thomas – G – comes through, and if we are going well we should reach the first Kilo in 1 min 03 secs. It is absolutely vital at this stage, indeed at any stage, not to be clock-watching, so we gauge our time by watching Shane Sutton 'walk the line' as we approach the finish after every lap. We should go through the first lap in 20.2 secs and once we hit top speed he will be taking half-lap splits on his stopwatch throughout; typically, on a world record schedule, that should be 7.2 secs per half lap. If we are on that schedule, or whatever schedule we are riding to, he will not move from that line. If we are 0.1 of a sec. ahead of schedule he will walk one step beyond the line, if we are 0.2 of a sec. behind he will walk two steps towards us. And so on.

So everybody has done their first turn and that sets the pattern. Ed, still blowing from his massive first turn, comes through for a second stint, then Paul, and suddenly I find myself in front again. This can sometimes be an important turn for me. If we are on schedule, great, it will be more routine and I just try and pile on more of the same, but if we have slipped behind now is the time to make the correction. I should still be in relatively good shape but must be careful to nudge us back up to speed rather than surge there with one big effort. G comes through again and he will have the same responsibilities. We should flash through 2 km in two minutes flat after a 57-second Kilo and it's beginning to hurt now.

Extra concentration in the third Kilo. Don't let it slide. I'm head down trying to suck in even more air than normal because the third turn is often when I have to earn my corn and make an extra big effort. Ed and Paul will be digging deep now, after their earlier heroics, and everything is getting critical, on the edge. Hopefully they are still feeling good enough to do a full lap, but if they feel their speed dropping they just have to swing up half a lap earlier. The big thing is for the man at the front never to let the speed drop, there is no point being a hero and battling on because the more the speed drops the harder it is to regain. No heroics. The only thing that counts is getting the third man through the line as quickly as possible.

Paul swings up and now is usually my big moment. I've been psyching myself up for the last minute of so for this. As the 'strongest' individual rider I am going to put in a lap and a half now, really grit my teeth and make it the best and smoothest stint possible and give the others just that little bit more time to recover. If we have dipped on the schedule this is our last realistic chance to get back on terms. The crowd will be roaring and the adrenaline pumping and still the runaway train rattles along. Keep that body position, hug the white line, corner in sympathy with the man in front of you, keep the aerodynamics sleek, move as one, lean as one. Nice, very nice.

The third kilometre came home in 57.5 secs. We are still on it. The last kilo now and it is killing us, we need to come home in just under 59 or thereabouts. The pain is indescribable – you start seeing black spots in front of your eyes – but we have trained like dogs for years and this is where all that endurance work on the big Tour or on camps in Australia and Majorca kicks in. You can keep going to that finish line. Extra concentration on technique, that is the first thing that goes when you are knackered and feel like you might black out. Ed comes through, Paul comes through but we need to stay alert. Any of us could feel the pace at any time and need to swing up early or simply crack, in which case you could suddenly be down to three and be prepared to do your turn that bit earlier.

If the team is reduced to three you have to stay cool. It is then, if you want to somehow stay competitive, that the strongest individual rider has to do a lap and a half each turn and the other riders half a lap each. It is not ideal but if you ask one of the guys who is blowing – perhaps the number one man – to do his full turn under those circumstances he will blow as well and then you will be disqualified because you must have three finishers.

We are hanging on in there. Concentrate, guys. Watch the wheel in front of you. No looking over to see how your opponents are doing, the crowd noise will tell the tale anyway. Keep those changes safe. Again, years of practice kicks in. You swing up – pedalling all the time because you must never lose speed. Because of centrifugal force you are now on the fastest part of the track but you are also now travelling further than the other riders so you keep pedalling flat out. The banking is the only place you can change; if you try and change on a straight it won't happen, you just will not have the speed to get back on.

After a lifetime of racing you just instinctively know when you have reached the sweet spot, that point on the banking when the bike doesn't want to go up any more, it wants to come down. Mostly, when you come down it is absolute perfection and you slot straight in, but when we are playing safe, because we are particularly tired and stressed, you will see that the rider coming down will deliberately overrun the third rider by a couple of inches and hover for a fraction of a second before he is in the perfect position to slip in. For a few seconds everything goes quiet and the pressure on your pedals eases as you take the tow, but if you miss that tow you are dead, there is no way you will ever catch the train up, no matter how strong a rider. I can do 4 km on my own in 4.15, the GB quartet does 3.56 – 19 seconds difference over 16 laps, over a second a lap.

We are nearly there now. We have survived as a four and are on schedule but need to keep our wits about us. Cycling gold medals are won by fractions and the time of a quartet is always taken as the third man crosses the line so we need to be organised as we go into the final straight otherwise we could clutter the place up and there could be an accident. Keep thinking, lads.

As we go into that last bend the lead man takes the sprinter's line, number two follows him and number three follows number two until coming out of the last bend when he goes a bit wider to avoid any possible clash with one and two. Ideally, number four stays back a little to keep out of trouble in case one of the bikes ahead of him should go down. A sort of backstop. It's rare but it can happen. Ten years ago we made a Horlicks of the last bend at a World Cup meet in Valencia and I ended up catapulting into the inside of the track. No damage done, but a bit embarrassing.

Back to the Team Pursuit in Manchester. I felt entirely different from Athens, when I had doubled up, but although the mood was great, qualifying was not entirely straightforward. The Danes – always good and looking particularly strong as they started their Beijing build-up – blew qualifying apart with an unbelievably quick ride of 3.57, the third quickest time ever, which definitely threw the gauntlet down. Going last we knew exactly what was required, basically anything under four minutes, and we had no intention of trying to match the Danes' time so early in the piece. A long 58 would do us fine and we were pretty much on course when we encountered a minor problem – Geraint Thomas, our number two man, blowing up at the end, reducing us to three men. As we have seen, this can happen very easily when you are operating at the speeds we ride.

We got home fine with a long 3.58, but it was a timely reminder to concentrate at all times on our pacing. We knew exactly what had happened within seconds of coming off the track, with our splits and speeds there for everybody to see. G, in super-aggressive mood after seeing the Danes go so well, had taken it out a bit too hard after Ed swung up the first time, and then when his turn came again he had ridden at the front too long and allowed the speed to dip before swinging up. That, in turn, means the next man to hit the front had to put in a burst to get the speed back up and the cumulative effect of that is very significant.

There were no recriminations; it can happen to any of us when you are operating at such levels. We hurried off to the gym and sat down with Matt Parker and Shane Sutton to talk things through, though we knew instinctively what had happened. There were two considerations. It was undoubtedly a shock how well the Danes had gone – we really didn't expect them to be that quick – but again, using the Steve Peters adage, their performance was completely beyond our control. I had very grave reservations as to whether they could back it up, but we had to assume that they were capable of coming out that evening and repeating the ride, in which case we, as we had always trained and planned for, would have to ride 3.56 something, and possibly dip below the world record. That was fine, we were well capable of that. I had confidently spoken before the Championships of our potential to beat the Australians' mark from Athens. We had the record well within our compass.

What to do about the line-up? G is extremely talented and there is no reason to suppose he would get it wrong in the final, but he is also a very fiery and emotional rider and his inclination is possibly to overcook it, so the logical thing was to move Paul – always the most consistent and calm member of our team – along to the hot seat at two, for me to slot in at three and G to act as tail-gun Charlie. It was a great compliment to Paul that we could move him there with such confidence, and a wonderful tribute to him that he pulled it off with such expertise.

Even if things had gone a little smoother in our qualifying ride I believe we might still have made the change. Ed and G are young tigers and the fact that Denmark had reeled off a 3.57 had got their nostrils flaring. We had to avoid blasting away suicidally quick.

And it wasn't that big a risk; in fact we were reverting to the exact order we had used to win the Worlds in Palma, the only reason we had been experimenting so much with G at two is that, potentially, if we absolutely nailed it to perfection, that was the order within the quartet capable of producing our fastest time. I firmly believe that if we get it right one night we can record a time in the region of 3 mins 52 secs, which is a sentence I never thought I would find myself writing a few years ago.

The final itself was a complete dream. We put in a beautiful, beautiful ride and it felt superb from start to finish. We had set the schedule at world record pace and Shane didn't deviate an inch from start to finish as he walked the line. I sat in at the back on the last lap and began to celebrate. I punched the air down the home straight – as we qualified second we started and would finish down the back straight – and coming off the final bend I came off the bars and started punching the air again and generally lost it. An absolutely unbelievable moment. The roar of the crowd told us instantly that we had broken the world record with 3 mins 56.322 secs, as well as won gold, and we milked it a bit, going around for four or five laps of honour.

An incredible ride on a very special night for Great Britain. Rebecca Romero had won a sensational gold in the women's 3000 m pursuit to add to her rowing gold medal a few years earlier, and Vicky Pendleton and Shanaze Reade had taken the women's team sprint. The velodrome was buzzing like never before in my experience.

It was wonderful to enjoy the moment with the lads and we were a happy bunch as we did the medal ceremony and dope control before heading back to the hotel. The other three headed straight for the bar, for their first decent drink since the new year, but reluctantly I went up to my room and locked the door. If I had stayed down for the 'one' that would have developed into a happy kick back for a couple of hours, but I was still hungry for that third gold in the Madison. Steve and I had anticipated this moment –

the feeling of wanting to relax completely and 'declare' after two golds, and the need to remain focused and start thinking about the Madison. Among other things, I owed it to Cav who, as usual, was already asleep. Although riding in the Points race the next day as well, he was only really concerned about the Madison. That was his gold medal shout and he needed me at my best.

I got it dead right the next day, Friday, which was a rest day for me but a potential banana skin. I had to come down off the huge high of my two gold medal days but remain ticking over mentally and not go into celebratory mode. This was going to be a key day.

I decided to get up and about pretty early and go down to the track and do an hour on my Madison bike during the practice period, just getting the feel of it. Hugh Porter and Garry Sutton were doing their notes and preparation up on the TV gantry so I wandered over for a natter. Between them they gather all the titbits and gossip, so in no time at all I felt I had caught up with all the news from the event. A nice long massage and soon I was back in the hotel, watching a few DVDs and the night's action from the velodrome which garnered another two gold medals for Britain to maintain the momentum.

Wendy Houvenaghel, Rebecca Romero and Joanna Rowsell created a new world record of 3 mins 25.725 secs in the women's 3000 m Team Pursuit, a relatively new event which unfortunately is not yet in the Olympic programme. And then Chris Hoy blazed his way to his first ever World Sprint title, defeating France's young gun Kevin Sireau 2–0 in the final, having accounted for Roberto Chiappa from Italy in the semi-final and, crucially, the mighty Theo Boss in the quarter-finals after being outfoxed in the first of their three races by the Dutchman. Chris is a quick learner and poured on the power in the final two races, leaving nothing to chance, to take Great Britain's first spring gold medal since Reg Harris in 1954. Chris is a powerhouse of a cyclist and that win completed a unique career grand slam in World Championship sprint events – the Individual Sprint, Team Sprint, Keirin and Kilo. Extraordinary effort. Just before I went to bed I shaved my legs for the day ahead, a little ritual which in my mind brought my day off to an end. I was back in action tomorrow and I needed to get my race head on.

For the first time that week I got a really good night's sleep, woke up feeling rested and went straight into Madison mode. This was a big day for myself and Cav. We had become great mates and enjoyed each other's company, but we are both competitors and we wanted a gold medal. Things can go wrong in the Madison; it's all a bit frantic and you can get caught up in another team's crash, but we fancied our chances. Shane was insisting that chance and luck shouldn't play much part in the Madison. We were the best team and if we produced we would win.

There was a bit of a scare first thing because Cav was feeling an annoying dragging pain in his groin, a pulled muscle or something, which he suddenly felt come on during his Points race the night before when he had been taking it fairly easy. We didn't panic; these sorts of pains are commonplace in cycling. Sometimes they simply come and go, the body reminding you that we make a lot of unreasonable demands, on other occasions they can persist and become a problem and need treatment. Cav went to the GB medics and physios for some treatment while G was put on alert that he might be riding with me that afternoon. G has all the weapons to be a brilliant Madison rider in the future – world-class endurance and the ability to put in a fast burst off the back of a good pace to score points in the sprint – but we hadn't practised together and it would have been a big ask. Not totally beyond us, but a big ask.

As the morning wore on, Cav began to smile again. The pain

and discomfort were easing considerably – it was a short-term niggle rather than an injury and by late afternoon when we raced he would be fine. Game on.

We started as marked men. I enjoy a reputation of being an exceptionally strong Madison rider and I was clearly in form, and Mark had all the potential and was a World Champion as a teenager in 2005. True, things hadn't gone wonderfully at the Ghent Six Days and in the World Cup round in Australia, but the opposition had quickly sussed out that there had been valid reasons back then and now we were definitely one of the form teams. They weren't going to make it easy for us!

We chipped away early on, accumulating a few points, but Germany, Denmark and Belgium had got away and put a lap into everybody so, as we always suspected, there would come a point when we had to rev it up and get that lap back to stand any chance of taking the title. Of course everybody else knew that; on a couple of occasions I pushed for a break but the main bunch were straight onto us. We had to bide our time but in a way that suited us as well, because the later in the race you make that big decisive surge the more devastating it can be. There is less time to react and recover.

Forty laps to go and the moment had come. Now or never. I took a couple of extra deep breaths – apparently the big screen was on me at that moment and Cath says I was gulping like a fish – and I hit the turbo. This time a gap did quickly develop, not absolutely decisively as I had hoped but something to work on. This was going to be a long haul. Head down, I went for it, piling on the speed. Denmark and Spain roused the bunch and tried to chase – they had no intention of rolling over – but the Saturday afternoon crowd, pretty well lubricated by the sound of it, was going berserk and I could feel a great surge of energy. At one stage I even got out of the saddle and up on the pedals, straining at the leash, and the crowd roared like I had scored a goal. They were really getting into this and loving it.

Still we hadn't cracked them and for the next 15 laps or so Cav and I had to work our socks off, Cav putting in some excellent turns as we went for that lap. People forget that, although one of the road world's great sprinters, he used to be a member of the GB Team Pursuit squad; in fact I think he even took a first once, at a World Cup meet down in Australia. There is an endurance element to his make-up as well – he showed that this year in the Giro when he did superbly to get through some horrible days in the mountains – and he really knuckled down as we went for it.

Eventually the judges decided that we had nicked the lap as the bunch cracked to pieces and stragglers fell off the back. We were in the lead and in the final stages had to cover moves and attacks to preserve our place. There was a late scare when Germany got back on our lap and could have taken gold if they had won the last sprint, but Cav was aware of the danger and raced hard to take second in the final burn-up and the race was ours. He seemed to know instantly that we had won and started celebrating; on the other side of the track, I was knackered and wasn't quite sure of the maths, but as I rolled around and looked infield Jamie Staff – who had been helping out with the BBC for the afternoon – gave me the big thumbs-up and a huge smile. We were home and dry, my third gold medal in four days. And yes, it felt bloody marvellous.

I was as excited and animated as I can ever remember, and the TV and press interviews came and went in a manic blur. On the spur of the moment I decided to dedicate our Madison victory to Garry – it seemed the right thing and I wanted to make a gesture. By now you have will have gathered that my relationship with Garry was hugely complicated, marked mainly by anger and bemusement on my part at his behaviour, but at that moment I wanted to honour him very publicly as a great Madison cyclist.

Garry had lived for the Madison and was European Champion at a time when really that was the World Championship – every team that counted was there back in 1985. One way or another thoughts about my father had woven their way into my entire World Championship campaign from the moment I had taken that fateful call from Shane in the middle of the night. That was the backdrop to Manchester 2008 and making a heartfelt dedication gave me a feeling of closure.

That night we were on it big time. After we did the medal ceremony, Cath and I celebrated with family friend Terry Dolan, a noted frame builder, and then had a few more at the Hilton. There was a feeling of massive release and plans for a big night were soon hatched with G – always a thirsty drinking companion when let off the leash – and Cav, who isn't such an Olympian drinker but enjoys the craic. A fair few of the Aussies were up for it as well – when aren't they? – and we ended up in some cellar-type nightclub off Deansgate, which seemed to still be filling up at about 3.30 a.m. when I started to lose the picture and Cath suggested it was time we headed back.

Sunday was mellow, wandering around the velodrome with Cath and the kids after a later start soaking it all up. What a week. Nine golds and two silver medals – at the World Championships! This was new territory for Great Britain in any sport, but frankly I wasn't surprised. I had us down for seven or eight before we even started, we were so up for the Champs and our preparation had been so good.

As I chewed the cud with coaches between races and chatted to experienced campaigners like Chris Hoy, there was a reassuring feeling around that this was just phase one in the master plan for a huge year. Nobody's celebrations were over the top. The Worlds are great but unfortunately nobody remembers them in Olympic year; on this occasion they really were just a staging post. Phase two commenced the following morning when we started our four-month build-up to Beijing, and phase three would start when we stepped off the plane in Beijing.

Phase two started for me when I nipped back down to the velodrome early on the Monday for my regular blood test and on the big message board in the office DaveB had written in large capital letters: 'Great effort everybody, much appreciated.' It had been a great triumph for the backroom boys as well – every single one of them – and typically most of them were already back at their desks or out the back tinkering with the bikes. It had also been a great triumph for DaveB and it was only when I read a press interview he had given on the final day of the Champs that I realised how badly the entire Rob Hayles affair had hit him, and how close he had come to resigning on the Thursday when he began to feel it had undermined everything he and his team had achieved.

Common sense prevailed, not least because Rob was innocent and has always been a clean rider as all the following tests demonstrated. The team had achieved so much at Manchester, something DaveB demonstrated on the Saturday night at a meeting of the riders and back-up squad when he asked anybody born in 1954 or before to stand up. Just two of the assembled party got to their feet. 'Well, you are the only two who were even alive when Britain last won the Men's Sprint Championship with Reg Harris in 1954 before Chris took it the other night. We have been making history this week.'

While everybody else went back to work I needed to kick back for a while after all the excitement and dramas. There was a long summer ahead so I packed the car – and managed to lose my mobile phone in the process – and drove home for a couple of weeks of R&R and very little time on the bike. I didn't envy Cav, heading off back to Europe for a heavy racing schedule, but he is addicted to racing and winning and was having the time of his life.

My schedule was a little flexible – High Road had been excellent in that respect – and knew I wouldn't be up to much for a while. The basic plan, however, was set in stone and it all revolved around the Giro d'Italia in May. That was going to be my major Tour, with the Tour of Romandie as my warm-up, and the last thing Shane Sutton said as we said our goodbyes was to bloody well make sure G and I got around. It was absolutely essential that we got those 3500 km in our legs before we returned to the fold and started back on specific track work. 'Just remember that when you are clawing your way up those mountains. Every yard and every ounce of effort will reward you come the Olympics. Just don't quit on the Giro, Brad. That's where you can win your gold medals.' Message received and understood.

—

Chapter Nineteen

Marking time

was much more tired than I expected after the World Championships, even though I established in my mind that it was only a stepping stone to Beijing. It was still a big physical effort and, although I was delighted at how I coped mentally with the challenge, there was extra pressure appearing in front of a home crowd. I had kept on top of it but there has to be a release afterwards.

The next week or two was a huge downer – inevitably, I knew exactly how I would feel – but I struggled a bit. I didn't go near my bike for a week and decided to spend the time usefully thinking about this book and the recent developments in my life. It was good therapy, unwinding mentally and physically, and soon enough I felt the need to go out and do a few miles. Although I was exceptionally fit in track terms I needed to get my road legs back for the Giro, which had a massive significance for me in terms of Beijing.

There was no great debrief or anything after Manchester. Everything had gone as planned and everybody had always appreciated that it was only a stepping stone to the Olympics. We were on the way and it was time to step back a little and go into road mode for the early summer.

Or rather, to go into Mark Cavendish support mode. My

'roomie' and Madison mate was on fire and at Team Columbia our tactics had become very simple indeed on a flat day. Get 'Cav' into the sprint finish, peel off and watch him do the rest. It was a brilliant time, one of the most enjoyable periods of my cycling career.

I warmed up in the Tour of Romandie and got a little form back before hitting the Giro, exceptionally fit but well undercooked in terms of road racing. My objectives were simple, keep clear of trouble, help Cav and get through all the mountains to the finish in Milan.

The Giro was great; I appreciate it more every time I compete. It is a magnificent, tough, arduous race but very low-key compared to the Tour de France. There are only crowds at the start and finish really – no madness in between except on top of one or two of the classic mountain climbs – and the press and media is low-key. There is a more relaxed atmosphere and if you are feeling good it is a beautiful riding arena.

The weather on this occasion was cool and showery – the start of a disappointing summer all round for northern Europe – which was a nice change but also made for a very nervous opening five or six days with the main objective being to avoid crashes and spills before the race finally began to settle down. Brad McGee went down heavily and badly damaged his shoulder and I didn't want to join him. An injury could disrupt all our carefully laid plans.

After we emerged unscathed from the first week it was a fortnight in the service of Cav, who pulled off two stage wins and finished second in two other stages. He fulfilled everybody's predictions and showed that over the final 150–200 metres of a sprint he is the fastest roadman in the world. A great spirit built up in the Columbia team and morale was very high. We worked our socks off to deliver Cav in good shape at the finish and he usually produced the results.

I was completely delighted for him and not remotely surprised. The great thing about Cav is that he is exactly the same as he ever was. Yes, that means he can be a little feisty and hot-headed – some describe him as cocky, I prefer ultra-confident – but that is the sprinter in him. If you took that out of Cav, he wouldn't be the performer he is.

Apparently, when Cav first presented himself to DaveB a few years back for an interview with a view to becoming part of the British Training Academy, the man himself was asked what ambitions he had. The young tyro, more than a few pounds overweight, didn't miss a beat. 'I'm going to become the fastest sprinter in the world.' DaveB was a bit taken aback. 'Bloody hell, what have we got here?' was his exact comment.

As a teenager, Cav used to finish a training run with colleagues in traditional fashion with a sprint to a nominated lamp-post down on the seafront on the Isle of Man: 'I'll be Robbie McEwen,' said one. 'I'll be Zabel,' said another. 'I'll be Mark Cavendish,' came a third voice. No surprises who won. Then and now.

My own form started to get much better and, although I had to dig deep to get through the mountains, I was pleasantly surprised to bag a fourth position in the time-trial on the final day – I was dead to the world the previous evening after getting through the final mountain day.

I said goodbye to the team a little reluctantly after Milan. That was my road season effectively over although there would be one final swan song in the Tour of Britain after the Olympics. I suddenly realised I would miss the Tour de France, despite the madness and the pain it has caused me. I also knew with some certainty that Cav was going to blast his way into the record books and the team were going to have a fantastic three weeks. I would be lying if I denied that a part of me wanted to be involved in that.

But it was Olympic year and I had to focus. First came a couple of days at home and then a family holiday in Majorca, which is like a second home these days. I was a bit wound up to be honest, feeling that my Olympics was under way, and couldn't resist nipping out early every morning for an hour or two on my bike before spending time with the family. Beijing was beginning to loom large.

I was eager to get cracking and once we got back it was straight down to the velodrome and the old routine. Everything was on track and I was very happy the final haul was under way.

I was back in the groove immediately. I had great legs and was feeling very sharp. Everybody was sharp, there was a fantastic atmosphere at the camp and everybody was flying. One afternoon, after a couple of hours' pretty strenuous work, Shane said it was time for a timed run just to see exactly where we stood.

We got the gate out and from the buzzer I felt superb, very controlled and hardly breathing. I came home over a second and a half inside my Olympic record, which was in itself the second fastest time in history. Just for a second I was in shock; it was scary how well I was going. But then I thought, no it wasn't that strange. I had been the top Individual Pursuiter in the world for five years now, I was fitter than ever before, highly experienced in all aspects of the event and of course I should be hitting those sorts of numbers.

Privately, I decided that not only was I going for Olympic gold but, if I got just a sniff of a chance, I was going to have a crack at Chris Boardman's all-time world record, even if he did achieve it in the 'Superman' position. Now was the time, I might never have a better opportunity.

Everybody was riding out of their skins. One afternoon I was having a breather on the side of the track for half an hour and the 4 km squad, with Chris Newton on board as well – they rode as a five – did a 2 km time-trial that equated to a 3.50 in the 4 km. Incredible stuff. You could sense Shane and others trying to rein everybody in. We had to avoid peaking now, we needed to be at our best between 15 and 19 August.

Meanwhile Cav, as predicted, was filling his boots on the Tour de France and there was a rush to watch the highlights every night when we had finished our work. There was a lot of pride in the camp that one of our own was emerging as almost the biggest name of the Tour de France. You could see the look of awe on everybody's faces.

The first stage win was the big one. Once he got that out of the way – and there was a bit of a false start on Stage 3 when the peloton dithered around and miscalculated the chase – he was always going to bat on and he simply got better and better. Four stage wins in the Tour de France, absolutely amazing. Just to write it down like that brings a bit of a tingle. In my opinion it is one of the greatest performances by a British sportsman in recent years. And he bailed out at exactly the right time. There must have been a temptation to try and get through the Alps for the final day on the Champs Elysées because that stage was there for the taking, but he was getting tired and had suffered a crash early in the second week and cut a knee. It was a good call to stop. Cav was constantly in touch with Shane and they and Columbia made the decision together. Everybody was happy. Columbia had gone into the Tour targeting stage wins and it worked out perfectly.

Then it was down to Newport, which felt homely and familiar after our successful stay there four year earlier. The velodrome is a great facility, the gym is good and there was loads of space for out technical staff to set up the heat chambers to replicate the conditions we were expecting in Beijing. As was the case four years ago, we were put up in five-star comfort at the Celtic Manor – the resort venue for the 2010 Ryder Cup – whose staff, again, couldn't have been more helpful. Top nutrition and chance to relax, and although it was hard being parted from Cath and the family, it offered the best possible chance of keeping clear of bugs. Nobody is fireproof and when you are extremely fit you are also, ironically, on the very edge of illness most of the time. All you can do is pay extreme attention to your personal hygiene – DaveB even organised for a top surgeon to show us how to wash our hands properly – avoid crowds and keep your fingers crossed.

Arriving in Wales I felt relaxed and controlled, in vivid contrast to four years earlier when, in retrospect, my life was all over the place and I was experiencing all sorts of emotional ups and downs – although luckily I had pulled it together physically and managed to focus just long enough to succeed in Athens.

Checking in was a strange feeling. It felt like barely four months ago I had been doing the same, not four years. Yet so much had happened in the meantime.

Since Manchester I had been seeing or talking to Steve Peters fairly regularly and reaping the benefit, feeling very motivated but relaxed. Arriving in Newport I went to see him again for a proper sit-down chat. I was slightly concerned that perhaps I felt too good, in the best form of my life, and wanted to avoid any complacency. There wasn't any real danger of that – after Athens I knew that there were so many pitfalls, ahead no matter how in shape you were – but, as ever, I wanted to hear that message from Steve. It was a way of reaffirming what I knew to be true. It was important and settling for me mentally to hear Steve spell it out.

'Brad, it's great you are feeling so good physically,' he would start. 'You are looking incredibly lean and sharp and I can hardly believe the figures you are posting in training. But you know better than me that the job is not even half done. Confidence tempered with realism is good, that is a very good place to be and that is exactly where you are. But confidence leading to a little complacency – overconfidence – is not good. That would be dangerous and worrying. Nobody at the Olympics is so good that they can just turn up and win the gold medal. And I mean nobody.'

The press day was a good-natured zoo, held within the track, and a massive demonstration of exactly how far our sport has progressed. In 2004 it felt like a quiet sideshow, this time it was the full Hollywood production with over 100 media in attendance. It really doesn't bother me much – there is now so much 'positive' pressure to succeed from within the group and management that the public's expectations simply feed into that equation.

There was much interest among the press when Shane Sutton let it slip that Cav was going to ride a couple of 4 km trials after he had rested up from the Tour to challenge for a place in my event! G had already gone extremely quick in training – 4.17 at the end of a strenuous session – but the management were very loath to have two of us involved at the sharp end of that event the night before the Team Pursuit began the following morning.

So the theory was sound. If Cav shaped up he could ride the IP with no pressure and enjoy a really strong workout on the Beijing track ahead of our Madison.

As for his chances of challenging me? Well, Cav is absolutely the best sprinter in the world and had nearly 6000 km of endurance in his legs after the Giro and the Tour, so theoretically he could ride a very fast 4 km; but there is a world of difference between having the raw materials and using them to best advantage. Hopefully you will have gathered by now that IP is a little more complicated than it looks. It is all about the timing of pace, the gradual squeezing out of your effort, the ability – normally gained after years and years practising the event – to ensure you don't overcook the ride early on and that you save something for the final stages.

You wouldn't put anything past Cav these days but the 4 km is not his event; frankly, I never expected to see him lined up against me in the finals and wasn't surprised when GB quietly shelved the idea. Not that it would have bothered me if he had ridden. I know what I am capable of and was capable of seeing off all comers. As ever the trick in the 4 km is not to get involved in a *mano a mano* race with the other guy, but to ruthlessly organise and execute your own ride.

Sitting around in the evenings I had a chance to reflect on what I really wanted from Beijing. You have to have your own goals and having accepted that I am never going to be a Tour de France winner – although a stage before I retire would be nice – the Olympics has massive significance for me. I want to achieve performances and records that will stand for ever. I feel slightly self-conscious writing that, but just about every sportsman I know sets themselves targets and knows exactly where they stand in the scheme of things. I know, because riders have told me that I have been the target they have shot at, so I need something to aim for myself to be able to raise the bar.

Going into Beijing I had done my research and knew exactly where I stood. Sir Steve Redgrave leads the way with five golds (and a bronze that everybody seems to forget), with Matt Pinsent in second place alongside Palo Radmilovic, who won three water polo golds and one swimming gold early in the twentieth century. I knew that if I pulled my triple crown off I would join that duo behind the great Sir Steve and that would mean an awful lot to me. In the back of my mind I also had the fact that if I won

The Awesome Foursome. The world's best Team Pursuit squad – now and perhaps ever. *Left to right:* Ed Clancy, myself, Paul Manning, Geraint Thomas. This after winning the 2008 worlds (*PA*).

Myself and the Cavman celebrate winning the 2008 World Madison champs in Manchester. Happy days, a great team ride (*Getty*).

The sun shines on the righteous. Getting back in the groove in Beijing after my nasty illness scare in Newport (*Action Images*).

Laoshan Velodrome was powered by its solar-panelled roof. The GB squad was powered by self-belief, talent and supreme preparation (*Action Images*).

Follow that line, Brad, there's a gold medal at the end (*Colorsport*).

Steven Burke and New Zealand's Hayden Roulston join me on the podium after the 4 km final (*Getty*).

Poetry in Motion. Our World Record ride in the final against Denmark was sporting perfection, one of the great moments, I believe, of Beijing 2008 (*Getty*).

Winning is addictive and we sportsmen live for moments like this (*Action Images*).

GREAT BRITAIN

Lottery money well spent! Myself and Chris Hoy have garnered seven golds between us at the last two Olympics. And neither of us are finished yet (*Action Images*).

An incredibly proud moment – being awarded the CBE on 11 June 2009 (*Photo by Anthony Devlin/WPA Pool/Getty Images*).

Nearly there. Near the top of Mount Ventoux with Tom Simpson providing the inspiration (*Associated Press/ Stephane Mantey*)

Happy days, cruising around the Champs Élysée on the final day. Job done (*Associated Press/Bas Czerwinski*)

a medal of any sort in all three events that would give me a total of seven in all Olympics, a new British best. There was everything to aim for.

Chapter Twenty

Beijing

With the media day out of the way we really went to work with a vengeance down at Newport and I have rarely felt so invincible on a bike. Everybody was flying but I was in unstoppable form and, yet again, our only worry was that I might be peaking too early. On the Sunday – that's 27 July, with the Olympic track meet less than three weeks away – we turned the temperature in the velodrome up a bit; I warmed up as if for an Olympic final and gave it the full Monty in an unofficial 4.5 km interval session during which I rode above Chris Boardman's all-time record of 4 mins 11.114 secs. I was totally elated but also just a little in a state of shock. This was scarily good form but I badly needed this situation to last another three weeks at least. When you start falling off your form it can all happen very quickly and you go into decline, sometimes sharp, sometimes gradual.

The next morning – Monday – I woke up in my beautifully appointed room over looking the golf course and I couldn't move. I don't mean I was sore and stiff after an unofficial world record ride the day before, in bits physically and needing a two-hour massage – I mean I simply couldn't move. I felt paralysed, with no feeling or strength in my legs. I thought perhaps I had somehow ended up lying in an awkward position in an unfamiliar bed and had a really severe case of pins and needles so, very gingerly, I manoeuvred myself to the side of the bed and hung my legs over, waiting for the blood to return in that painful way it sometimes does. I went to stand up but there was no power, no strength; my mental commands ordering my legs to move weren't getting through. Shit, this was very serious, my worst nightmare was coming true. My first race in Beijing was two and half weeks away and I couldn't even walk to the lavatory.

I called the team doc Roger Palfrenan and, trying to stay calm, asked him to look in. While I was making the call I noticed that I had a sore throat and felt a bit feverish as well – or was that my imagination playing tricks? He came in and gave me the once over. It was pretty clear from the start that I had been struck down by a virus of some sort, probably precipitated by my maxed-out world record pace ride the day before. You destroy a lot of muscle tissue when you take the body to the limit like that, and somehow a virus had infiltrated the muscle and the muscle nerves themselves as they began to recover and regenerate in the night.

That was the theory, but this is a bit of an unknown grey area and I was frightened. It certainly seemed like the end of my Olympic hopes for sure and the priority now was to contain the problem and make sure it didn't spread. Somewhere in the back of my mind I recalled morbid stories of aggressive infections and viruses eating away at athlete's bodies, depriving them of limbs. Apparently the fitter the athlete the quicker the virus devours the muscle.

Roger and the medics tried to put it into perspective. It was a virus; 99 per cent of the time they are self-containing and, given time, will just blow through, but in my pre-Olympic panic I didn't have time on my side. They started taking blood samples every three or four hours and in the meantime I was ordered to take complete bed rest. For the next three days the only time I got up was to drag myself over the loo.

Dark, dark days. Somebody up there didn't like me, what with all the Garry stuff at the start of the year and now being struck down by a mystery ailment while in the form of my life. I wasn't a good patient and fretted non-stop. Some of the boys called in to see me before and after their training stints and I tried to put on a brave face. 'I needed a rest anyway, this is the body's way of saying slow down, a blessing in disguise and all that.' But all the time I was wondering if the feeling would ever come back into my legs, if this was something very serious indeed and possibly permanent. I would read through the papers and there, mocking me, would be various feature-length stories from the interviews I had done just the previous week, stating how I was gunning for three golds and I was a stronger and more resilient athlete these days than in Athens.

Somewhere in the middle of the Wednesday night to Thursday morning my legs started feeling normal again and I heaved a huge sigh of relief. It had been very frightening. By Thursday morning I felt completely recovered – the ailment had disappeared as quickly as it had arrived – but it was clearly best to err on the safe side and, although I was allowed to get up and potter, Roger and his team still strictly banned me from my bike.

Having turned the corner my improvement, glory be, was rapid and by the weekend I was feeling absolutely fine although still a little concerned. I had been off my bike for six days now and we were leaving for Beijing early the following week. It was agreed I could ride a 3 km trial on the Sunday on the understanding I would bail out immediately if there were any unusual sensations.

I rolled out cautiously but soon hit my stride and was on a really good solid 4.15 pace when I pulled over after 3 km as agreed. I had lost that incredible edge of sharpness I enjoyed the previous Sunday but essentially I was fine. I would be going to the Olympics after all and the dream was alive, even though the bug had frightened me witless.

So off we headed to Beijing, the moment I had been quietly working towards for a very long time. In anticipation of the heat and humidity ahead I had even reverted to my Athens short back and sides haircut – the 'prisoner' look to signify the hard labour ahead. I wanted to feel as comfortable as possible so the locks had to go.

I was a senior figure now, undertaking my third Olympic campaign, and was determined to take everything in my stride. The main Olympic site in Beijing was incredible, something from a 22nd-century sci-fi scenario, but the bottom line always is how you perform, not where you perform and the stadiums, no matter how great they look. It is the performances and the medals that go down in the record books.

We had arrived ten days before the track cycling started so had time to get our bearings a bit in the athletes' village. Some of the team seemed a bit disappointed, as if they were expecting six-star luxury, with diversions and games to play 24/7, but I've never looked on the village like that. They are places where you sleep, eat, rest, get your evening massage and keep in touch with home. As long as I can do all that, I'm happy and the Bejing village was absolutely fine. The Olympics is not a holiday or a tourist trip and it always alarms me when some athletes start talking about 'chilling out' and embracing the Games, Chinese culture and all that stuff. The way to do that is to roll up your sleeves and bloody well get stuck in, produce the performances of your life and hopefully come away with a few medals. That's how you enjoy an Olympic Games.

We headed off down to the Laoshan velodrome soon after arriving and were pleasantly surprised by the transformation since we had last been there. It had always looked magnificent, with its huge space-age solar-panelled roof, but this time it also felt extremely comfortable and used. During the World Cup test event, there were still thick layers of dust and cement around, and lots of industrial taping and building materials lying around. Now, everything was squeaky clean and new. It felt complete, with a nice smooth running track, carpet fitted around the offices, and posters and flags everywhere.

It still lacked a little atmosphere by European standards, but that was because the cycling had generated such interest that one whole side of the stadium had been given over to press tribunes and TV, meaning there was only noise down one straight – and even then, the Chinese don't have the most sophisticated knowledge of track racing, and weren't really sure when to shout. No matter, I was sure it would warm up as the track meet progressed and the atmosphere would build as cycling folk dropped in and GB competitors from other sports came up to cheer once their events were over. The Chinese had generally made an excellent job of the entire Laoshan cycling complex, with a real fun BMX track built along one side of the velodrome – which was very tempting, but I resisted on the grounds that I would probably crash – while out the back they had laid down a demanding mountain bike circuit. It was all there – the envy of the cycling world really – and if they persevere with these facilities in years to come I can see a new wave of young Chinese cyclists coming through.

So we started rolling around, or rather the others did. They were well into their taper and, except for one or two short sharp passages of exceptional work, nobody was overcooking it. I was going at it pretty hard, however, feeling I had a week's training to recoup though I was beginning to feel very confident of my form again. The illness was a bit of a reality check – if I pushed things to the very limit there was just a thought in the back of my mind that it might come back and I started to step back a bit from my plans to smash the world record in the Individual Pursuit to make my definitive statement on the event. I was going to have to race seven times at the very limit of endurance in five days. There was going to be no rest day like at the Worlds in Manchester, as there was an extra round in both the individual and Team Pursuit before the Madison. Still, it was me who had taken the challenge on. These were the events I excelled at. Nobody had taken this on before, basically because they didn't think it could be done. I was going to try and prove something different, but I began to put my sensible head on. I had to box clever.

Steve Peters, as ever, was a big help and I was talking to him daily in the build-up to the start of competition. He knew instinctively that the illness had worried me and was in the back of mind. On the track, the numbers had quickly stacked up again, but the thought of what happened – and what might happen again – hadn't gone away. I needed a bit of nurturing and reassurance, I suppose, and Steve provided that. He also shared the view that I should do what needed doing to get the three golds and not get diverted by chasing world records and a slice of additional personal glory.

Training was smooth enough, although DaveB was a bit worried that the stadium authorities seemed to be keeping the air con on high, which was pushing the temperatures inside down – so much so that occasionally it felt a bit chilly. It wasn't what we had expected but it didn't worry me – I would have ridden through two foot of snow on the track to win gold – but it was irritating Dave and the number crunchers a little. It meant that none of their readings could be usefully compared with their readings from Manchester and Newport. Essentially they still knew – could see with their own eyes – who was flying. We all were. But the GB success has been built on our unswerving reliance on the numbers, who is performing and putting the effort in and who isn't, and for a few days the backroom boys were denied that data. Come competition time the air con had been sorted and conditions were perfect. Hot but not too hot, humid but not stifling. Ideal for going seriously quick.

Competition day dawned – Friday 15 August. Everybody seemed in good shape and the squad were in excellent spirits after the success of the women in the road races earlier in the week. Nicole Cooke had stormed home in the torrential chilly rain up at the hilly circuit by the Great Wall in Badaling, after fine self-sacrificing rides by Emma Pooley and Sharon Laws. Nicole really finished in style, getting in the final five-rider break at the end and taking it nice and easy around the final treacherous corner on her light wheels before unleashing an unstoppable finish up the steep sprint.

It was a very classy moment indeed from Nicole and had the immediate effect of kick-starting the most incredible Games for Great Britain. You could hear the cheers going around our block in the village – an uplifting moment. Lest we forget, things hadn't gone that smoothly in the lead-up. Gold medal hope Frankie Gavin had failed to make the weight in the boxing and our judo players had complained of being under-prepared on the first day. On the road, our lads, led by my old mate Steve Cummings, had endured an absolutely torrid day – 94 degrees of heat and 98 degrees of humidity – which proved intolerable for northern Europeans and none of them finished.

And then Nicole and that last corner. I know for a fact that many commentators and fans back home thought she had blown it as she appeared to lose contact on that final corner. Groans went up around the nation. Go on, admit it. Another Brit falling short when the heat came on. Far from it. This was a Brit showing ultimate class and coolness when the pressure was at its greatest.

Brilliant stuff. It showed exactly what was needed and plenty of others followed from all sorts of sports.

My mind went back to Jason Queally in Sydney, when his kilo win galvanised a great effort by the GB team, and Chris Hoy in Athens when his victory got the show on the road. Cycling has been contributing mightily to the GB effort for a while and it felt good. Emma produced a storming ride a few days later to take silver in the women's time-trial and all the indicators were good. The GB cycling squad were clearly in great shape and now it was time for us 'trackies' to join the Beijing party.

Friday evening and it was the start of something amazing. In quick succession we had Super Saturday, Superlative Sunday, Magical Monday and Terrific Tuesday. When Chris Hoy and his team sprint guys took to the track on the Friday evening – Fantastic Friday? – GB were postioned on two gold medals, seven medals in total, and we were lying a respectable but not mind-blowing 11th in the table. By the time the cyclists, rowers, sailors, Beccy Adlington and Christine Ohuruogu had done their stuff and finished five days later, we were third and heading for our greatest ever modern Games. It gives me goose pimples just thinking about it.

It was Chris and the lads who kicked the weekend off with a bang. Back at the Manchester World Championships they had been defeated by a convincing margin by the French – over half a second – with the French smashing the world record in the process. GB seemed like sound silver medal candidates but, frankly, a gold looked one step too far – although they never accepted that for one moment. As a squad they had not enjoyed the margin of defeat in Manchester and set about rectifying the situation with the sprint coaches.

The sprint squad took their lead from Chris and had been working like never before. Jamie Staff was enjoying an Indian summer to his career and was reeling off world record pace 17.2 second opening laps, while at the Newport training camp the important decision had been made to ask young Jason Kenny to fill the important but troublesome number two slot. Chasing Jamie and then having some gas left to take it to another level on lap two is an awesome task and, right at the death, Jason seemed to grow into the role, which says a lot about the talent of the young man. Chris obviously was in the form of his life and would always add his finishing power at the end, but GB needed to be in contention going into that last lap if they were going to pull off a major upset against the French.

I was warming up at the time, but I could feel the electricity in the air from the sprint qualifying as the big teams entered the fray. GB went second last and blew the competition apart with an incredible world record ride of 42.950 secs, a time they had been peppering throughout training, although they had tried to keep the lid on that news so as not to alarm the French and put them on their mettle. Jamie produced the fastest start time in history – 17.198 secs, Jason weighed in with the fastest-ever second lap (12.555 secs) and Chris brought it home with the fastest-ever final lap (13.197 secs). You could see the entire GB squad pump their chests out. This was fantastic, we were on it big time. The unsuspecting French were shattered mentally, and I suspect one or two other squads went into shock as well. Even with their World Championship trio of Gregory Bauge, Kevin Sireau and Arnaud Tournant on board they couldn't really respond and, going next, their time of 43.541 secs was down on their ride in Manchester. The gold was effectively won there and then.

We were next on in the qualifying of the Individual Pursuit, which was a curious and nervous affair. As defending champion and world ranked number one I spent most of the time waiting for somebody to come flying out of the pack to post a really quick time to which I would feel obliged to respond. It just didn't happen. I thought Jenning Huizenga from Holland, who went so well in the Worlds, might be the man, but he had a nightmare time after apparently falling foul of the scrutineers and having to change his riding position the day before competition.

There had been big rumours that the Aussie Brett Lancaster was flying. Shane used to egg me on in training, telling me he'd heard 'Big Bird' was going well, but he only posted a workmanlike 4.26, while I was sure Brad McGee would try to sign off with something special in his last Olympics, but he missed out on the top eight with another 4.26. All pretty military medium to be honest.

None of the big names seemed to be stepping up to the plate and young Steven Burke – announced as Steven Burkey to our general amusement – must have been wondering what all the fuss was about. A routine training session at the GB camp would have been harder than this. He had only heard the day before that he was to get the ride and started very cautiously with a slow opening kilometre before he suddenly got the taste for it and brought it home beautifully with a screaming 62-second final kilo to record the fifth fastest time in 4 mins 22.260 secs.

Only New Zealand's Hayden Roulston – a really strong and improving rider – really raised his game with 4 mins 18.990 secs, so down in the pits I was faced with a real dilemma. The adrenaline was still flying around from the team sprint guys and the alpha male in me wanted to go out there and produce something very special of my own. I had already decided that an attempt on Chris Boardman's outright world record would have to wait for another day when my racing programme wasn't so heavy but the compromise – the deal I had made with myself – was that I would give it a bit of whirl and post a long 4.13 to lay undeniable claim to the 'non-Superman' world record.

But now, down in the pits, I was thinking where is the opposition? I was assuming that at least one rider would have come out of the woodwork and posted a 4.15 and my reply would have to be to slap them down with a 4.13 to show them who was boss. But none of this had transpired. Just before I went out onto the track I made a very late call and told Shane to alter the schedule for a 4.15, just inside my Olympic record but not killer pace. He immediately nodded assent – he had probably been thinking on the same lines but hadn't wanted to deprive me of my fun and a 4.13 ride – and he immediately altered his calculations as he placed his white towel down by the finishing line from where he walked the line one way or the other.

After going out fractionally slower than normal – probably overcompensating after lowering my sights – and Shane making one step towards me, I got back on track immediately and he didn't move a muscle for the remainder of the race as I roared home in 4 mins 15.031 secs to break my own Olympic record and to put over three and half seconds into Roulston. I rolled around a happy boy after that. Illness scare or not, that felt a whole lot easier than my record ride in Athens. My basic fitness was excellent, I just had to take care not to abuse it.

I headed for a relaxed warm-down in the pits and thereby hangs a tale. We occupied position A1, the biggest area on the top rank, right next to the track as you came off. It could not have been more convenient. This allowed perfect access for warming up and instant recovery and attention post-race. No wending your way in and out of the maze clustered behind, getting into tangles with other riders or diverted by people wanting a quick word.

A good while back the Chinese authorities, anxious to organise the best possible cycling meet, asked if they could send a delegation to Manchester to earnestly study how it is done.

Rather than treat such a visit as an imposition, DaveB and British cycling laid out the red carpet, went into minute detail on how to get these things right, organised a minibus for the tour party and, in traditional style, the GB meeters and greeters ensured that copious food and ale were available 24/7 along with a couple of big nights out in 'Madchester'.

Firm friendships were formed and, when GB were in Beijing for the World Cup meet earlier in 2008, DaveB casually dropped into conversation that Pitt A1 would be very much to Great Britain's liking. The Chinese, with their well-known aversion to losing face, but also with gratitude for Great Britain's recent hospitality still coursing through their veins, happily obliged. A great result – and, if you keep getting the edge like that in everything you do, I suppose eventually the result will be eight Olympic gold medals in one historic Games.

Anyway, I was down there on the rollers when the Team Sprint squad finished the job with another two incredible rides in round one and then in the final against France, when Chris produced an amazing final surge to comfortably defeat the shell-shocked French. Like Nicole, he seemed to be holding off a bit going into the final lap, and one or two observers were worried, but Chris was using all his experience. He had been riding at incredible pace all night and, as the man going the full distance every time, was getting tired. There was no need to break the world record a second time, so he stood off a bit in lap two and then just burned the French into the ground on the final lap. *Chapeau!*

With Rebecca Romero and Wendy Houvenaghel looking highly impressive in the qualifying of the women's pursuit, and myself and Steve Burke, the GB show was well and truly on the road.

One slight irritant was that, as a new Olympic record holder, I was automatically required to attend dope control. Obviously I have no trouble with that per se – we must never drop our guard in the fight against drugs – but rather against the general well-run nature of the Beijing Olympics, dope control at the velodrome was chaotic to say the least, with nobody there talking English and some of the extraction of blood being somewhat crude. Vicky Pendleton and others had the bruises to tell the tale. The main point, however, was that it was an hour or more wasted before you could set off back to the village and that in itself was a 40-minute drive – more if you hit traffic. By the time you got back, piled into a mountain of pasta in an empty dining room and had a massage, it was well past the midnight hour. Believe me, the Olympics is not all glamour and glitz, and I often think it is those who think it will be special and different who sometimes trip up.

Saturday dawned and it was the moment of truth as far as the Individual Pursuit was concerned. To be honest, the only danger was complacency. I knew I had the beating of the field; there was nobody there who could match me and that is being objective, not arrogant. But I still had to concentrate and go out there and execute. I had to guard against all possible accidents and make it happen – prove my superiority beyond any doubt.

As the fastest qualifier, I had the 'luxury' of sitting back and watching the others post their times in round one, which decided the four riders to contest the medals. Steven Burke did another nice ride – 4 mins 21.588 secs to qualify fourth fastest, and by the time of my ride against Alexander Serov, the fastest time to beat was Roulston, who had come in at 4 mins 19.232 secs. He had backed up pretty well but it looked a pretty maxed-out effort to me.

A quick word with Shane and Steve and we decided that the logical thing to do was to schedule a ride no quicker than 4.17. It went slightly against the grain – I was riding for a place in the Olympic semi-final and I felt I should have been going quicker and producing something epic, but the logic was there for all to see. In actual fact, to qualify for the final all I needed to do was go quicker than the second-fastest qualifier – at that time Alexei Markov – but I absolutely drew the line there. I was the reigning Olympic champion and I refused to even consider only qualifying for the final as the second-fastest qualifier. That simply wasn't an option.

So we scheduled a 4.17 and it was one of those occasions when, from the moment I got on the race bike, everything felt settled and perfect. It was completely effortless, I felt I was at about 60 per cent gas and have worked up more of a sweat cleaning my teeth in the morning. If I had been in world record mode mentally, I would have taken it there and then that afternoon as Laoshan. At least, that's what I tell myself. The body is a funny thing though. If I had set out for the world record perhaps I would have tensed up and lost that magical feeling of freedom in my body. Perhaps it was the relaxation of 'only' going for a 4.17 that made me feel so good. It almost felt like an afternoon off. Anyway, having resisted the temptation to give it the gun over the last 2 km, I rolled back into the pits feeling like I had done a gentle four-lap spin by way of a warm-up rather than a world-class 4 km Individual Pursuit – I actually came home in 4 mins 16.571 secs, which was a full two seconds quicker than anybody else rode all week.

For a brief period of time it felt great, but then I had to get my Olympic final head on. Steve and Shane gathered around as we discussed the ride against Roulston. There was only one person who could defeat me and that was Bradley Wiggins. And there was only way that could happen and that was by Roulston somehow getting me to ride a race I didn't want to ride. Ninety-nine times out of 100 I would definitely beat him in a 4 km Individual Pursuit, but he is a tough Kiwi and there was no way he would lie down in the final. As with McGee in 2004, we correctly anticipated that he would come out all guns blazing and try to draw me into a race over the first 2–2.5 km, with the very slight outside chance that he could get me to 'blow'. In fairness, they are exactly the same tactics I would employ in such a situation.

So again it was a case of brain ruling heart. This was turning into a very thinking Olympics. I still hadn't really been let off the leash yet. I knew I could defeat Hayden under any circumstances – early burn-up or not – but the only chance he had was to force a mistake from me and the professional thing to do was to deny him that chance. Slam the door in his face. So Steve sat there quietly going through things with me in the pits, just gently spelling it out: 'It's McGee again, Brad, he will come out hard but you are going to ignore him. The race is over 4 km not 2 km, don't be bothered if he is still in contention or even ahead at 2 km. That will be his plan. Ignore him. Ride your race. This is all about you doing exactly what needs to be done to retain your Olympic gold. This is what you do better than anybody else in the world, Brad, just go out and do it. Don't do what the Kiwis want you to do.'

We scheduled a 4.16, which I reckoned would be more than enough. In the unlikely event of Hayden still being neck and neck in the final kilometre, I knew I could still find plenty more to see him off. But, frankly, I just couldn't see Hayden, on his third ride in 24 hours, improving on the long 4.18s which are his outer limit at present. One day, perhaps, but he was riding on the limit every time.

So that was the theory, but this was still an Olympic final and I still had to go out and execute. They don't give Olympic medals away and, for all the talking and common sense, the only person who could win the thing was me. Nobody was going to do it for me. I was nervous, despite all my experience and despite the fact I knew I should win this with something to spare.

Steven Burke rode off first for the bronze medal and nailed it with a fine ride, bringing his personal best down to 4 mins 20.977 secs. What a great moment for the young man, who only learned 48 hours before that he would be riding. It can be a thankless task being the fifth man in the Team Pursuit – doing all the training and always being on call but rarely getting the credit and glory, but this was a lovely moment all of his own. What a talent he will be for 2012. I remembered how I had felt on the podium in Sydney collecting my team bronze, and how it had fired me up like few events in my life. Hopefully Steve feels the same thing and will go on to enjoy an epic Olympic career.

And then it was me. My mental preparation was much the same as in Athens. I quietly went over the race I intended to ride – how to nail that 4.16, which I had done literally hundreds of times in training – and visualised how I would bring it home in the second half. Don't go chasing him early doors, Brad. That is his only hope, the only way he can get to you. Concentrate. No looking up. No screen gazing, no looking for Cath in the crowd. Follow that line and watch Shane like a hawk.

And off we went. Hayden went out really hard and had nearly 0.3 secs on me at the Kilo, which I took out in 1 min. 8.794 secs, nearly one and a half seconds slower than my Olympic record ride the day before. I was playing this one really cautiously. Oh so gently I began to squeeze it out. By the 2 km I had just nudged ahead and by the 3 km I was a full second ahead, although finally I was just beginning to feel the fatigue of riding the three fastest times in the competition in the space of 24 hours. I would like to tell you it all felt effortless and in control, like it had two and half hours earlier, but the truth is I had to keep pressing on, keep doing the work. Some rides you just fly and you are touched by genius or magic, and others you have to grind out and take a tradesman's pride in doing a job of work. No alarms though. The finish hoved into view and again I was under 4.17 – 4 mins 16.977 secs – and nearly three seconds ahead of Hayden – and my second Olympic gold medal in the same event was in the bag. Not many British competitors have done that in any sport and I was certainly the first cyclist. Did it feel good? What do you think?!

Job done. It was a really nice moment, with none of the emotional angst of Athens. My life was much more in control and – mystery illness apart – my preparations had been much smoother. In 2004 I was breaking through new ground and fighting Chris a little, although in retrospect I realise I needed changing and sorting out. It was a tough process. This time I knew exactly how much work and professionalism was required and, with Shane and Matt there constantly fine-tuning my approach minute by minute, it felt almost routine – and I mean that in a positive way. I had been the class Individual Pursuit rider in the world since 2003, the gold medal should have been routine. Eliminating any chance happenings or complacency was half the battle.

This time I savoured every moment on the podium. In Athens it was a blur. In Beijing I took a deep breath and had a long look around for ten seconds or so and recorded a snapshot of it all that will stay in my mind for ever. I don't need any photographs to remind me of Beijing 2008. The moment the Union Jack went up – in fact two Union Jacks because Steve was on the podium with me – will be with me for ever.

All very satisfying, but the fun and games soon started. As the gold medallist, I had a pile of obligatory media stuff to do and, in fairness, they had all given me a wide berth since Newport. I know one or two had sat on the illness rumours a little to give me breathing space, which had been much appreciated. So I plunged into that – TV and press – and gave it my best shot for an hour, despite a rather comical Chinese translator trying to steal the show at the press conference. He seemed to be under the misapprehension that it was cabaret time! I enjoyed a good natter with all the British press and there was a great atmosphere on a highly successful afternoon – Chris Hoy had taken the Keirin and Chris Newton had ridden a brave race in the Points to win the bronze. The cup was overflowing already. At one stage somebody asked me to try and describe the difference between Athens and Beijing and I suddenly had one of those rare moments of clarity when I could describe it perfectly. 'In Athens I was a mature rider but an immature bloke. Here I am still a mature rider but I've grown up as a bloke as well.'

On that note I took my leave and tried to be this new mature bloke! As prearranged with Steve, I immediately tried to put my gold medal celebrations and emotions on the top shelf. To an extent I managed that, but there was so much else to deal with. There was the usual agony of dope control and trying to produce urine samples when severely dehydrated, and again it was midnight before I got back to the village and made my way to the food counter. By the time I had eaten and had a massage it was very late and, having been busy, I was very much awake and buzzing with general excitement. Eventually I got off to sleep about 3 a.m., having remembered to put the alarm on for 6.30 a.m. for breakfast with the Team Pursuit boys and an early start down at the velodrome for our warm-up and morning qualifying. Well, nobody ever said it was going to be straightforward chasing three Olympic gold medals, but the organisers certainly weren't making it easy for me. It was a bit bizarre really. There were only ten golds available at the Olympics compared with 18 contested at the Worlds and the programme in Beijing seemed really light most days, which is something the sport needs to address, yet I couldn't have been busier or more stretched. All in all it was a bit unfortunate, a rare slice of bad luck entering the equation.

—

Chapter Twenty-one

The chain gang

At breakfast I spoke to Shane and Steve. I was more tired than ideally I had wanted to be. Although at various times in the previous two days I had felt great – that blissfully easy 4.16 round one ride for example – the fact is that I had still nailed three rides beyond anybody else's compass in the field in a tad over 24 hours. In the very short term you can deceive the body into thinking that is entirely normal, but there is always a consequence to pay and I felt bloody tired that Monday morning. A good honest tired with the prospect of a quick recovery, but tired nonetheless.

But presumably so did Steven Burke, who had recorded three consecutive personal bests in the Individual Pursuit, and Chris Newton, who had ridden really hard the previous day to earn that well-deserved bronze medal in the men's Points Race. One of us had to double up and all the objective evidence showed that, in past years, despite my occasional reservations, I had done all right the morning after the night before, even if I had dipped below the levels I expect of myself.

Shane took me to one side. 'Look, Brad, all I want you to do is give me three turns at 100 per cent and then you bail out at the 3 km mark, don't go digging too deep. The boys are going off the bloody Richter scale at the moment, they will bring it home no bother at all. Not only do you not have to finish, I don't even want you trying to finish. No heroics, we don't need that from you at all. Save those for the final. Just give me three turns at 100 per cent and we will be home and dry.'

Very wise words, which had the advantage of letting everybody know exactly what the score was, which is how we have operated for two or three years now in the Pursuit squad. We weren't just going to go out there and give it a blast and see if Brad could hang on the morning after the night before. We had a game plan and were going to execute, and nothing was going to be left to chance.

And early in the morning at Laoshan that's exactly what we did. Once into the race the adrenaline kicked in and I felt better than when warming up and gave it the full treatment on my three big turns before swinging up and away as ordered to let the lads complete in 3 mins 57.101, a seriously quick time in qualifying with just three men finishing. We were well pleased, everything had gone as planned, no real alarms. Ed, Paul and G were riding brilliantly, with the latter in the form of his life. You do wonder what he might have done if let loose in the Individual Pursuit against me – a silver medal at least! – but in the end G made the call himself. He was thinking only of Olympic gold and his best shout at Olympic gold was undoubtedly the Team Pursuit; he had no intention of doing anything to endanger that. Wise man, because ultimately he was part of a ride that will go down in history and be talked about for years to come.

The rest of the field were a mixed bunch and hard to read. New Zealand, resting Hayden, still posted a low 3.59, so were obviously an up and coming quartet, but Australia and Denmark – who we had earmarked as our most serious rivals – came in with sluggish times in excess of 4.02, although Australia did lose Mark Jamieson after 2 km, which didn't help their cause much. I wasn't fooled though. They could both go much quicker and, to my eyes, were trying to save something for the evening.

In between the qualifying and our eagerly awaited round one contest that night was the highly enjoyable spectacle of Rebecca and Wendy riding off for the Women's Individual Pursuit. I had long thought Rebecca was just about the strongest favourite GB had for gold in any event in any sport in Beijing, but it says a great deal for Wendy that she had upped her game tremendously in training and, come the final, even though she went a couple of seconds down early on, she was really tough and hung on like no other rider in the field had been able to do. Rebecca duly won gold but knew she had been in a fight, but she's a fighter herself and knew it would be a battle. What an achievement, rowing silver in Athens, cycling gold in Beijing. As an Olympic buff I love these kind of stories – there has to be inspiration there for young-sters watching. Who knows what Rebecca will end up doing in London 2012 but I fancy her real genius lies in riding bikes. She has discovered her sport. Stirring stuff, and a great story for the press to get stuck into, even on such an epic weekend.

So the final event of the day and the all-important first round of the 4 km Team Pursuit. This was always going to be the big session of the Olympic Games as far as I was concerned, the one we knew from way out that we had to get absolutely right. This was going to be the most nervous and exciting ride of them all. Denmark would be flying, I had no doubt about that, Australia wouldn't be far behind and the Kiwis had upped their game and emerged as a pretty special squad with vast potential. There was room for error in qualifying, and I knew in my heart of hearts that the final would take care of itself if and when we got there because we could back up every time we rode, but this round one was going to be big. Banana skins everywhere and GB were on such a roll that all the opposition were hoping to put one over us. There was a lot of emotional energy going into this session.

I felt much better than in the morning, much stronger, but still tired if that makes sense. Four rides down and I was fatigued but thus far 'managing' the situation, but I knew there would be no hiding in this session and had to let everything out.

Denmark were first up against France and from the outset it was clear they had only been in second gear in the morning. They had played a clever hand and were saving their best for when it was needed. Fair play to them, it was good thinking and showed exactly how serious they were. Despite our tag as favourites, Denmark were chasing gold and I applaud that. It is teams like them that have pushed us on. They posted an extremely rapid 3 mins 56.831 secs, not so very far outside our world record in Manchester and, to use cricket terminology, they had the runs on the board and were safely in the clubhouse. The state of Denmark was excellent.

Then came the Aussies, who were much improved on the morning but not quite so on the money as Denmark – still, a 3.58 showed just how classy this competition had become. New Zealand brought Hayden Roulston back into their quartet and they immediately responded to his extra strength and inspiration, roaring home in 3 mins 57.536 secs. That was the time we had to beat to be sure of riding in the final, and if we wanted to make absolutely sure – and finish ahead of the Danes – we would have to schedule a 3.56, i.e. a world record. It is a measure of the extraordinary leaps forward we have made physically, and in terms of confidence, that we didn't consider that remotely intimidating. We had always assumed we would have to ride 3.55 to win the Olympics and trained accordingly. We had gone inside the world record regularly in training, certainly so often as to not even cause a comment when our time was shouted over at the finish. World record pace had become our default setting and that's exactly how it has to be when you turn up at the Olympics.

But the big factor missing in training, as every athlete knows, is the competitive element, the nerves that can creep in and the tiny mistakes that nerves can cause. That is what makes world records in Olympics or World Championships so special: the greatest ever performance under the greatest pressure. There could be no second chance this time; we had to nail it like we had nailed it countless times before in Manchester and Newport.

Everybody was on it. Ed and G had grown immeasurably in the last two years. Initially they were young tigers and slightly volatile – remember G pushing it a bit too hard too early in qualifying in Manchester? – but in that Manchester final, and in the last four or five months, they had matured beyond all recognition. They were now hard core, absolute rocks and among the very best track riders in the world full stop – as reliable at their jobs as the vastly experienced Paul Manning and myself. I looked around as we warmed up, along with Steve Burke in case one of us fell off or suddenly fell ill, and I found myself smiling. This was a bloody magnificent squad. There was none better in the world, now or ever. I was so proud to be a part of this. Riding in this quartet has been just about the pinnacle of my career as a track cyclist. Rattling along with these guys was the greatest feeling in the world, moving as one, thinking as one, winning as one.

We had trained like dogs all year, in fact the last two years. Those bastard sessions in Majorca nearly killed me and the others. I thought of all the sacrifices people had made. G giving up a chance at personal glory in the individual, Paul doing me a huge favour in 2004 and dropping out of the running for the individual, Ed giving up on other individual track projects he could be excelling at to concentrate on this one event. And personally I had dug deeper than I ever have before to make sure I didn't let these guys down after my individual efforts. I had dedicated equal, if not more, time to the Team Pursuit than my own specialist event. I had religiously done every session, no matter how knackered I was. I badly wanted to be part of their dream and they wanted to be part of my dream to win two or maybe even three golds at one Olympics. We were in this together.

We absolutely rocked around. We hammered it from start to finish to smash the world record: 3 mins 55.202 secs, getting a nice tow from Russia in the final stages as we closed in to overtake them. We had taken well over a second off what was already a superb world record. We rolled around and I felt the happiest I had in a long time about my sport. I had loved that ride from start to finish and I didn't want it to end. It was the end of the session and we spun around and around warming-down as the crowd left. We must have been out there for 30 minutes or so, just chatting away, our voices beginning to echo in the emptiness. The Danes came out at one juncture, to enjoy a little down time of their own, and we yarned away, comparing notes and admiring each other's rides. Tomorrow's gold medal ride-off was put to one side for a few minutes. There isn't a whole load of time to kick back and 'enjoy' the Olympics in the heat of battle but for half an hour that Sunday night everything was mellow.

The press corps had gathered in the mixed zone for 'news' on our world record and, as they'd had to wait while we rolled around, we pulled over to oblige even though my inclination – in fact my original intention – was to get on with the dope control formalities – mandatory for world records – and head for the hills. I was absolutely thrilled but also relieved at getting through a very taxing day. It is not often you put in two competitive rides like that in two consecutive sessions, especially after four hours kip the night before and on top of three world-class Individual Pursuits in the previous 24 hours.

We tried to play the world record ride down a little and I

remember hearing myself explain that the 3.55 was the best we had and that the final would be slower because the opposition would be so much better and you don't get close enough to get a tow. I heard myself say all this but didn't believe a word. We were on fire. Of course we could go quicker. We had done 3.53 in training and we could do that again in the final. One day we will do 3.50, I am convinced of it. Ed and G are just going to get better and better, Steven Burke will come in and do a Paul – and there are others in the wings – and one day I won't be compromised by having ridden the Individual Pursuit the day before. This event is going ballistic at the moment, with GB in the vanguard, and with three outstanding teams chasing us who knows where it could end up?

The others kept to the party line, insisting the final would be a tad slower, but our attempts to contain everybody's excitement were rather undone when a beaming DaveB, adrenaline still pumping, told the gathered hordes that if you thought that was good, wait for tomorrow. 'You ain't seen nothing yet' was his message. No wonder the secret Squirrel Club don't entrust him with their innermost secrets. Oh well, he was only saying what we were all thinking.

Time for dope control and the long journey home. The fatigue hit me like a sledgehammer but I was a bit more relaxed. Although it was late again and I had to do the normal refuelling down the canteen and massage, I had the Monday morning off – my one mini-break throughout the five days – and I could sleep for England, which is exactly what I did. Eight hours solid and I woke up feeling considerably better.

Monday 18 August. Two days to go. Could I keep it all together? Mentally I was coping much better than Athens. No question. I was totally absorbed by the Team Pursuit competition and giving it my all, I didn't feel detached like I did in Athens. I would have been absolutely suicidal if for any reason we didn't win the gold whereas in Athens the silver was like a nice little bonus, the icing on the cake after the Individual Pursuit. I had definitely got that part of the campaign absolutely nailed on.

Yet physically I was feeling the strain. Strange, I had always assumed that it would be the other way round, but perhaps the virus had taken more out of me than I thought. I knew I had one more big ride in me but did I have two? Privately, that was my worry, and inwardly I was more than a bit concerned about the Madison, but I was so engrossed by the Team Pursuit that I couldn't look beyond Monday night's final for the minute. That's how you become as a professional cyclist, especially somebody like myself who has got around and finished the big Tours. Sometimes the next 30 seconds is the only thing in life that counts, getting over the next hill, cresting the next mountain, beating the cut, reeling back the break. You learn not to look too far ahead because that future you are worrying about might not even happen. Your next race, your next day, your next hour is the only thing that counts. Tunnel vision, perhaps, but most top sportsmen I have chatted to seem to share it. The Madison would take care of itself one way or another.

We arrived mid-afternoon and started going through our own warm-up routines before hitting the track for some squad drills. Everything was smooth, no alarms, you could feel something special building. We were firing on all four. G and Ed were in the zone and Paul was absolutely determined to finish his career on a high note – he had already made the decision to retire and get the proper grown-up job his intellect and talent demands. I plugged into Oasis down in the pits and felt a surge of confidence and well-being. Sometimes, even when you are in good form, you dread race time and would give anything to be a million miles away – Athens, for example. It can feel like that wait before you go to sit an exam. But this time I was in clover. I wouldn't have swapped those pre-race minutes for the world. There are Olympic medals and world records – they come and go a bit – but we were going to hit the world with something very special. Usain Bolt had done his stuff in the 100 m in the Bird's Nest, and Michael Phelps had astounded the world at the Cube, and all this brilliance was infectious. Now we wanted to make a mark and make people look up. We were an awesome quartet and last night's world record was just a taste of things to come. Bring it on. Bloody well bring it on!

We were perfection. Absolute bloody perfection. Paul thought afterwards it wasn't quite perfect but I think he was trying to gee us up one last time as he headed off into retirement. On the day, in my opinion, it would have been impossible to ride a better, faster race. We took it out in a long 62 and brought it home with three consecutive 57-second Kilos. We smashed our own record of 24 hours' standing by nearly two seconds and, from a standing start, averaged 61.719 mph for the entire race. The time flashed up on the scoreboard – 3.53.314 (WR) – and I just couldn't take my eyes off it for a while. Every change was perfect, every descent was perfect, our pace judgement was spot on. We were on automatic pilot, it was familiar territory, we had been here before in our dreams.

I have watched many fine rides across all the track events from opponents over the years and I have been lucky enough to be involved in a few decent ones myself, but take it from me, considering that was an Olympic final, our Team Pursuit was an absolutely astounding, nigh on miraculous ride. It is all very well me telling you we had cracked it training many times, but here it was in black and white for the world to wonder at. No dispute, no grey areas. We had occasionally talked the talk but now we had walked the walk. Twice in 24 hours. In years to come, I know for sure, long fragments of that ride will come flashing back into my mind; it will always be with me. You spend your entire life as a sportsman training and seeking perfection and just occasionally it's as if perfection finally seeks you out. And when that happens, although wildly exhilarated, you also feel a little humbled. This sporting life can be wonderful but I can't think of anything that will beat the feeling of that night in Laoshan as we rode around in a state of awe at what we had pulled off together.

I wanted to go out there and then to celebrate, it felt right, but this is where the logistics of completing such a tiring treble kicked in. First, to try and buy an hour or so I excused myself from all media except the flash BBC interviews, which was a shame because I wanted to tell the world how incredible my team-mates were and what an amazing team they had been over the last couple of years. Hopefully I have rectified that a bit in this book. I then tried to get dope control over and done with asap, but these things can rarely be rushed and always take an hour or more;   finally, it was back to the village. Making the ultimate sacrifice, the other three lads, with no other racing required from them, still swore off the celebratory swill for the evening. All for one, one for all. Despite their hard-earned gold medals and world record they would join me in alcohol-free purdah for the night by way of solidarity.

It was a fantastic gesture; I was touched and vowed we would make up for it in the weeks to come. But back at the village, as I stuffed the pasta down me and went for my nightly massage, I was feeling tense and, unbelievably, suddenly a bit down. I had clamped down on the euphoria and members of the GB team seem to have been briefed not to mention the Team Pursuit but to look ahead to the Madison at all times. The full enormity of tackling this triple was coming home with a vengeance. What had I done? I was taking on too much. Nobody could be expected to go again tomorrow surely? Already I had been part of six winning races, all in world-class times.

Physically I was in bits and, frankly, I hadn't reckoned on that. I had been convinced that I could get through the race programme like I had in Manchester, but those extra rounds – I hadn't realised what an extra burden they would be – had taken their toll, and the intensity of the Team Pursuit had left me thoroughly drained. I knew it would be hard but I didn't know it would be that hard. I was lacking energy and strength and didn't sleep well that night. I mulled things over and kept trying to justify things to myself. You don't know what you can achieve unless you try, that was the entire philosophy behind GB under DaveB. We go for it and push the outer limits of what people believe is possible. We go for gold at all times. We are not afraid of failure. Later in the week we saw Shanaze Reade give up a certain silver medal in the Women's BMX while attempting to pull off a radical overtaking move in an attempt to win gold. Good on her. It's how British cycling works at present. We aim for the stars all the time and that means occasionally we will fall flat on our faces. We try to redefine what is possible and there are no comebacks if we fail.

But I was still fretting. This was Cav's only Olympic event. He had bailed out of the Tour de France early to prepare. He had gone under the radar to prepare in Manchester at a time when he could have been making a small fortune on the Continent as a four-time stage winner on the Tour de France. Our Madison team worked if both made their contribution – I press the pace and make the break, he delivers the finish. We were a great team, we had proved this before, but we both had to be in perfect working order for it to happen. I had been absorbed by the Individual and Team Pursuit, and we were going to need a bit of help and or luck tomorrow to pull this off.

After finally dozing off I woke up early and felt rubbish. It was all a bit worrying but I have ridden well before after feeling rubbish, and I have been in bits before and suddenly felt okay the moment I climbed on the bike in earnest. These things happen. Anyway, I took myself off down to the velodrome very early to try to spin the lethargy out of my legs, and perked up a little, although not as much as I would have liked. It was too late for any dramatic changes. We had worked hard to qualify for this final – in fact I had ridden like two men here in this very velodrome in Beijing in that World Cup meet when Cav was off colour – to make it happen and I wasn't just going to give it away. We always knew it was going to be incredibly difficult, that was part of the challenge and attraction. Who could we bring in anyway? Only G of the riders still in camp had any previous in the Madison and, although he had stayed off the grog, he had certainly started to wind down – and rightly so – after three magnificent rides in the Team Pursuit.

It was all a bit edgy, none of the normal banter. Cav was tense because it was his first Olympics, his one shot at glory, and also this was his first track race since March. The transition from road to track takes time even after regular practice. It doesn't always happen first race up. And I was tense because I wondered if I had one final big race in me. Having warmed up above and beyond the call I found myself a quiet chair and, as a last resort, plugged into Oasis and Weller for inspiration, as I had done the previous afternoon.

It just never happened. We were heavily marked for a start and I couldn't begin to get into a position to make a break, and there were all sorts of mafias working against us, notably the tried and tested Spanish and Argentinian teams, regular medallists on the circuit, who recognised our threat and decided to join forces early on. Not that I blame them for one minute, it was always going to be like that, after the way we won in Manchester. Argentina and Spain got a lap on the field, Italy perished trying to do the same, but although I was hanging on to the pace OK I couldn't mount that decisive break we needed. Cav was getting pretty exasperated and I was getting pleading looks when we changed and shouts of 'Now, Brad, go, you've got to go, now' but some days executing what you want to happen isn't easy. Other days you just hit the accelerator and move away. In fairness he looked a little track rusty as well, and I had thought we might have picked up a few more points in one or two of the early sprints to keep morale ticking over. I tried to rev myself up one final time with 30 laps to go and hit the front hard. Just for a few seconds I thought I had got away and it was 'Game on', but again they closed it down. There was no way back into medal contention after that. Me and Cav then missed a change right in front of the VIPs box – Princess Anne, Tony Blair and all sorts – and they copped an earful of some very industrial language from the two of us. The race was gone, Argentina and Spain were away and fighting for gold, we were among the also-rans, which was not a position either of us had occupied much in recent years. It really hurt.

We were both disgusted in our own ways and hurtled down the tunnel and out of the stadium not saying a word to each other. Mark then disappeared for a bit; I think he had to go back up to the pits to collect some personal gear. By then I had calmed down and would have had a chat with him had he been there. No sign, so I went out onto the track seeking Cath. Things were building to a magnificent crescendo for GB, with individual sprint titles for Vicky Pendleton and Chris Hoy, the latter making it three at one Games. Awesome. I can safely say that I appreciate his achievement more than most. But for me it was time to get out of town. We were booked on the 7.30 a.m. flight – that was always our intention and nothing to do with any disappointment over the Madison – and after months and months of good behaviour I had a big night planned. The net result is that myself and Cav never got to talk it all through and, at the time of going to press, we still haven't. No calls and no texts.

There's not much I can say, really. I am not going to apologise for reaching out to the stars and falling short at the very final hurdle. Everybody knew what I was attempting and everybody was behind me. The time to raise any serious objections was much earlier in the process and I don't remember anybody kicking up much of a fuss when we won so gloriously in Manchester.

Yes, I am disappointed, falling short of my target of three golds, and I'm sorry Cav's first Olympic experience was not a good one, but we all knew the score. We weren't great but actually looking back at the video of the race there wasn't much more we could have done, we got marked out of it by a bunch of clever Madison riders who were on our case from the start. It happens. You could also argue that after both enjoying stellar seasons we both endured a bad day at the office together. That also happens, sport can bite back at you. We try to make winning an exact science – and we have come closer than most to that at Team GB – but occasionally it doesn't work out and you lose.

We'll get over it. In fact, by the time this book comes out, hopefully we will have piled into a couple of beers and said what needs to be said. Cav has had a magnificent historic year, the like of which we have never seen by a GB road-rider before. He has been at the very heart of the greatest year in British cycling history. Nothing can take that away from him. He is a star with an incredibly bright future and at least a couple of Olympics ahead of him, but sometimes sport can pull you up with a nasty jolt and this was one of those occasions. As the 'older bugger' of the duo,

I know this from bitter experience, and the only thing you can do is learn and move on.

Cav will move on to even bigger and greater things, rest assured.

I brooded for about an hour but then the realisation that I had won two Olympic gold medals and was on the first plane home the next morning to see my beautiful kids kicked in. I had been away from home way too much this year and, although Beijing had been an extraordinary experience, I didn't want to spend another minute longer there than was strictly necessary.

It was time to celebrate. The entire squad was on it but of course the first ones I sought out were the Team Pursuit squad, who had manfully kept their thirsts under control by way of solidarity to me. Needless to say, they were making up for lost time and I started playing catch-up. The pints just poured down my throat, reviving nectar, and my spirits rose with each drink. Beijing. The Olympics. Two more golds added to the collection; six medals in all, now level with Sir Steve, although of course the great man has five golds. All the more reason to absolutely cane it in London 2012. Bring on London 2012. My home town Olympics. I'm not finished yet, no way. Yes, I'll have another lager, thanks very much, G ,if you are going that way, in fact make it two, they seem to be hitting the spot tonight. Rock and roll, it was turning into a great night.

It was getting late and for some reason we decided to pop into London House, where the London Olympic people had set up shop for the fortnight – possibly the offer of unlimited free booze had something to do with it. Anyway, it was all extremely high-spirited and loud but, hey, it's not every day you have a pile of Olympic golds to celebrate. A team decision was made to move on to a highly recommended nightclub/late bar, after which I needed to be thinking about getting myself and Cath to the airport.

We rolled out and, as you do when you are both intoxicated with booze and high on life, I rolled over the bonnet of the first car that got in my way. Unfortunately, it was a taxi and the driver was not a happy camper. Unused to British-style celebrations, he went completely bonkers and a situation developed. Luckily, and thinking back this was lucky, a Chinese policeman saw the entire 'incident' and immediately recognised it as a bit of drunken horseplay and nothing more. He stepped in and handled the situation very well. For appearances sake he had to let the driver have his rant, and made a big play of taking down all the details and nodding sympathetically; then he also made a big play of radioing a situation report to his bosses and taking me to one side for an 'interview'. He had very little English but was clearly okay with everything, and in his own way was calming everything down. I remember BBC commentator Steve Cram arriving at one stage in another taxi – possibly after free booze like us? – and coming over to see what was happening and me telling him I thought it was all under control. It was getting a bit surreal but eventually the policeman reappeared and indicated that it had all been sorted and, if I would step this way, all that was now required was a picture of him and me with my gold medals. Very happy to oblige, officer. Incident over.

We even managed a final couple of quick pints at the nightspot, as arranged, before Cath and I headed for Beijing's incredible airport – the biggest in the world – where our BA flight awaited. Still buzzing on adrenaline and nervous energy I seemed to have sobered up and was in good shape when we checked in. A pleasant surprise awaited us there: the BA check-in girl was all smiles and uttered the immortal words: 'We have been waiting for you, Mr and Mrs Wiggins, many congratulations on behalf of all of us at BA and the country back home. We have all been very excited by the Games. I trust you will accept our invitation for an upgrade to first class for the flight home. Please tell us straight away if there is anything else you need. Many congratulations again.'

Way to go! I think perhaps I was the first GB gold medallist to head for home and BA, one of the official team sponsors, were determined to make the occasion. As upgrades go it was by far the best and most enjoyable of my life; there followed 12 hours of complete bliss and pampering as I got my head back together, dozed, chatted with Cath, posed for a few pictures with crew and the medals, and generally tried to take it all in. It was just so nice and perfect at the end of an amazing season and a huge effort. All my sporting career I and many other cyclists, and indeed other athletes from less fashionable sports, have had this chip on our shoulder about not being appreciated by the wider British public and not having our achievements recognised. Natural, I suppose, but from the moment BA started treating me and Cath like royalty I began to realise that finally, at Beijing 2008, the GB cyclists – and others from the less 'glamorous' sports – had cracked it. The British sporting public had been won over.

The next couple of weeks – months, no doubt – I knew were going to be fairly mad, but this time I could cope. I had grown up beyond all recognition as a person and, although I had no intention of becoming teetotal for the celebrations ahead, it wasn't going to jolt my life off track like it did last time. I had a wife and two children now, and loads more ambitions to fulfil on the track and on the road, and in particular at the Tour de France. Life was very good indeed.

Epilogue

I suppose this is the warm-down, the chance to roll around the track for a while, to take stock and put everything in perspective, not unlike that Sunday night in Laoshan after we had broken the Team Pursuit record for the first time. And a chance to look again to the future and exactly what I want from cycling and life. At 28 there is still so much to aim for, with London 2012 clearly the biggest carrot in track terms.

The first thing I noticed getting off the BA plane at Heathrow – and thanks again, guys, for a memorable trip home – was the true arrival of cycling as a proper big-time sport in Britain. It's been building steadily since Athens with a bit of attention for our exploits at various World Championships, and Cav made a big breakthrough on behalf of the sport with his four stage wins on the Tour de France in July, but this was something else. The Olympics is what really counts for the British public and cycling had definitely hit the jackpot in Beijing. The Great Haul of China, as our medal haul was quickly dubbed. Eight gold medals, two silver and two bronze. You just can't argue with that and I like to think also that we provided the full range of excellence, world records, thrills, spills, drama and, yes, the occasional disappointment to keep everybody back home on the edge of their seats.

The full impact of our exploits – and of course the GB team generally – hit me the moment I got through customs, when I was informed by my management company that there had been a change of plan and they had booked me and the family into a top London hotel – the Landmark – for the foreseeable future – because the media demands were so massive. I was probably the first of the gold medallists to wend their way home, and was first in the firing line to speak – not that I am complaining. Cycling has craved a higher profile and publicity for years – me included – so this was the moment to roll my sleeves up and enjoy it. Which I did.

It was full-on-though. BBC News, BBC Sport, Radio Five, Radio Four, BBC Children's TV, Sky News, Sky Sport, ITV News, Breakfast Time TV, Morning Time TV, *The Times*, the *Sunday Times*, the *Sun*, the *Telegraph*, talkSPORT and so on, You name the organisation and I gave them 20 minutes or more of my time. The media fest lasted for five days and was punctuated most nights by a fair few celebratory beers, although nothing remotely as manic as post-Athens. In fact, the media barrage worked very much in my favour: I had to keep my wits about me and a reasonably clear head for the long day ahead. Looking back, one of the contributing factors to my post-Athens binge is that – apart from family, friends and cycling nuts – nobody really took much notice, not compared with 2008. Although I was a busy racer there was lots of time in 2004 just to drink, which I did with a vengeance.

One of the most enjoyable functions was the televised 'Handing Over' party on the Mall on the Sunday, to coincide with the Games being closed in Beijing at the same time. Over to you, London, as it were. There was a really nice atmosphere, Katherine Jenkins entertained the crowd and myself and Phillips Idowu, who proved to a real character and great fun, did various live interviews as London lads looking ahead to our Games in 2012. It was great crack and the whole event was unexpectedly moving and inspiring. Even just a few days after a Beijing, with all the joy, fatigue and a little disappointment involved in 2008, I was already thinking that I had to be part of London 2012. There is no way I cannot be involved and competing for gold medals on my own patch. It has to happen and, no matter what life throws at me in the next four years, I will find a way of ensuring I am involved big-time.

There are targets to aim for everywhere. I am on six Olympic medals now, equal first with Sir Steve in the all-time GB list, but he has five golds to my three. So my first target, of course, has to be two more Olympic golds so I can look Steve in the eye. But despite that I am not even the leading gold medal winner of current GB competitors, such is our growing Olympic pantheon. Chris Hoy with his three in Beijing and one Athens is on four, so obviously myself and Ben Ainslie – who is also on three – will have to chase Chris as well. The Real McHoy will be 36 in London but Chris is a phenomenon, a truly great athlete who takes care of his body and I don't see him going any slower in four years' time, do you? So take it from me, he will still be the man to beat. although with Jason Kenny going like a bat out of hell at the age of 20 in Beijing I can see Chris encountering some unbelievably tough opposition in London.

There is a big part of me that still wants to aim for the treble, simply because it is so bloody difficult. I fell one race short this time, which is frustrating but possibly understandable. I dedicated myself to the Team Pursuit in a way I hadn't before and it was incredibly draining. Looking back, the mystery virus so close to Beijing probably didn't help, although you can't quantify these things. I read an article featuring David Hemery just before the Games and he was explaining how top athletes pushing the frontiers back live at the edge of illness and injury all the time. It's a fact of life, you just have to deal with it.

It's way too early for any decisions. We will need to have a look at the programme first and that doesn't get finalised for a couple of years. With such a light track cycling programme generally in Beijing there seems no reason why I wasn't permitted a rest day, as was the case in the Worlds, but there is a lot of politics that goes into the drawing up of these programmes. In fact, the whole thing needs looking at urgently. It can't be right that there are only three gold medals for women in track cycling as opposed to the men's seven. Can you imagine the fuss that imbalance would cause if transferred to the athletic stadium or the swimming pool? Actually, it doesn't bear thinking about.

I am sure Vicky Pendleton is delighted with her gold medal in the Individual Sprint, but in fairness she should have been allowed to compete for another two – in the Keirin and the Team Sprint with Shanaze Reade. Both events are well established World Championship disciplines, and both events could have been effortlessly slotted into the Olympic programme. That programme was so thin in Laoshan that they had to eke out Vicky's sprint event over three days. That is clearly a complete nonsense, not to mention unfair on the competitors. All the athletes are there on the grounds, it involves no extra expense for the IOC, so let's give cycling the full programme it deserves. Heavens above, they dish out enough swimming and diving medals, and you only have to look around to see that more people in the world cycle for pleasure than swim for pleasure.

Sorry, that was a bit of diversion there, but as I am on my 'warm-down', it's a heaven-sent opportunity to sort a few things out in my mind. The bottom line is that the Olympics should never be a lesser event than the Worlds; sorry, that just cannot be the case, ever. I don't see the Olympic athletics cutting their programme by 40 per cent or more from what occurs at the Worlds every two years. No way, there would be a riot. In which case track cycling should not be expected to do likewise.

So we want and deserve the full programme, which would result in more fun and excitement but, strangely, would also result in a more streamlined meet. That's the way forward and if the Worlds programme was replicated it would mean dropping one of the Individual Pursuit rounds and one of the Team Pursuit rounds. Being entirely selfish about it, that would mean my treble dream would be very much back on.

So, until they shut the door on a rescheduling, the treble dream lives on. There is definitely unfinished business as far as the Madison is concerned.

The Individual Pursuit is my baby, I have dominated the event for five years and it is my intention to dominate it for another four years and make it three in a row in London. Nothing would give me more pleasure than completing the hat-trick on home turf. I want to achieve a Redgrave-type domination of this event. Very few Olympians in any event win three consecutive titles. In all honesty, since the head to head with Brad McGee in 2004, nobody has emerged to seriously challenge me, but that might not always be the case. Somebody might post a 4.13 one day – who knows, maybe even G or Steven Burke – and I will know when that happens I will respond. In fact, I would welcome that new challenge, it would sharpen everything up.

As Shane and DaveB both tell me, important decisions should never be made when you are either on a high from victory or a low from defeat. All this lies a long way in the future. One day, probably sometime in 2010, the think tank will gather around a pot of tea in one of the Velodrome offices in Manchester one rainy morning and we will make the call. But already I am beginning to play out certain scenarios in my mind. You have to keep the circus going in your head.

As for the next year, I'm tossing a few balls in the air at the moment and will have to make a couple of quick decisions. Basically, I am looking for a long busy road season but I am also very tempted to keep in track condition – and help keep the momentum going for GB – and compete in the 2009 World Track Championships in Poland, which come early in the season in March.

As for the road I am anxious to plunge back into the Tour de France again. I liked what I saw in this year's Tour very much. The peloton was slower, clearly much cleaner, and the racing much more unpredictable and fun. The authorities are still on the case of the pond-life who continue to take drugs; soon there will be none left and the rest of us can stand and fall by the merits of our riding. And, you watch, the Tour will become even more popular as a result. Mark my words.

I'm switching from High Road to Garmin for 2009 – no great dramas, just a couple of things that suit me better contractually. What I do know is that I will be moving from one 100 per cent clean team I believe in to another 100 per cent clean team I believe in, which is the most important thing. It will be riding with the Garmin guys, and in particular Dave Millar, who is a bloke I have really warmed to recently as you have probably gathered during the course of this book. Dave is a guy whose personal experience and fight against the drug problem mirrors road cycling's fight against drugs. Despite his two-year ban, Dave had the great merit in my eyes of coming totally clean and swearing to help a sport he is patently in love with. I now look on him as one of the good guys; he is as bright as a button and a good spokesman for a sport trying to get its act together. He never hides from his past and has taken a big lead in cleaning road cycling up after he hit rock bottom personally, and I support him all the way. He is always good for a bit of chat and gossip as well, and it will be fun riding in the peloton with Dave.

As for the pure riding, although always mindful of my team role, I want to be a bit more ruthless in picking off possible stage wins. It's time I started clocking a few up. I am going to target specific Prologues and time-trials, and I am going to be more aggressive and adventurous in getting into the breaks and making a bid for glory during the slower non-mountainous days. One of my favourite all-time riders is Fabian Cancellara. I love the way he sometimes gets in a break and then takes off with, say, 3 km to go, and uses his time-trialling ability to jump ahead of the sprinters and kill off their finish. Fabian is a one-off, but there is no reason why I shouldn't try that occasionally. If my legs are good and our GC rider is safely looked after, I should be able to give anybody a run for their money from 3–4 km out.

The exciting prospect of a Team GB on the Tour de France, possibly from 2010 onwards, has sprung up with DaveB – where does he get his energy from? – pulling the strings and putting the very considerable finance and commercial programme required together. Basically, I am wholly supportive but have got too much on my plate to get involved with any pre-planning in the next 12 months. My priority in 2009 is to re-establish my credentials as a road-racer pure and simple. When DaveB gets the entire commercial deal in place – and realistically that needs to be by mid-2009 – then is the time to start talking and thinking. Riders like Cav command huge financial clout now on the Continent; G is a much sought-after young gun with incredible potential on the big Tours; Ben Swift and Jonny Bellis will probably get contracted rides this year; Steve Cummings is a widely respected peloton rider; and I've knocked around a fair bit on the Tour and the Giro and have my own qualities and commercial value. The only way a GB team can be formed is if those riders involved are made an economically viable bid for their services. The patriotic card can only be played if there are two similar bids on the table – then of course you will look at the extra honour of riding in your national colours every day. The basic concept is absolutely brilliant – a once-in-a-lifetime project – but the fine-tuning and logistics are going to be difficult.

Still, if there is one organisation in the sporting world that seems to have a handle on fine-tuning and logistics at present it is GB cycling. It has underpinned everything we have done. If you have got this far in the book you will know exactly how much work and expertise goes into everything we do. Natural talent can take you so far, and I would suggest I am the perfect example of that. I would have achieved a fair bit on my own – my natural aptitude and competitive nature took me a long way down the road in the early years – but ultimately I have achieved so much more with absolutely everybody at Team GB behind me all the way. It is the X factor that marks us out and I have no doubt that if DaveB can take that X factor into his Tour de France project – and given the young talent coming through – then one day we will see a GB rider on the podium on the last Sunday in July in Paris.

It will take time. It has taken probably ten years, starting with Peter Keen and his vision, to get British track cycling into a position of world dominance. And you won't see a British yellow jersey coming down the Champs Elysées in the first few years. But one day it will happen, and when it does it will be one of the greatest days in our proud sporting history.

It would be the ultimate example of what can be done if a small group of people have a dream and the dedication to carry that dream through. And if the country supports them in that dream – in fact shares the dream – and helps them carry the project through with a bit of financial assistance and patience when things occasionally go wrong, then a little slice of that glory will be yours as well. How good would that be? Fingers crossed all the way. My gut feeling is that it is going to happen.

It's nearly time to pull over now, this warm-down is coming to an end, but it's been good, the perfect way to end the book. I have got so much to be grateful for over the years and especially over the last two or three years. Where would I be without Cath and the kids? I don't even want to think about that one. And then there is Shane and Matt Parker, who have been with me all along the way since I picked up the pieces after Athens and got back on track at the 2007 Worlds in Palma. Nothing is too much trouble for those two, they never have a bad day at the office or are in bad form. Never, or at least not when you are in their company. They raise the bar all the time. You look to them for the smallest thing and they are there instantly. Every time you go to them for something you leave believing you are the most important cyclist/athlete in the world and there is nothing they wouldn't do to help you.

And that is exactly how it is. They leave all their own personal worries or tiredness behind to serve you. I owe a huge debt to their unswerving loyalty, patience and good advice. Thank you so very much, guys. And they are the tip of the iceberg. From DaveB and his canny management skills to Scott Gardner, the best sports scientist and number cruncher in the world, down to the *soigneurs*, mechanics and physios. These guys are gold medal winners in their own right, believe me.

There is a strange poster in DaveB's office in Manchester, a huge picture taken from behind Chris Hoy as he receives his gold medal in Athens. It is not, it has to be said, Chris's best side by any means. Apparently it puzzled Sir Clive Woodward for a good while before one day he plucked up courage and asked DaveB what it was all about.

'That is it to remind people why we are here,' said DaveB. 'We are all behind that bloke and any rider in GB kit who goes onto the track. We are here totally to serve and to make sure they have everything they want. Any of the backroom staff who can't accept that are in the wrong place and the wrong job and need to remove themselves immediately. Or I will remove them.'

Fantastically talented people, but honest, straight-talking and humble. I've tried to learn from them, especially the honest and straight-talking bit, and reviewing my scribblings over this last seven months or so I am very aware that occasionally I have been pretty blunt, especially with regards to my feelings about Garry and his death, my insane drinking and irresponsible behaviour after Athens, and my sometimes spiky relationship with Chris Boardman in the early days.

It's tempting, even with the deadline pressing, to review everything and tone certain passages down, to settle for the quiet life and offer you a sanitised version. But to what end? For the last four or five years now I have been in an environment with Team GB in which honesty and confronting the issues is everything. Obviously that has worked in a sporting context, but one of the big lessons of working with Steve Peters in particular is that I realise you must be honest in assessing your own non-sporting life as well.

My drinking was exactly as described, from what I can remember! It got wildly out of control after Athens and was something I had to deal with. Most cyclists, having lived like monks for months on end, enjoy a good gargle off season, but this was something altogether different. It was going right off the Richter scale, as Shane would say. It was mental as much as anything; I was all over the place and out of control, letting myself down and testing the patience of friends and family. Sorry one and all. Cath's love and the birth of Ben pulled me out of it eventually, and now I can enjoy a good piss-up for what it is and not feel the need to do it again and again. It was a massive warning and hopefully I know the signs now.

With Chris, I had to learn to take fairly harsh but objective criticism from somebody who knew exactly what he was talking about and, at that stage, had achieved something I had not, i.e. had won an Olympic 4 km pursuit title. There was no room for bullshit, messing around or pulling the wool over the coach's eyes and relying on natural God-given talent. This was new, uncomfortable, territory for me and there were bound to be a few sparks. I used to curse and swear to Cath about Chris and his bloody red-inked emails – God she took some ear-bashing – but as I hope I have acknowledged earlier, it was an absolutely crucial part of my development and I have much to thank Chris for. He stuck with it and together we got the job done. Sometimes I think it was a bit like breaking a wild horse in. Chris drummed into me, literally sometimes, exactly what was required in terms of dedication and attention to detail if I wanted to become the world's best, not just for 2004 but for the rest of my career. The lessons remain with me to this day.

With regard to Garry, I had no control over our relationship for my first 18 years on this planet. He buggered off, broke my mum's heart, left me with a picture at the zoo, left me and Mum potless, made no effort to get in touch for 15 years and then tried to crash back into my life when it suited him as he grew morbid and regretful. They are the facts, I can't change any of that – all of that was beyond my control.

When I was old enough I took the initiative and went to visit him. I tried to understand this serial bolter who thought nothing of quitting on three separate wives and families and leaving a trail of devastation behind him. I made every effort, but the plain truth is, related by blood or not, ultimately he had caused too much damage and he wasn't somebody I would ever choose to spend time with.

Part of the pleasure of doing this book is the therapy value it has offered. When I write down the facts – the truth – about my relationship with Garry, it's like getting the data feedback from Scott and Matt after a ride that didn't go so well, or having a one-on-one with Steve when I'm in a state about something. It's all there in front of you, the entire scenario, but you have to look and understand. You can either choose to ignore the facts and the logic of a situation – or you can accept the way it is and move on accordingly.

I did appreciate Garry's class as a rider and his pioneer spirit, his determination to make a career for himself as a professional cyclist. I quite liked his hard-man of the track image, a sort of anti-hero, anti-establishment figure. All that struck a chord with a fellow cyclist and competitor, but not the other stuff. I hate all that. We were never close – how could we be when he disowned me? – and although his unexplained death came as a shock, if I am honest I didn't grieve a great deal. His life and death had a tragic element. He was clearly a lonely and troubled man and it brought a lump to my throat when I learned about the scrapbook and photos he kept of his three children in his 'unit' – but basically his life was so unconnected with mine. I can't dredge up emotions that aren't there.

None of that is meant to cause offence to his friends and his family – my family for heaven's sake – it is just a statement of the truth from my end. They will remember the Garry they knew and I am telling you about the Garry I knew.

As you will recall, I didn't interrupt my preparations for the World Championships one bit when I heard the news of his death. In fact, if anything, I trained with more venom than ever before. Training was a brilliant balm and perhaps the one positive I can take out of Garry's death is that he somehow concentrated my mind on achieving like never before in 2008.

Was I trying to prove something one last time? Perhaps, I don't know. But what is certain is that the fitness base I established during those long months in February and March created a platform to launch me into a season that resulted in three World Championship gold medals and two Olympic gold medals. I like to think Garry – hard man that he was to impress – would be forced to acknowledge that his son had enjoyed a half-decent season on his bike.

Chapter Twenty-two

—

Beijing Launch Pad

The aftermath of Beijing was nothing like Athens, which affected me so badly in many ways. It's not that I suddenly developed teetotal monk-like tendencies or anything – I necked my share of celebratory beers and the awards/dinner circuit seemed to continue apace until Christmas – but this time I was much more in control. I knew what was coming and what the potential pitfalls were and was able to enjoy it much more. As far as my whole outlook on life was concerned, I was in a much better place.

Those months immediately after the Beijing Olympics were a golden time for British cycling, with thousands of column inches and everybody singing the praises of the sport in general, and it was nice to be part of that. Nicole Cooke kept the momentum going with a gold medal in the Women's World Championships in Varese – and what a double to take Olympic and World golds in the space of seven weeks – and, of course, Chris Hoy was the name on everybody's lips in the lead-up to the BBC Sports Personality of the Year Awards, which I am delighted to say he won. The GB cycling team took the team award and Dave B walked off with the coaching prize. Job done and plaudits all round – a very pleasing evening after fighting for recognition for our sport for so long. The Great British public got it absolutely right on this occasion! Then came the New Year's Honours list, and with it the news that I was to get a CBE to add to my OBE from Athens. Happy days. Very happy days indeed.

Although I was in a much better place mentally, it was still a tricky period from the point of view of developing my cycling career. So much of my focus had gone into the Olympics that really my season ended right there and then after the Madison in Beijing, in the middle of August, which is a little early, to be honest. My move to Garmin was signed, sealed and delivered, so that was good and gave me peace of mind, but I still had to keep busy. I had intended to spend some time, on the six-day circuit – which I always enjoy and pays well – but that fell through for various reasons. Not for the first time the excellent family atmosphere within the GB camp kicked in and, despite resolving to concentrate on my road-racing career for the next couple of years, I found myself training with a group of us, including 'G', based mainly at the velodrome in Manchester.

We got into a nice groove in the months heading to Christmas. As well as my own road work, I would head down to the velodrome early on Monday mornings and join the endurance squad, doing four or five rolling 5 km pursuits, which is high-quality work. Then in the afternoon we would head up into the hills for a four-hour ride, come rain or shine. When the weather is rubbish – which is most of the time during our winters, although those occasional cold crisp days make up for it – it can be tempting to sit at home or just go on the rollers, but when there is a group of you it doesn't seem to matter so much.

There is always a bit of craic and banter and, before you know it, you have got your wet-weather gear and you are spinning away. I remember on one such day the Beeb came along to film their prepiece on the GB cycling team for the sports personality of the year show. Without really noticing it, on those Mondays I would log up 100 high-quality miles, and it would be much the same every Friday when we would begin the day back down at the velodrome doing some pacing work behind the derny before again heading off as a group at lunchtime for another long ride.

In the New Year I also went off to a week's training camp with Team GB to our old haunt in Majorca and went through their drills with them. It was very enjoyable, if hard work, and gave me a sense of déjà vu. Exactly a year earlier this was where we laid the foundations to what I believe was one of the greatest rides of any description ever seen on a track. For some of the lads, the World Track Championships in Poland were beginning to loom large and, noting the time I was spending with the track boys, one or two journalists put two and two together and came up with the theory that I was going to defend my world titles in Prushkow after all, but that was never the case. While I was pedalling away all my concentration was on new road projects and, of course, the Tour de France in July.

I had been keeping my hand in on the track firstly because I simply love riding a bike around a velodrome – it makes me happy – and during those dog days of winter, it was contributing significantly to my fitness regime. Secondly, I'm not so arrogant as to think I will be able to parachute back into elite track cycling sometime in 2011 ahead of the 2012 Olympics and just pick up where I left off. Absolutely no way. Unlike some road professionals I have the greatest respect for the athletes who compete on the track and know just how high the standards are that they set. The sport will advance steadily as it heads towards 2012 and I need to keep my hand in. I might not compete at the Worlds for a couple of years, but I certainly intend to drop into the odd six day or do a few six-dayers in the winters. You can't afford to get too rusty in this business.

While all the time my focus was on the road, I intended to have another go at living the dream by basing myself abroad from the start of the road season, this time with Cath and the kids. Garmin were based in Girona, a lovely small city on Spain's northern Mediterranean coast, so we started laying plans to get an apartment there. It was now or never really – the kids needed to start school in September and be settled and that was an absolute priority so we were spending quite a lot of time getting all that sorted.

Suffice to say, it was worth every minute of our time. Girona is a great place, a real mini centre for cycling, the weather is good, there is all sorts of training terrain and always a mob to train with. Brilliant. Looking back, I get a little bit irked thinking of what might have been if I could have had all this ten years ago instead of 'existing' in some freezing, grotty French basement flat where I had to put the milk out on the patio overnight because I had no fridge and if my bike went wrong or I needed a new wheel I had to sort it all out myself. These days, when I go for a training ride with the Garmin boys, we will have a team car and mechanic behind us looking after our every need and Cath and the kids are there to welcome me home in the evening. What a difference. If nothing else, those tough lonely years early in my career make me appreciative of everything I now have. They were a hellish testing ground. Did I really want to be a professional cyclist or not? I did.

I was preoccupied with my weight, not obsessively so, but I wanted to shed 11 or 12 lb intelligently and sensibly, because I knew deep down that is what was needed to start maximising my potential on the road. I don't think I can ever be accused of having been 'overweight' at any stage of my career – well, during the season anyway – but I'm a pretty tall bloke with a big frame and when I'm heavy into track racing I need to keep feeding the engine with fuel, so to speak. You ride on the track at a weight consistently above that which you would naturally be on the road and, of course, if you are doing World Cup meets you have ride and recovery cycles that see your weight yo-yo, plus you have a lot of travelling, jet lag and so on, which can see you balloon or comfort eat. For the 2009 road season I wanted to get completely on top of this, which I did without too much pain – sensible eating, no track racing during the winter, though some nice high-quality training and, once we started using our Girona base, a much healthier lifestyle. I can give you no little secret tip other than it was gradual – no crash diet or anything daft. I just decided that I had to shed the weight.

Myself and Matt Parker – who was from the GB set-up and was helping with my conditioning – had the theory that being lighter would radically improve my climbing. In terms of output and wattage, I have always produced the numbers that suggest I should be a more than adequate climber, but two things had been working against me over the years. Firstly, I could and should have been a bit lighter, and secondly with my specialist time-trailling and team duties, there had never been an urgent need for me to thrash myself in the mountains and go out of my comfort zone. Survival was the priority, alongside helping my colleagues and leaving enough in the tank to compete in time trials and prologues.

It was high time to come out of the comfort zone and set my sights a little bit higher – this was one of the reasons behind my move to Garmin, where I was being encouraged to expand my repertoire, have a go at everything and push the boundaries back a bit. Really have some fun! It was a win-win situation and, if nothing else, an improved ability in the hills and mountains would see me suffer much less on tough days – and recover more quickly for the stages when I am meant to be competitive and busy. That was the theory as we started out.

The early season, therefore, was all about having some fun with half an eye towards the Giro but at the back of my mind was the thought that I wanted to arrive at the Tour de France in the best shape of my life. So first it was off to Qatar where we started our season-long rivalry in the team time trial with a nice win that saw me take the leader's jersey. There was an encouraging second in the Paris–Nice Prologue – I thought I had won that but Alberto Contador produced an amazing ride and I just had to put up my hands up and say well done – which was followed by an enjoyable day in the Milan–San Remo, won so memorably by Cav, only the second British rider ever to take one of the great one-day classics. Great ride. I was a solid second again in the time trial at the Criterium International and then won the time trial at three days of Panne, by which time I was in exceptional early season form, flying actually.

Originally none of the spring classics was on my schedule, for no other reason than they can be pretty hairy races – crashes and injuries are frequent, and the last thing I wanted after everything had gone so well was a needless injury. However, I was loving being on a bike racing again and decided to have some fun at Ghent Wevelgem and Paris–Roubaix. Needless to say I did crash in both – you almost take it as read in those races – but I felt good in both races finishing in the middle 20s. It was very enjoyable mixing up my racing routine, finding myself in race scenarios I had never been in before and stretching myself. And of course it was terrific all-round preparation for the Giro.

After some quality time in Girona, training and resting, the Giro came around very quickly and it was a superb fun event this year. The organisers had really pushed the boat out to celebrate the centenary with a mouth-watering itinerary taking in Venice, Milan, Turin, Florence, Naples, Rome and just about every tourist sport you care to think of. There was even a climbing stage up

Mount Vesuvius – passing Pompeii en route – and best of all, the sun shone virtually from start to finish. Offhand I can recall about an hour's rain in total.

There was loads of British company in the peloton – there were a record nine of us riding the race, which shows the strong depth that is beginning to develop and why, long term, the Sky GB road team has such potential. What with all the Americans and Aussies in the race, there were plenty of English voices – on my debut a few years back, I'm pretty sure myself and Charlie Wegelius were the only British speakers. How times have changed.

There was a big race feel from the start – unusual for the Giro which, although a magnificent bike race, always tends to be low-key and intimate, travelling along the back roads of Italy rather than heading straight for the centres of population. But this year everything was cranked up by the arrival of some big-name riders – Tour de France winner Carlos Sastre; Denis Menchov, who had been looking in great early season form; Levi Leiphheimer, who was also going great guns and a certain Lance Armstrong who had done exceptionally well to get to the start line after badly breaking a collarbone in a crash at the end of March. The Armstrong legend lives on and there is not the slightest doubt in my mind that his presence, and the fact that the racing was celebrating its centenary, boosted the crowd numbers to near those seen at the Tour de France.

Going into the race I was in a bit of a dilemma in that I felt in the best form of my life but I didn't want to thrash myself and end up leaving in a coffin. The Tour de France was still my main focus so, although feeling great and wanting to do well on specific days such as the team time trial and the two individual time trials, I wanted to leave plenty in the tank and ride with a little in reserve.

The team time trial was good fun – on a pancake-flat course up and down the Venice Lido – although it ended with a tinge of disappointment when we lost to our rivals Columbia with Cav geeing them up. There had been some mainly good-natured banter between the two camps in the lead-up – as rival American sponsors it does no harm and generates a few column inches – although one comment of mine was a little misconstrued when I said I didn't mind what happened as long as we beat Columbia. The meaning of that was, of course, that we knew only too well if we beat Columbia we would have won the race – our two squads, with Astana as very useful outsiders, were clearly the best in the field at team time trialling.

I was very pleased with my form in the team time trial; I put in some huge turns at the front and could feel the engine purring over in full working order. The course possibly suited Columbia a little more than us – and their win at least gave Cav the opportunity to wear the famous Maglia rosa, the first Brit to be so honoured. We all knew, however, that bragging rights for the season could only be claimed after the much tougher, lumpier team time trial on the Tour de France down in Montpellier. That would be the day of reckoning when both squads were at full strength.

After the time trial it was time to get my head down in the race. It was gratifying to find myself pretty effortlessly near the front of the peloton most days and, by my standards, floating up some of the hills and climbs. On one big day I even found myself riding alongside Lance and eventually opted to step on it and overtake. Mind you, for a guy racing so soon after a major op and with just four races in his legs since his comeback, Lance was going pretty well in my opinion. He got noticeably stronger as the tour continued, really going through the pain barrier on some tough days to get those hard miles in his legs. By the end there was one climb when he hung back to help Levi – usually a really top climber – up a big ramp, which is pretty impressive. By the time the Giro finished Lance looked in pretty good shape to me and ready to challenge hard in the Tour de France, which was always going to be the centre point of his comeback.

I continued my steady progress and although I did occasionally drop back into the grupetto, it was due to a conscious decision not to flog myself. I still felt great within myself and I wanted to give it my best shot in the two individual time trials, which were very different and challenging in their own ways.

The first, the Cinque Terre TT, was a brutish 60.6 km climbing, twisting ride, which even a couple of years ago would have brought me out in a cold sweat and would have seen me trail home 40th or something, thoroughly intimidated by the climbing involved. Not this time. I knew I was never likely to win but I fancied giving this very unusual stage – as testing an individual trial as there has been in modern years – my best shot and find out exactly where I stood as a bike rider compared with the rest of the world. The race of truth rarely lies.

Among the 180 or so riders competing, I came home seventh and was pretty satisfied with that. This was terrain that would have psyched me out a few years ago. I took it on and emerged with honour amongst the heavyweights of world road-racing, on a bitch of a day when even they struggled. In retrospect I went out just a tad quick, but over such a long course it was very difficult to judge. I went a little bit conservative around some corners and overcooked a few others but I went up both climbs – Passo del Bracoo and Passo del Termine – pretty easily. Initially I was even a bit disappointed with seventh but it quickly became apparent what a unique and demanding course it had been. Ultimately the fact that I was 18 seconds ahead of Ivan Basso, 27 seconds ahead of Lance and 48 seconds ahead of Michael Rogers – another noted hilly time trial specialist – meant a lot.

My whole racing horizon was beginning to expand. I would always have track but now I realised I could be competitive in a couple of one-day classics, very competitive in superfast prologues and conventional individual time trials, a dark horse in mad hilly 60 km individual time trials and I could also lead the charge for line honours in the team trials. It suddenly felt like I was beginning to find my true identity as an all-round road racer. That evening and on another evening on the tour, as I sat around chatting with the Garmin guys, it became evident they felt I should seriously set my sights in the future on some of the prestigious week-long stage races such as Paris–Nice, the Tour of Catalunya and the Dauphine Libere. Although I am still never going to challenge GC on a three-week stage race, I could take pride in my all-round ability. There was much to focus on for the future.

The immediate future, however, was all about the final stage of the Giro, a pretty quick but technical 15 km time trial around Rome that I quite fancied the look of. Cath and the kids came as well, and I very much wanted to present her with a win to mark the occasion. I started eyeing it from a long way out and throttled back during the final week of the Giro – it included a stack of climbing which, I was gratified to note, I was still taking in my stride. On some days I felt really good and fancied riding with the front group but again I reigned myself in a little. I wanted my first Giro stage, and to achieve that, I needed to be fresh.

So near but so far. I rode just about the perfect race but got unlucky and finished in second place. I couldn't have done any more, but got thwarted by the onset of rain right at the end when I was on the road. It made the final technical corners, which were mostly on cobblestones, very treacherous and I had to back right off, losing three or four seconds at a time. It was frustrating but I didn't throw a tantrum or anything at the end. I knew I had been unlucky and that speedwise I was the quickest rider on the course that day. These things happen. Physically I had been the best but the sporting gods were looking the other way. That's how it is sometimes. On other days it is me who has benefited from changes in conditions and a slice of luck. I recovered my sense of humour and perspective very quickly. It had been the most enjoyable of Giros, I had finished in bloody good shape physically and it was all to play for in the Tour de France. Life was good and I'd promised my boy a trip to the Colosseum to see the Gladiators.

Chapter Twenty-three

My 2009 Tour de France

As you will have gathered, after an excellent winter, encouraging early season and feeling great without overdoing it in the Giro, I arrived in Monaco for the Depart in the shape of my life – down to four per cent body fat, which is the perfect reading (any less than this and your metabolism starts eating into your muscle instead of your fat). I was in a pretty positive state of mind. I had told myself a top 20 finish and a shot at stage wins in all three time trials, including the team time trial, was a realistic target, but others who I respect such as Dave Millar, John Vaugters and Christian Vande Velde were telling me to aim higher still. Why not a top ten finish? They could see the shape I was in and had noticed the difference in my approach. The way they spoke gave me great confidence.

Telling the press that I, Brad Wiggins, a fully paid-up member of the grupetto in my two previous tours, was aiming for a top ten finish was probably asking for trouble, so I confined myself in public to less ambitious mutterings about a top twenty tour and a couple of dashes for glory in the pursuits. Privately though I was very excited, the Tour could not have been set up better for me: two time trials in the first four days, separated by pretty flat days, and then a couple of transitional stages to the Pyrenees, which weren't epic. They were tough, but the sort of terrain I was beginning to take in my stride. There was every chance I could be somewhere near the top going into the first rest day and then a relatively flat week in central France. After that it would be in the lap of the gods as we headed for the Alps and then Mount Ventoux. I would take it day by day, ride by ride and bring home the best finish I could. That was my game plan, nothing too complicated. You can have an overall strategy in the Tour but it doesn't pay to get ahead of yourself too much. Stuff happens and you have to react.

Having said that, I had no doubt from day one that Alberto Contador would win, barring injury or an act of God, because he is the class rider at present who has got it all and just operates at another level. And I was pretty certain that Andy Schleck, the only man who can consistently match Alberto in the mountains on the big days, would chase him home in second, although he would also have to keep it together in the time trials to fulfil his potential. But looking around the field after that, I reckoned I was one of a group of ten or fifteen riders, including Lance Armstrong, who could fill the positions behind that duo. And one of us would gain third spot and stand on the podium in Paris, something a British rider has never done for the GC.

Of course the return of Lance to the Tour and the rivalry within the Astana team – real or imagined – was the main talking point in the build-up and at least took a lot of pressure off other teams and riders. Cav was probably the other big story and whether he was or wasn't gunning for the green jersey. I fancied it might still be a year early for that – he had, after all, yet to finish a Tour de France – but I knew for certain that he would win a hatful of stages in the form he was in. He is going to bag three of four stages a year for a long while yet.

And so to Monaco for the Depart – it was glitzy and flash, but in the nervous days before a Tour starts you don't really notice much around you. It was all about good preparation, having a look over the opening time trial course and trying to rest and stockpile the sleep before we set off. The 15 km TT course featured a tough climb and a pretty quick descent and, to my mind, best suited Alberto and my old rival over many years, Fabian Cancellera. Realistically I had a pretty solid shot at third with my improved ability going uphill, perhaps better if my tips had a bad day for any reason, and that's exactly how it turned out.

Fabian won it and was as impressive as ever. He is a superb all-round time trialler, one of my fellow professionals whose talent I admire. He can cope with most terrain and invariably goes quicker than anybody in the descents. That's what happened in Monaco – we were about level pegging time-wise going up the climb but he came down quicker than anybody. He had been having a quiet season – illness hadn't helped – but he looked fit again during the tour of Switzerland moving into the Tour, and rode beautifully in Monaco. Alberto was virtually faultless and to my mind confirmed that he was in supreme form. I came home in a very pleasing third position and picked up useful time over the likes of Lance, who will probably admit that rediscovering his time trialling form has been the most difficult thing since his return.

One ironic consequence of finishing third is that with Fabian in yellow for the start of the next stage on the Sunday to Brignoles, and Alberto in the polka-dotted King of the Mountains on account of the quickest climb up the hill, I found myself in the fabled green jersey at the start line. Did we give Cav any 'stick' about it? Of course not! In all seriousness I knew it would be my one day in green because the run to Brignoles had Cav written all over it, and so it proved to be with a textbook ride from the Columbia boys. In any case I was hoping to top that with the big one – a day or two in yellow – if we could maintain the status quo up to the team time trial in Montpellier and then put a few seconds into the Astana GC riders. That was the theory but, like I say, it never pays to count your chickens on the Tour.

Looking back at stage three, the run across Provence from Marseille to La Grande Motte was a real low point for me – the only real negative of the entire Tour – although it didn't particularly seem like it at the time. It was a bloody tough day of hot mistral winds but I was riding strongly, feeling good and being as vigilant as possible as we headed to what would certainly be a sprint finish in La Motte. The peloton was moving quickly towards a sharp right-hand bend, a bit sharper than we had been led to believe on the route plan. As we got there and went around the bend, the wind, which had been a full-on headwind, instantly changed into a sidewind and the alarm bells started ringing as those at the head of the peloton and first to the bend surged ahead while the rest of the riders, including many of the big GC riders, got battered a bit longer by the headwind. It was a classic peloton fracture on a windy day and the result was a strong 29-man break, which included Lance Armstrong and the Columbia train that got 20 seconds clear, then 30 seconds and then extended that to 41 seconds by the time Cav took the sprint.

Once a quality break of that magnitude had gone, and by the time the rest of us realised what was happening and got organised, it was too late and virtually impossible to close in. In many ways it's one of those things, it happens all the time, and I tried to be pretty philosophical about it afterwards but, looking back, those 41 seconds that Lance gained on me cost me a yellow jersey the following day and, nearly three weeks later, a place on the podium in Paris. I was bloody annoyed with myself, it was the one moment I let my concentration slip in the entire three weeks. I wasn't the only one by any means, but I am usually a good rider in such conditions and it was irritating. Like I say, stuff happens on the Tour and you have to stay alert to everything.

The other great thing about the Tour is that there is no time to dwell. Tomorrow is another day and another opportunity, and the team time trail in Montpellier was certainly that. We had been down to ride the course a couple of times and knew it was tough – a nasty climb, technical, narrow roads in places and windy. We also knew that if Astana rode as a team they were the strong favourites; they had an incredible line-up and seven or eight riders who could stay with the pace and put in their tune.

Tactically we had a dilemma. We had four of the world's best time trial riders – Dave Millar, David Zabriskie, who was right back in top form, Christian Vande Velde and myself – and five riders who were not TT specialists at all. Did we ride conservatively and try and limit the number of our team who dropped off, or did the four of us give it full gas, effectively riding as a four-man pursuit team and hope and trust that one of the guys, probably Ryder Hasjedal, who is very strong, could hang on and be our fifth man home. The clock only stops when the fifth man goes through the line.

We decided to go for broke – if we rode conservatively we might finish a full minute or more behind Astana. Better to try and fail than not to try at all. In many respects it paid off. We tore off at a rate of knots, raced up the climb and, as anticipated, we were soon down to our minimum five riders with 27 km to go. It probably looked alarming on the TV but we were taking a calculated gamble. To a certain extent we knew what we were doing. We ploughed on with the four of us having the time of our lives, trying to do outdo each other with heroic turns and Ryder hanging on for dear life out of the wind at the back. The plan worked in every respect bar one: Astana, despite all the rumours of dissension, rode a magnificent race as a team and behind their four top TT specialists (Lance, Alberto, Andreas Kloden and Levi Leipheimer) so had much more strength in depth to just ease the workload a bit. They got home by 18 seconds but, if there had been just one mistake from them, or if a couple of their riders had dropped off earlier, we would have been right in the mix.

It was a big buzz and the fact that we beat Columbia – who had enjoyed their moment against us in the Giro – by 41 seconds showed just how well we rode. After the disappointment of being the wrong side of the split the previous day, the team time trial put me right back in the groove again. I had a good feeling about this Tour.

After the time trial we had two classic transitional stages to negotiate before the mountains moved into view, down to Perpignan and then onwards to Barcelona. I just got my head down and rode hard with the Garmin boys. Dave Millar, who showed some real class at various times throughout the Tour, got away in a great break on the Barcelona day when the heavens opened in the latter stages of the race. He went again on his own and was only caught with about 1.3 km to go – a brave, aggressive break that deserved better reward. Dave always rides with a bit of panache and imagination, and his awareness of everything that is going on tactically is one of the reasons the French fans enjoy his riding.

Then came the moment of truth, the first big mountain stage up to Arcalis from Girona, my new home from home and Garmin's base camp. We had enjoyed a relaxed night among friends and neighbours and were in good heart for the long climb up into Andorra. To be honest, I felt good and comfortable right from the start riding next to Lance with all the GC contenders. Although very high and long, Arcalis was the perfect start for me – it's not too vicious and is one of those climbs when you can get your head down and grind it out. I felt comfortable and in control, not too stressed or on the edge. I looked around and some big names were looking much worse than I felt, which was very encouraging. My confidence started to soar. I knew I had prepared well and was in good form, the numbers were adding up and the opening time trial suggested I was right in the mix, but until that first man-on-man contest up a testing climb, you don't really get a feel for it. From that moment on Arcalis, I knew for sure that I could, at the very least, compete against these guys.

Towards the top, Alberto suddenly sprung into life, got up on his toes and sprinted up the mountain to gain 21 seconds on all of us, just to show everybody who the main man was when it came to the mountains. It was a very impressive and a good riposte after he, like most of us, had been caught out en route to La Grande Motte and Lance had benefited. I never had any illusions about my ability in comparison to Alberto Contador. He was always going to win the 2009 Tour de France because, all things considered, in July 2009 he was simply better than the rest of us. That's not being defeatist, simply realistic, and I never wavered from that viewpoint. My task was simply to maximise my new fitness and form and finish as high as I could. Arcalis, however, was a big breakthrough for me; I had ridden the whole day on the mountain with the big-hitters and felt completely at home.

So far, so very good. Still nothing much untoward had happened and a couple of things conspired to keep my momentum going. Astana clearly had no great desire to gain the yellow jersey for the second week – it would have complicated things for them – so they were riding conservatively. Plus, as we always knew, the Pyrenees weren't quite so demanding as usual, although it's all relative – if you weren't in good form or shape, they could still stop you stone dead. Saturday's stage started with a long grind up to the Port d'Envalira, which topped out at 2408 m, but only a couple of sections were steep and there was a long descent before the Col del Port and Col D'Agnes, then a rapid 40 km descent down in Saint Girons. Toughish but manageable, with plenty of time on the descents to recover ground.

It was a similar story on the Sunday when there were huge crowds on the mountains. Normally you would expect a day featuring the Col D'Aspin and the classic Tourmalet climb at the end of an aggressively ridden first week would open things up but the potential advantage of the pure climbers was cancelled out because of the superfast 70 km descent down into Tarbes, a comfortable cruise home to the finish. Knowing that any major attack they put in would probably be chased down by a determined bunch meant that the very top climbers understandably became more conservative. All this, plus my excellent form, made for a pretty comfortable passage to be honest. I was feeling good and the dice were falling my way a little bit.

I arrived at the rest day in Limoges in very decent nick, still fifth overall, and there was a chance to take stock. I couldn't really see a lot of movement in the GC in the coming week until the Friday, which had the potential to be a tough old day in the Vosges Mountains, although I was still adopting my day-by-day philosophy. I would worry about Friday at breakfast on Friday morning. Let's get there first, I thought.

I'm not a big fan of rest days, they break up your routine and if things are going OK you just want to crack on, anxious that the form and magic don't disappear. You are into the race, the adrenalin is pumping and then suddenly you stop dead for 36 hours. I suppose it does give the body a chance to recover but, if you are not careful, what it actually does is just give it a chance to seize up and start shutting down. You have to put in a two-hour spin at the very least to prevent this, so 'rest day' is a bit of a misnomer.

You will excuse me if I don't dwell on the middle week too

much. While it was an important sector for Cav and his sprinting mates – and he duly bagged another couple of wins – it was very much a holding operation for me, riding in close contact with all the GC riders, guarding against accidents and mishaps as much as moves. There was very little potential on that flattish terrain for anybody making gains but you still had to stay alert. It was tiring mentally but physically it sometimes felt like a day off. This was all new territory for me and very interesting. Once you get yourself into the GC group – the yellow jersey group – the race changes totally from what you remember. Everybody shows you a little more respect and gives you a little more room; I particularly noticed this in the final week, when the peloton knows that you are at the sharp end of the race and allow you to move through more easily. On transitional days you don't have to worry at all about getting in the break or chasing it down, you just sit in, mark your opponents and let others force the pace. Another discovery was that the huge mountain days sometimes feel 'easier' when you ride them 35 or 40 minutes quicker than you would in the grupetto. You are alert and racing and going up much quicker. As the race moved forward I gradually grew accustomed to this race within a race.

You still have to be vigilant though. Stage Ten – from Limoges to Issoudun – proved tricky right at the end because in the lead-in to the sprint, a crash held up many of us in the peloton. At the end of the stage we were docked 15 seconds, which seemed pretty harsh and would have seen me drop down a few GC positions but thankfully the race jury thought better of it overnight and decided to revoke their own decision and restore my group to the same finishing time as the rest of the sprint bunch who came home behind Cav. It was a welcome reversal of fortunes. Just as 'missing' the break on stage three had cost me dear in relation to chasing Lance, getting those 15 seconds back was to prove very useful on the final day of reckoning in the GC.

On Stage 13, which was a filthy cold wet day in the Vosges, I survived intact. I had a puncture towards the end, which was not ideal, but a quick tyre change and a concerted effort saw me get back on easily enough and I even managed to get up and finish eighth in the bunch as we came in behind Heinrich Haussler who had broken with Sylvain Chavenal and then went on his own with 30 km to go.

Cav and Thor Hushovd, far and away the two best riders competing for the points competition, were having a real battle for the green jersey during this middle period of the race and it got a bit heated after Stage 14 when they were racing for points behind the break. Cav was adjudged to have obstructed Thor at the end as he tried to go up on the inside by the rails. Cav was docked 13 valuable points – he eventually lost the competition by ten – and the spat lingered for a while, with Cav saying the green jersey would be 'tainted' if Thor won. Thor responded by riding a blinding race on the final Alpine stage in the third week to hoover up the intermediate sprints and virtually clinch the issue. Peace broke out when Cav won his fifth stage at Aubenas on the Friday and conceded that the Thor had won the green jersey fair and square. Honours even.

The first Alpine ascent to Verbier, on the Sunday, was my next big test and the nerves started kicking in as the day got closer but, again, there was little to get stressed about. There was a reason that I was so high in the placings and that was because I was riding well and intelligently – and although it was a short, sharp test, it wasn't an epic. Alberto Contador rode it brilliantly, attacking early on with only Andy Schleck attempting to go with him. Even Andy couldn't get his wheel and eventually Alberto put 46 seconds into him. Meanwhile I was feeling good and just maintained my own tempo and eventually came home fifth, just

1 minute 6 seconds behind Contador. Just a year ago I wouldn't have thought that possible but it's amazing what the right approach and a bit of confidence does for you. Lance finished 25 seconds behind me but climbed to second overall behind Alberto, and guess who was in third place? One Bradley Wiggins.

This was all getting a bit heady. Officially I was working for top 20, secretly I was hoping for top ten and here I was in a podium position two weeks into the Tour de France. Great stuff but, of course, the media pressure was beginning to mount up. Could I beat Robert Millar's best-ever British finish of fourth in 1984? Could I become the first Brit to stand on the podium in Paris with the yellow jersey and runner up? I tried to play it all down, not because I was being coy or awkward, but there was still a very long way to go. I knew that just one really bad day would send me tumbling down the GC and, suddenly, any talk of top three finish would have looked very stupid and a bit egomaniacal.

It was exciting though – I was finally racing the Tour de France, not just getting through it and surviving. I was involved in the action every day. It was all a bit of an eye-opener, just how massive the Tour de France is, it just towers over everything else in cycling and I say that as somebody who has been privileged to represent his country in three Olympics and win three gold medals in the process. This was a different league, every day felt like an Olympic final, and I was loving it.

The second rest day saw another halt in proceedings but this time I didn't mind so much, with the two biggest alpine stages moving into view. At Garmin we organised a helicopter and went down to Annecy with our bikes to a have a look at the 40 km individual time trial course that could possibly come into play in the shake up for podium positions, and it was time well spent. The climb in the middle was much harder than we had been led to believe, and at almost double the length – 4 km, not 2 km as shown in the stage profile – it could clearly have a big role to play. Then it was back to Verbier to ponder the next two days.

One stage at a time, that was always my mantra, and the first of the two stages didn't send the fear of God down my spine. It was basically a shortish stage with two very long climbs: the Col du Grand Saint Bernard at 2473 m, followed by a descent into Saint Pierre and than a climb up the Col du Petit Saint Bernard at 2188 m before a glorious fast descent down into Bourg Saint Maurice. The first climb was where the famous mountain scene from *The Italian Job* was filmed, with the coach left hanging over the cliff with the gold about to fall into the valley below. Spectacular countryside.

The good weather was back with us for this one and I had good legs from the start. Mikel Astarloza eventually emerged from the day-long break to win the stage, but behind that in the yellow jersey group, it all started to go off going up the final climb, the Col du Petit Saint Bernard. The two Schleck brothers, Andy and Frank, started to attack really hard – this was their attempt to finally get into Alberto Contador – and they weren't holding back. I knew that this was one of those decisive moments when I had to hang on for dear life.

Alberto just started dancing on those pedals a little quicker and matched the brothers easily, but the rest of us were right on the limit. Initially only myself, Vincenzo Nibali and Andreas Kloden were able to stick with it, with Lance Armstrong, Cadel Evans and Carlos Sastre all beginning to lose ground. Bloody hell, what was happening? For a short period of time I was the 'virtual' second on the road.

It was a big moment and then, as the Schlecks slowed the pace a little having failed to shake off Alberto, Lance showed his class and great fighting spirit by upping his pace to a sprint and getting across the 40-second gap that had opened, bringing a fair few others with him. As we all came back together, the attack fizzled and effectively I had got through another massive mountain day without any damage, still in third place. From the top it was a glorious descent strung out like a massive team pursuit team, with a helicopter tracking us just above eye level in the valley, beaming live pictures. It was exhilarating and fun, and all my dreams were still in place as we sped into Bourg Saint Maurice.

We were now very deep into the third week and the final Alpine day loomed, the day I knew everybody has been describing as the 'Queen Stage' but a day I had been blanking from my mind until the moment arrived when I had to deal with it – just as I had dealt with every challenge so far.

When I started to study the race profile at dinner on the Wednesday night, I knew this would be a killer, whether I was superfit and a stone lighter or not. For me it was the very worst kind of mountain day: five separate climbs, including four Category One Beasts, with the last two being particularly steep as they headed towards the summit. There was hardly a flat kilometre to be had all day in the 169.5 km run from Bourg Saint Maurice to Le Grand Bornand. As we lined up that morning, Alberto was beginning to move clear of the field with Lance second at 1 min 37 and myself third at 1.46. Behind me came Andreas Kloden (2.17), Andy Schleck (2.26) and Vincenzo Nibali (2.51). At 3.25, Frank Schleck was still a danger to all except the yellow jersey himself, but the reigning champion Carlos Sastre was beginning to fade at 3.52 and had shown nothing to suggest he was ready to launch a big attack.

If I'm honest I knew it was a day on which I was going to have to limit my losses, especially as everything I had heard and read that morning suggested that Alberto – and I take this as a great compliment and a sign of how far I have developed – was wary of my time-trialling ability and with Annecy in mind wanted to 'take me out of the equation' as soon as possible.

Frank Schleck launched the first big attack of the day – after a doomed effort from Carlos Sastre – on the penultimate climb, the Col de Romme, which has the reputation of being very nasty and steep indeed. It was! Lance initially chased Frank down but in a classic move his brother Andy went straight after we had caught Frank, and inevitably Alberto was immediately onto the danger and tracking him, along with Andreas Kloden, who was enjoying a good day up to that point.

I couldn't live with them – or if I had tried I might have 'blown' – so I just kept going at my pace and found Lance by my side, which confirmed in my mind that we were absolutely level-pegging in fitness and form on this Tour. It was an interesting tactical situation as well – tough, given the reports of rifts in the Astana line-up. Working together we might have been able to cut into the time gap, but that would have been helping my cause visa vie the others, so I found myself doing all the work and Lance tucking in. No problem with that; it was a sound tactic from a guy who knows everything there is to know about racing the Tour de France.

There were thousands of words written about the situation within the Astana team during the Tour, and Lance and Alberto did have a major dig at each other afterwards, but I have to tell you that inside the race itself I thought everybody within Astana rode with the utmost professionalism at all times and I don't recall an occasion when Lance tried to 'flick' Alberto. The La Grande Motte day was a one-off and I defy any top road racer not to instinctively take advantage when something like that happens. Equally I felt Alberto attacked at exactly the points you would expect a Tour winner to attack and they were attacks intended to win the Tour de France, not to score any points off teammates. You don't have to be a happy crew to race well. That was my take on it.

Lance is the only rider I have ridden with who has an aura and presence; he is one of those guys you know has come into the room before you see him. To spend virtually three weeks alongside him, competing directly with him for a podium place was not something I had ever envisaged in my career, especially after he retired in 2005. It was the stuff of dreams and we began to develop a decent rapport, enjoying a gossip early in the day before the racing kicked off properly.

We were racing properly now and Lance was tracking me, making no effort to help bring us back to Contador group and I was to pay on the final climb of the day – the Col de la Columbiere, whose last 4 km are all at 9 per cent or more. We went up together but in the last kilometre Lance, who had been biding his time, attacked and I couldn't respond. There was a bit of a descent and although holding my own I couldn't eat into the advantage he had gained on me. Before the race, Lance had been talking about trying to lay down a buffer between himself and me before the time trial, and right at the death of a very long day he had done exactly that and you could only take your hat off to him. All the old racing skill and nous is there.

My eighth place in the stage was actually one of the very best rides of my life against all the best mountain riders in the world on a queen stage of the Tour de France with no quarter asked or given. But it had been a savage day and I owed a great deal to Christian Vande Velde and Dave Zabriske who had ridden superbly in support of me – great teammates. I was 3.07 down on the stage winner Frank Schleck, who had the same time as Alberto Contador and Andy Schleck, while Nibali and Armstrong had gained 49 seconds on me and Kloden 40. In the GC I had slipped down to sixth but it wasn't catastrophic, I was only nine seconds behind Kloden and 58 behind Lance and I fancied myself, all things being equal, to beat both in the Annecy time trial. By how much I wasn't sure.

There were a lot of very tired bodies among the GC riders warming up in Annecy on a muggy morning and I thought it unlikely that any of us, bar possibly Alberto, had enough in the tank to actually win the stage. Riders like Fabian, Dave Millar and Dave Zabriske – if he had anything left after his efforts on my behalf in the mountains – would have been eyeing this stage up from a long way out and as it happened, the earlier starters also got the best of the conditions with their runs fairly windless. The last group of 20 or so were hit by a blocking wind after the climb that slowed everybody down, except for Alberto, that is, who raced home in fine style. Sixth in the actual stage, I was second-fastest of all the GC contenders and climbed back up to fourth place overall, so although I didn't feel absolutely at my best, it was a very decent result. If you are contesting the GC late in the third week, you aren't necessarily going to be at your very best in the individual time trial but I wasn't far off it. By the close of play I was 11 seconds behind Lance who was in third, just two ahead of Andreas Kloden and 23 seconds ahead of Frank Schleck.

The end was nigh and thoughts were turning to Paris and seeing the family again but there was still work to do. Friday's 19th stage was another stinking hot windy day and ridden much quicker than I felt was strictly necessary! Rabobank had missed the break and rode hard to close it down and Columbia had decided that despite a category two climb close to the finish, they were going to put Cav in contention again, so we rattled along at a furious rate. Cav took the sprint, one of his best wins, and Lance somehow clung onto the sprint bunch to finish four seconds clear of the other GC contenders. We found ourselves baulked a bit by the various lead-out riders as they dropped off and cluttered the road up a bit as we rode in! C'est la vie, they were only doing their job.

And so to Ventoux on the Saturday with well over 750,000 fans expected on the mountain, a location which has a very special place in the hearts of British riders for the very obvious reason that Tom Simpson died there in 1967 trying to win the Tour de France. As I wrote earlier, when I made my long solo break in the 2007 Tour, it was not a conscious effort to 'celebrate' the 40th anniversary of his death; in fact, it was primarily a way of celebrating my wife's birthday. But this time it was very different. But from the moment I started considering the Ventoux stage, I had the Tom Simpson story very much in the back of my mind – the courage, raw guts and pioneer spirit to take on the world – which I knew I might be able to draw inspiration from when the going got particularly tough. I have read the book, watched the painful footage of his final ride and spoken to various people over the years who knew Tom, the man and the rider. Of course, I am not unaware of the other aspect of Tom's story – how he, like many others, seems to have resorted to taking the drugs of the day in an attempt to improve his racing. He was what he was, a product of his times and the sport was different then. What will never change is that he was a superb, gutsy, bike rider who took on some of the greatest-ever names in the sport and is Britain's only ever world champion. I wouldn't say I am an overly spiritual bloke but it was impossible, given the circumstances, not to feel his presence on the mountain; he was sort of riding with me and I would have hated to have let him down. He was certainly my inspiration. I was going to dedicate this ride to him and go to the limit in his memory.

It was another scorching hot day down in Provence with the usual perfect blue sky but, when we woke, the wind was blowing a fair old gale and threatened to make conditions very difficult at the top once you come out of the tree line at Chalet Reynard. For a while there was even talk of bringing the finish down the mountain a bit, but the forecast was for the wind to drop a bit during the day and that was, in fact, what happened, although it was still pretty blustery and uncomfortable at the top.

The stage was all about Ventoux and after from the break that went up the road – Juan Manuel Gaate and young Tony Martin from Columbia HTC – it was all eerily quiet on the approach. There was almost no banter whatsoever, which is almost unheard of; everybody was lost in their own thoughts and trying to summon up one final effort. A climb of Ventoux really does take you to the limit. We were all going to suffer, GC riders or those just riding for a finish. There is no easy way up. And the route in really does rub it in and build the tension – we spent most of the day, or so it seemed, circling the mountain, viewing it from various angles and sizing it up before the moment came to begin the ascent. This was the big one, the ride that would determine the final rankings in the 2009 Tour de France.

Ventoux is one of the great climbs of the Tour, considered by many to be the hardest, not just because of its 21 km length and gradient but because it can be such an uncomfortable mountain: windy, very hot, but sometimes very cold. Stark and barren with that strange white shade at the top, it can be very intimidating. I didn't necessarily feel that daunted – it was incredibly tough, but in many ways it was my kind of mountain: one big effort, very long and steady, a sort of extended mountain time trial. I had been up and over it on a number of occasions in the grupetto but I had never 'raced' up it in such elite company, which was the unknown for me. I had no idea how I would cope when it all went off, I was just determined to dig as deep as humanly possible on the day.

Which is exactly what I did. I went with the yellow jersey almost all the way to the top as we closed in rapidly on Garate and Martin and only started to yo-yo off the back a little with 2 km. I was gone at every level, operating on instinct and frankly can't remember going past the Simpson Memorial. I knew I would be out of it and had paid my tribute in advance by taping a picture of Tom to my top tube. Afterwards I heard that all the British riders paid their respects – Dave Millar threw over a cap with RIP Tom written on it, Cav took his helmet off as he rode past and Charlie Wegelius gently lobbed over his water bottle. All nice touches from the lads.

I was deep in the red zone now and hanging on for dear life – I had come so far I was desperate not to let it slip. Keep going, keep going, don't look up, Brad, just keep going. Eventually the final sharp right-hand bend came into sight, followed by that vicious last ramp to the finish next to that famous weather tower. One more effort, where's the bloody line? One more effort again. There it is, I've finished, I've raced up Ventoux!

It was all pretty emotional as I virtually fell off my bike into helping hands. I was completely out of it, fighting for air and thinking I had never felt so completely spent in my life. I had been emptying the tank all Tour in the mountains but this was a new level of fatigue. My first real conscious memory was Christian Vande Velve coming over after he had finished and saying: 'It's all over man, you've finished, you don't have to do it any more.' He was expressing the relief that every rider feels when he effectively finished the Tour, albeit for the formality of a promenade into Paris the next day. For us the Tour was over and it felt great.

Five minutes later it felt even better when, as I was sitting in doping control with Lance, it was confirmed that I had finished fourth overall, three seconds ahead of Frank Schleck and 41 seconds ahead of Andreas Kloden. Happy days. Soon after I free-wheeled down to the Garmin bus and we cracked open a couple of cold beers on the ride down to our hotel in Avignon. For a so-called team of time trail riders, we hadn't done so very badly with fourth for me in the GC, eighth for Christian Vande Velde, some great days on the road for the two Daves and good work from everybody else. There was a great sense of camaraderie as we slowly drove down the mountain with a beer in our hands and the sound system on. They are the kind of moments you remember for a long time.

That really was where my Tour ended. Paris was just fun, a gentle ride in, a sprint around the Champs Élysées and then the traditional lap of honour afterwards meeting family and friends and getting the beers in. A big team dinner and a very late night when I took on Jack Daniels and lost, and suddenly it was time to head for home and whatever the future held.

The 2009 Tour de France was an extraordinary experience for me and a pointer to what I want to achieve in the future. It came about for lots of reasons but the bottom line was that, after Beijing 2008, I really had to give road racing the attention and dedication I had given my track career. In many ways it was now or never. That added the edge and impetus and then other things fell into place – a sensible diet, rock solid training uninterrupted by illness and injury, and in many ways an experimental season that was fun all the way. I was allowed by my team to branch out and really discover what I am good at, apart from Prologues, and to the surprise of many we discovered that I was actually a GC rider all the time. Better late than never, I suppose! Actually, it's perfect timing. I'm 29 and Tour riders traditionally hit their peak between 29 and 33, so it's not to late to work towards the ultimate – winning the Tour itself.

An impossible dream? We will see. There is nobody who admires Alberto Contador's talent more than me, and I also rate Andy Schleck enormously. They are both young and I doubt if they will be going away any time soon, so it's a monumental task, but in many ways I have been here before. This is not unknown territory. There was a time when Brad McGee seemed simply untouchable in the individual pursuit, at least to me, so much so that I was often beaten before I even lined up against him. But I overcame that and eventually started reversing the role.

And then there were all those years when the GB Team Pursuit squad could never beat the Aussies or break through the magical four-minute barrier. For a long time it all seemed pretty hopeless and pointless but we had a major rethink, went to work and eventually cracked it. If you want it badly enough, these things can be achieved – just don't expect it to be easy!

There is so much more I can do in the Tour. In 2009, for example, because I only belatedly felt I could make the top ten, I didn't recce a single big climb in the months before the race. That could make a huge difference. Also I deliberately 'over-raced', if you like, in the early season, packing in various road experiences to help find what really suited me. I had a ball but next year perhaps I won't race quite so much; instead I will concentrate a little more on specific preparations for next year's Tour.

The bottom line is that 2009 has to be a start, not an ending. After the pain of my debut in 2006 and the humiliation of 2007 when I left the Tour under a police escort, I have belatedly discovered that probably the greatest thrill in cycling is 'racing' the Tour de France and fighting for the yellow jersey in the high mountains against the legends of the sport. Sometimes your dreams come true and my dream is still to win the world's greatest race outright.

Palmarès

OLYMPICS

2000 Sydney: bronze medal: Team Pursuit

2004 Athens: gold medal: 4 km Individual Pursuit; silver medal: 4 km Team Pursuit; bronze medal: Madison

2008 Beijing: gold medal: 4 km Team Pursuit; gold medal: 4 km Team Pursuit

WORLD CHAMPIONSHIPS

1998 U19 World Track Championships (Cuba): gold medal: 3 km Individual Pursuit

2000 World Championships (Manchester): silver medal: Team Pursuit

2001 World Championships (Antwerp): silver medal: Team Pursuit

2002 World Championships (Copenhagen): bronze medal: Team Pursuit

2003 World Championships (Stuttgart): gold medal: 4 km Individual Pursuit; silver medal: Team Pursuit

2007 World Championships (Palma): gold medal: 4 km Individual Pursuit; gold medal: Team Pursuit

2008 World Championships (Manchester): gold medal: 4 km Individual Pursuit; gold medal: Team Pursuit (world record time); gold medal: men's Madison

COMMONWEALTH GAMES

2002 (Manchester): silver medal: 4 km Individual Pursuit; silver medal: Team Pursuit

VARIOUS

1998: stage win Tour of Lorraine (4th overall); two stage wins Tour of Ireland (2nd overall)

1999: Tour of Guadeloupe, two stage wins

2000: 3rd Six Days of Grenoble; 7th Six Days of Ghent; 1st U23, Circuit des Mines (7th overall); 1st Grand Prix Mol-Rauw; 1st Grand Prix Harlebeke (U23); 2nd Grand Prix Merelbeke; 3rd overall, Centurion Tour of Majorca; voted 'British Cyclist of the Year' by readers of *Cycling Weekly*

2001: European Individual Pursuit Champion; 1st, Tour of Majorca; 1st, Flèche du Sud; 2nd, Prologue Tour of Rhodes; 3rd overall, Tour of Rhodes.

2003: Stage 1 ITT, Tour de l'Avenir

1st Six Days of Ghent (with Matt Gilmore)

2005: Stage 2 ITT, Circuit de Lorraine

Stage 8, Tour de l'Avenir

2007: Prologue, Critérium du Dauphiné Libéré

Stage 1 ITT, Four Days of Dunkirk

Stage 4 ITT, Tour du Poitou-Charentes et de la Vienne

Stage 6 Combativity award, Tour de France

Duo Normand (with Michiel Elijzen)

Glossary of cycling terms

abandon: when you are forced to quit a race, either through injury, exhaustion or mechanical failure.

arrivée: the eagerly anticipated finish line.

Benjamin du Tour: the youngest rider in the race. In 2007 it was Britain's Geraint Thomas.

besoin naturel: how can we put this? The art of completing a comfort break while still riding at pace on the hoof. Extremely difficult and spectators beware.

bidon: a water bottle.

Blue Train: an elite group of track riders who receive automatic and lucrative invites from the promoters to all the big Six Day event races on the Continent. To book your place on the Blue Train was to guarantee a certain level of income for the winter.

broom wagon: see voiture balai.

caravane publicitaire: a huge parade of commercial floats – it can take nearly an hour for all the vehicles to pass through a village – generally staffed by nubile young French students earning their summer holiday money as they throw trinkets and souvenirs to the crowds. The *caravane* will proceed an hour and half ahead of the race. Fees paid by the sponsors of *caravane* vehicles are the primary source of revenue for the Tour organisers.

chasseurs: the 'hunters' who chase down breaks.

Classement Générale: the General Classification or GC, the overall standings in the race. The rider at the top at the end of a stage race wins the GC.

col: a mountain pass rather than a mountain summit. Cols frequently feature in the middle of a stage and can prove every bit as stressful and exhausting as a summit finish.

contre la montre: a 'time-trial'. A race where each rider rides alone and is timed individually as in the short prologue, which often starts a major tour, or the more traditional time-trial stages – normally two – that often prove vital during a closely fought Tour.

coureur: a rider.

Criterium: a Criterium race consists of numerous laps around a short circuit based on a city or town. Popular in France, Holland and Belgium, especially towards the end of the season after the big Tours. Exciting for spectators but a mixed blessing for the cyclists – they can be unpredictable and dangerous, but they also pay well with decent appearance money and prizes.

décrocher: to be 'dropped' – left behind by the stronger riders.

Derny: small motor-powered bikes which are used in speed training and also to set the pace in a Keirin race, increasing it by a fixed amount each lap, before pulling away with three laps to go to allow the race to develop.

Directeur Sportif: the head coach/general manager of a cycling team, very often a distinguished ex-racer. He will ride in the team car during a stage, issuing tactical orders.

domestique: literally, a domestic servant dedicated to serving the needs of other racers in the team. This may include shielding them from the wind, chasing down breaks from opposition GC contenders, dropping back behind the peloton to collect extra water and food bags, dropping back to help the big-name rider if he is struggling with a bad day or has crashed and needs pacing back. An unglamorous, unenviable task but no big tour winner could ever manage their victory without them – which is why the winner of a big tour traditionally divides the prize money among all his team.

dossard: one of many derisive terms used to describe a rider who never takes a turn at the front, but always allows himself to be pulled along by the other riders. A wheel-sucker.

étape: a stage of the Tour de France.

flamme rouge: a red flag situated 1 km from the finish for the benefit of the sprinters as they time their finish in a mass finish.

Giro d'Italia: cycling's second most famous stage race or major tour, every bit as gruelling as the Tour de France. It can be even more testing in the mountains and the weather can still have a wintry feel.

grimpeur: a specialist climber and nearly as mad as the Directeur Sportif. A guy who actually enjoys going uphill and is good at it.

groupetto (autobus in French)**:** a large group of 'non-climbers', who negotiate their way through the huge mountain stages together and aim to finish within the cut-off time each day – usually 10 per cent of the winner's finishing time, although it is at the discretion of the Tour officials.

hors catégorie *(HC)*: a climb so

bloody severe and long that technically, and verbally, it is beyond description or classification. A Category 1 is the next toughest climb – calculated on steepness and distance – followed by a Cat. 2, Cat. 3 and Cat. 4, with the latter the smallest classified climb.

lanterne rouge: the rider in last place on the Classement Générale during the Tour de France. The *lanterne rouge* is often rewarded with some of the largest appearance fees at the various post-Tour Criterium races having become something of a personality during the Tour. Don't go thinking this rider is a mug – remember he will have got around the Tour, whereas 70 or 80 of the world's best cyclists will have failed. In addition he will almost certainly be a *domestique* who will have dedicated his three weeks on tour to serving his team leader in his fight for GC honours.

Keirin: a sprint event which originated in Japan where it is almost a national obsession and the basis of a $7.5 million betting industry. Typically on a 250 m track a field of between six and eight riders will follow a Derny for three and half laps, with the Derny driver steadily increasing the pace, before swinging up with two and half laps to go. After that it is a traditional flat-out high-speed sprint with a large potential for crashes.

Kermesse: not unlike a Criterium but generally held at smaller venues, often coinciding with a village fair or fête. Used to be very popular in Belgium, when professionals and talented amateurs alike would race in midweek Kermesse races, but in decline now although still popular in Holland and parts of northern France.

Madison: probably my favourite event, a lot of fun but also a huge test of your bike-handling skills. Originated in the very early days of Six Day racing in America, when it proved very popular at Madison Square Gardens in New York. It is basically a two-man points race over distances between 50 and 70 km, although the World and Olympic events seem to be standardised at 50 km. Points can be won at sprints after every 20 laps but a team can also wipe that advantage out by gaining a lap on the rest of the field. If a number of teams are the same number of laps then the points come back into play to decide the winner. One member of the two-man team will be riding in the race at any one time with the other circling high on the boards trying to take a breather. The team can 'change' at any time and this involves the resting rider coming down off the boards and completing a hand-sling with the rider who is about to take a rest.

With 11 or 12 teams on the track this can prove a spectacular and dangerous business. The decision when to change is entirely down to individual teams. The endurance man may do a longer stint when they are looking to gain a lap, while the sprinter will invariably be brought into play as a sprint looms.

maillot à pois: a white jersey with red polka dots worn by the leader of the 'King of the Mountains' competition.

maillot jaune: the fabled yellow jersey – worn by the leader of the Classement Générale in the Tour de France. The only British riders ever to wear it are Tommy Simpson, Sean Yates, Chris Boardman and Dave Millar.

maillot vert: *t*he green jersey – worn by the leader of the points competition in the Tour de France.

musette: a shoulder bag containing food and drinks for the riders that is handed to the riders as they pass through the *zone de ravitaillement*.

Palmares: the French expression for your Honours list and career achievements.

patron: literally, the 'boss'. The rider who has earned the respect of the peloton to the extent that he is placed in charge of the day-to-day running and internal discipline of the riders. Self-policing. Merckx, Armstrong and Hinault are the obvious examples, with the latter

ruling with a fist of iron. Normally a distinguished yellow jersey rider but not always, longevity also counts. The *patron* will decide when a humble *domestique* is allowed to ride ahead of the peloton to stop in his home village and enjoy a glass of champagne with family and friends, or when a rider celebrating his birthday can enjoy a spell 'up the road' to pose for a few press pictures and gain his team valuable exposure. More importantly, he will take soundings and decide if there is to be a go-slow or even a strike in times of turmoil within the race. The Tour is in a state of flux at present and no obvious *patron* exists, but one will probably emerge.

peloton: originally, a military term meaning a 'platoon'. Used to refer to the large bunch of riders as they contest the race.

pistard: the general term for a track cyclist – a cyclist who rides on the piste.

Points Race: a bunch race on the track with points awarded in descending order for sprints at various stages of the race (normally between 50 and 70 km). Riders lapping the field can be awarded extra points or, under some local rules, automatically be declared the winner.

Pursuit: pursuit racing is my speciality. It is essentially you against the clock and not, directly, your opponent. The men's pursuit race is over 4 km or 16 laps of a standard 250 m velodrome. Very simple to follow, the two fastest riders from the qualifying process meet in the final and then the fastest in the final wins. The Team Pursuit is just an extension of the Individual Pursuit with a team of four contesting the issue. The time of the team is taken when the third man crosses the line. Generally speaking a Team Pursuit squad can lap one second quicker per lap than an individual.

remorqueur: used to refer to a rider – the long-suffering *domestique* – who rides in the front to protect his team-mates from the wind. There is 30 per cent less wind resistance if you tuck into the slipstream of another rider and therefore you have to expend 30 per cent less energy.

ravitaillement, zone de: a designated section of the race where riders pick up *musettes* from the *soigneurs*. The end of the *zone de ravitaillement* is a good place for spectators to pick up discarded water bottles and *musette* bags.

soigneur: the rather mystical background figure – a butler almost – who takes care of the physical needs of the riders, from distributing *musettes* to giving massages and the distribution of

les préparations although the latter is hopefully in decline.

sprint: a mad dash for the finish line or some other designated point on the stage. Some of the most exciting moments of the Tour are the mass sprints that conclude many of the flatter stages in the first week of the Tour.

sweet spot: the point on the banking of a track when you just know it is right to come back down. Will differ according to the angle of the banking. This knowledge only comes with experience; technically I suppose the description is that part of the banking where the momentum to go down outweighs the momentum to continue upwards. You just know.

tête de la course: the head of the race – in the lead. As in: 'Lance Armstrong *est tête de la course.*'

vainqueur: the winner.

vélo: a racing bike

virage: a switchback or hairpin turn on a mountain road. There are 21 of them on the Alpe d'Huez.

voiture balai: the broom wagon. A van that follows the race picking up the riders who have abandoned the stage or have fallen so far back as to be unable to finish within the time limit. Not a fun place.

Index